Languages in Competition

THE LANGUAGE LIBRARY

EDITED BY DAVID CRYSTAL

Languages in Competition

Dominance, Diversity, and Decline

RONALD WARDHAUGH

Basil Blackwell
in association with
André Deutsch

British Library Cataloguing in Publication Data

Wardhaugh, Ronald
    Languages in competition: dominance, diversity
    and decline. — (The language library).
    1. Language and languages — History
    I. Title
    409   P61

    ISBN 0–631–15744–1
    ISBN 0–631–15745–X Pbk

Library of Congress Cataloging in Publication Data

Wardhaugh, Ronald.
  Languages in competition.
  (The Language library)
  Bibliography: p.
  1. Language spread. 2. Linguistic minorities.
3. Languages in contact. 4. English language—Social
aspects. 5. French language—Social aspects.
I. Title. II. Series
P40.5.L37W37 1988   409   87–10312
ISBN 0–631–15744–1
ISBN 0–631–15745–X (pbk.)   7/514

Typeset in 10 on 12 pt Sabon
by Photo·graphics, Honiton, Devon.
Printed in Great Britain by Billing & Sons Ltd, Worcester

Contents

Preface

Language has become a burning issue in many parts of the world today. Passions are aroused as some languages spread and others decline, and, on occasion, these passions lead to violence of one sort or another. The spread and decline of languages is not a new phenomenon; there is every reason to believe that it is as old as language itself and that competition between languages is to be expected when their 'territories' impinge on one another. What makes the phenomenon so interesting today is that in a world of well over five billion people who speak several thousand languages among them but who are organized into less than two hundred states the opportunities for competition to turn into conflict are considerable.

This book is about language spread – or dominance – and about various languages that have found themselves in competition as a result of that spread. Dealing with every aspect of such a topic would require an encyclopedic treatment. In order to make the topic manageable, I have concentrated on the spread of English and French, on competition between them, and on the way in which each has been imposed on speakers of other languages both within the British Isles and France and outside. I have also included a discussion of a variety of other linguistic situations in the world in order to show how states other than the United Kingdom and France have tried to deal with competition among languages and problems of language dominance and diversity. Finally, I have felt it necessary to mention certain developments that have created recent complications in several more or less stable linguistic situations in the world.

In discussing particular cases, I have tried to indicate trends when these are apparent but have deliberately avoided adopting either a position that language loss is to be deplored in any circumstance or its opposite that states are best served by unilingual populations. I believe that these are opinions not facts, although they are often stated as facts. Readers can let their own personal opinions guide them in this matter, if necessary to conclusions different from mine when I have drawn conclusions.

Facts are themselves, of course, relative. They must be selected and that selection must be motivated by a theory of one kind or another. I have tried to provide a wealth of facts but the selection is mine, guided by what I have attempted to do, which is to show some of the forms that language competition takes and some of its consequences. Sometimes it has been necessary to state a fact one way rather than another, for example, to choose one version of a name rather than another, e.g., Bern or Berne, Ireland or Eire, etc. The choice I have made implies no political judgement, for in most cases I might just as readily have chosen the alternative.

A book like this should also encourage readers to delve further into the various issues that it raises. Consequently, each chapter ends with some suggested further readings. These are not meant to be at all exhaustive for the topics are vast, but the suggestions should provide the reader with an opportunity to go further into the issues discussed in the book so as to form an independent judgement.

Finally, this book is written by a linguist, a professional student of language and languages. Much of the literature on the topics contained within it has come from historians, political scientists, sociologists, educators, etc. rather than from linguists. It is my belief that linguists must be more prepared than they have been to treat 'real-life' language issues such as those I have dealt with here and I hope that this book will provide a further stimulus to that end.

1

Language Dominance

It is a well attested historical fact that languages are born and die and experience periods of ascendancy and decline. Today, some languages appear to be prospering: they are acquiring many new speakers and extending their influence far beyond their original bounds; however, others appear to be in retreat before the advance of rivals who may eventually overwhelm them. There is little that is new in this process – it seems to have existed since time immemorial – except the emphasis that the modern world places on language. People seem now to be more conscious than they once were of the importance of language in daily living; language loyalty is associated with ideologies of various kinds; and states now have resources they may use to deal deliberately with matters they heretofore left largely unattended. Some people are also actively concerned with spreading particular languages at the expense of other languages, while still other people concern themselves with attempts to preserve these threatened languages from the effects of such dominance.

The scope of the problem is easy to illustrate. Estimates of how many languages are spoken in the world vary widely – from 4,000 to 8,000 – and 5,000 appears to be a not unreasonable number. Each of these languages offers those who use it a unique way of looking at the world and unique cultural opportunities. However, a very few languages are dominant in the world in terms of the numbers of people who use them. Five languages account for 45 per cent of a world population estimated to reach some six billion by the year 2000: Chinese, English, Spanish, Russian, and Hindi. Altogether a dozen languages account for 60 per cent of the world's population, 25 languages for 75 per cent, and about a hundred languages for 95 per cent. Within even these few though some are currently prospering and others declining. But outside, among the several thousand that exist, many are in serious jeopardy. Essentially what we will be concerned with in the pages that follow are the tensions that are created by situations in which one or more members of the few compete either with one another or with one or more members of the many and the various types of linguistic competition and accommodation that have occurred in the modern world.

LANGUAGE SPREAD

All languages are constantly in a state of change, a fact that does not go unrecognized but one which is nevertheless hardly acceptable to those who make part – or the whole – of their living by warning us against the evils they perceive to be inherent in change. But languages also change in their attractiveness to speakers: they change the uses to which speakers put them; they sometimes retrench, losing speakers either entirely (and, of course, 'die') or only for certain functions; and they sometimes spread or expand, gaining more uses and users. Most of the factors bringing about change, retrenchment, or expansion are unconscious ones: generally, speakers are not aware of what is going on. However, some changes are conscious: when a government decrees that one language rather than another must be used in certain circumstances, then that is a conscious decision affecting both languages. Language planning, that is deliberate government intervention in language matters, is therefore a factor that must be considered if one is to achieve an adequate understanding of the phenomenon of language spread and how languages gain or lose speakers.

A very first prerequisite to the spread of any language is a base from which to spread or to dominate others. Such a base is also critically important when one language comes under attack from another, that is, when it is threatened by one or more other languages. The larger and more populous the base the greater the degree of security, initially at least, and possibly the most secure base of all is a territory in which the language has exclusive domain. In this way a language may maintain its vitality, particularly if those who use it do so for a wide variety of purposes: they should speak it, write it, work in it, govern themselves in it, publish books in it, use it on radio and television, and maintain contact with those who use the language elsewhere in the world if such people exist. It helps too if the population is an expanding one and if it exhibits considerable resistance to learning other languages. If these conditions are present, the language should at least hold its own. If, however, the language is to spread outside the territory some additional factors must undoubtedly come into play.

The boundaries of a state often appear to offer a language a 'natural' area to dominate, particularly if the state is at the same time a nation-state. As we will see in Chapter 3, it is common in the modern world to equate the terms *nation* and *state*, but the equation is scarcely valid, for few indeed are the modern states which are also nations. Most states are composed of several national or ethnic groups and even states such as the United Kingdom and France enclose groups that sometimes present themselves to others as nations that are more or less 'captive'. However, the equation of nation and state does persist and nearly everywhere language is regarded as a potent unifying and integrating force within the bounds of the modern state, which is seen as the natural domain of a particular language. In those cases in which a state has had to recognize more than one language the resulting situation is often fraught with danger. A single language appears to offer people who must live together under a single government a system for achieving a shared set of beliefs and a common ideology and, of course too, a shared medium for pursuing the mundane matters of everyday life. Many states are engaged in the active promotion of one or more languages within their territorial bounds in order to foster the creation of a 'national' identity and this even in cases when all that really exists are states that are but the chance creations of political 'accidents', as are many of the states of modern Africa. We may even view the United Kingdom and France as states which are in the late stages of becoming nations, with pockets of resistance on their geographical peripheries, pockets which continue to resist, although not very successfully, the dominance of the English and French languages respectively.

If the authority of a state is to apppear legitimate to those who live within its bounds, certain basic issues must be resolved during the state-building or nation-building process. Individuals must achieve some sense of common identity or membership in a single community. They must also come to recognize the legitimacy of the state's authority over them and comply with its edicts. They must feel a sense of involvement in the affairs and decisions of the state rather than a sense of isolation from what happens and a resulting powerlessness. There must also be a feeling that rewards are fairly distributed and not dependent on inappropriate factors. And, finally, where a person happens to live should not affect the life chances of that individual: peripheral geographic areas should be treated equitably with those that are more central. We can easily appreciate how important a factor a common language or, when there is more than one language in the community, an equitable language arrangement is in achieving these goals and why those who seek to develop a sense of belonging to a particular state promote the kinds of language policies they do. That there should often be resistance is also not surprising as people reject those policies or realize that they fail to meet many of the objectives for which they are apparently advanced. In the modern state language can therefore easily become a symbol of either unity or resistance.

It is probably only in the modern world that language has become such a powerful political symbol. Language has become symbolic of nationalism, and nationalism is a modern phenomenon. In the pre-nineteenth century world languages diffused and contracted as empires expanded or fell, or religious systems flourished or declined, or mercantile patterns changed. There was little direct management of language affairs by states and empires. Directives, orders, and laws there were, but these tended to affect the few rather than the many and to guarantee administrative convenience rather than define long-term policies. It was only with the rise of nationalism in the late eighteenth century that language became symbolic of nationality and could be used as a focus for political and cultural struggle. It could also at the same time be used to expand a state's power both within and without and to resist similar expansionist policies of other states. Language diffusion could be managed and, because it could be, it was.

Sometimes that management has been quite brutal. In France one politician, Barrère, declared that 'fanaticism speaks Basque, hatred of the Republic speaks Breton'; he was prepared to tolerate only French, 'the language of reason'. In Spain Franco once dismissed Catalan as the 'tongue of dogs' and excluded it, along with Basque, from public life. But even in the anglophone world there has been little tolerance of languages other than English as the Welsh or Irish can readily attest, or the French in Canada, or most immigrants to North America. President Theodore Roosevelt was not alone in believing that there was room in the United States for only one language; indeed his sentiments are still echoed as we can see in recent attempts to have English declared to be, by constitutional amendment, the official language of the United States.

Some states try to resist allowing language issues to dominate the political agenda. As events in countries as disparate as Belgium, Switzerland, Canada, India, Sri Lanka, the USA, and the USSR have shown, language can be a divisive, even explosive, issue when people are allowed to align themselves for political purposes according to the languages they speak. Modern political life favours arrangements which encourage the formation of political parties along social or economic class divisions and discourages those made to support linguistic, religious, or regional differences. The latter are seen as direct threats to the state itself. Consequently, attempts may be made to take these out of politics through the imposition of a single language in the first case, separating matters of Church and State in the second, and adopting regional equalization programmes in the third. Thus people can be safely left to organize along what are considered to be the rational dimensions of class and economic interests and discouraged from employing their 'primordial' feelings for like ends.

Speaking a particular language is also often closely related to expressing a certain nationality or identity. With change of language may come a shift in nationality or identity. In fact, there is a widespread belief that a shift in language often brings about a shift in identity and there may be resistance to adopting a new language because the new identity is unwelcome. Of course, the opposite can happen: the new language and the new identity may be actively promoted or pursued. On occasion people may go so far as to fear that taking words into their language from another language will weaken their identity and pose a threat to their continued existence. They may strive therefore to maintain the 'purity' of their language and keep it 'uncontaminated'. In contrast, still others may willingly learn a pidginized variety of a language or a lingua franca for the usefulness it will have in their lives and feel no identity crisis at all. The options available to individuals are many: English is resisted in Quebec because it is perceived to threaten French identity there; immigrants to the USA often willingly surrender the languages they bring with them in their quest for a new identity; the use of pidginized English in Nigeria and of Swahili in East Africa creates few problems of identity; and in Ireland there is only the most tenuous connection between the Irish language and identity, the Irish variety of an adopted language, English, having come to serve the Irish people quite well.

Today, states and groups within them deliberately promote languages and/or raise barriers to the diffusion of languages: they encourage the use of one language at the expense of another or others; they deliberately restrict the uses of one or more languages; they employ special alphabets or writing systems; and so on. They do all of these things in attempts to encourage the use of one language while discouraging the use of another or others, and a move to increase the dominance of one language may well be met with a move to try to ensure that the existing diversity remains. Furthermore, as we will see, not all the attention is given exclusively to their internal linguistic affairs. Modern states are not completely independent entities; the nature of the modern world requires of states a considerable interdependence and few are the states that have not recognized this fact. Therefore, most states are likely to feel the effects of decisions made in other states; and a decision made about language in one part of the world may have consequences in distant places. The modern world may not yet have become a 'global village', but certain events in it do not go unnoticed and certain kinds of language events have become particularly noticeable in the last several decades.

FACTORS IN SPREAD

Just as states are interdependent so are languages; they too influence one another. Languages expand and contract both within states and without. Many different factors influence such expansion and contraction; nor do these factors remain fixed. As we will see, factors including religious expansion, migration, economic policies, geographical isolation, urbanization, administrative convenience, and so on, all or separately or in some combination, can affect what happens to a particular language. The effect itself may be limited to a specific part of a state, or it may extend to the whole state, or it may be felt far beyond the bounds of a single state or even a single region of the world. As we look at how languages have spread or are spreading in various parts of the world, we will see that, as times and places change, so the factors responsible for the spread either change or relate differently to one another. However, the factors themselves seem to cluster into a few broad areas.

A necessary but apparently not sufficient condition for a language to spread is that there be the geographical opportunity for one language to spread into the domain of another language or other languages. There must be routes of some kind into the other. These can be the routes that rivers and seas provide or historic trade routes. They can also be the routes of migration and conquest, routes which also often have serious consequences for the movement of whole populations. Languages have spread and come to dominate new areas because of various invasions of Europe and Asia, the movements of populations in Africa, the 'opening' of new continents, and the establishment of patterns of trade in areas like the Mediterranean, Southeast Asia, the coasts of Africa, and, in recent decades, across the whole world but modified by an overriding political allegiance to either the 'East' or the 'West'. The Ancient Greeks spread their language through their colonization of the Mediterranean; their language went along with their trade, religion, and culture. In the nineteenth and twentieth century speakers of Amharic spread themselves through Ethiopia largely as a result of military conquest but it was the availability of road systems and towns on those systems that enabled them to spread their language and consolidate its position in the newly acquired domains.

Towns and cities are very important factors in achieving language dominance, particularly capital cities and trade and commercial centres. Towns tend to dominate the surrounding rural areas and their influence radiates out to those areas. They also become interconnected in the transportation systems that develop and achieve additional strength and influence from the resulting cross-fertilization. They become government, social, cultural, and economic centres. They attract people, particularly in the modern world where urbanization is an almost universal phenomenon. Cities are viewed as progressive and the countryside loses its attraction, particularly to the young and mobile. Consequently, it is in cities that languages come together, solutions are often found to problems of language diversity, and then these solutions held out as models to surrounding areas. We cannot ignore the influence of London in the United Kingdom or Paris in France as urban centres from out of which English and French were promoted. Nor must we fail to appreciate why the French of Quebec moved in the 1960s and 1970s to preserve Montreal as a French-speaking city and reverse the movement toward English there. Likewise, we can appreciate why the Welsh and Bretons view as disastrous the loss of towns in their midst, both big and small, to English and French respectively and why many Ukrainians deplore the fact that Kiev has become a Russian-speaking city. What happens in urban areas seems critically important to what eventually happens to a language: its ultimate prosperity, its holding its own, or its eventual demise.

Military conquest appears to be one of the most important factors in accounting for the spread of languages. It is often the 'motor' that drives a language along a particular route that is available to it. Latin, Greek, Arabic, and Turkish were all spread by military conquest. As Brosnahan (1963) has indicated, each of these languages was imposed over a particular area as a result of military conquest and, once imposed, maintained by force there for several centuries. Eventual survival of a language imposed in such a way may well depend on the linguistic characteristics of the area under control. If that area is multilingual in nature, then the imposed language may well take firm root: it is promoted as a necessary unifying force. That was certainly the case with Latin, Greek, and Arabic, but not entirely the case with Turkish in the Ottoman Empire for there serious competition came from other languages, particularly Arabic. We can contrast the above situation with that of French in England after the Norman Conquest or of Swedish in Finland; in each case an attempt was made to impose a new language in a monolingual area but the attempt eventually failed.

It is also instructive to compare how the French and English went about spreading their languages as they became involved in imperial adventures in the nineteenth and twentieth centuries. To the French an important part of their imperial misssion was the *mission civilisatrice*, (civilizing mission), the desire to create yellow, brown, and black French people having the same ideals and views as those of metropolitan France. At that time many people – not just the French themselves – gave a supremacy to French culture in the world; consequently, the French were determined that their language should be given a special place in their imperial possessions and that local languages, no matter what their historicity, were to be ignored or spurned. French colonies were to be regarded as parts of France in certain respects, even in some cases as *Départements d'Outre Mer* (Overseas Departments), e.g., Algeria. Still, today, many of the leaders of the post-colonial francophone world accept the validity of some of these claims about French linguistic and cultural preeminence; it is an important residue of earlier military conquest and one that continues to have a profound influence on what is happening to languages in various parts of the world, particularly in Africa.

In contrast, the British were much more pragmatic as they pursued their imperial ambitions. They spread English along with their empire but they did so for pragmatic reasons. They were also prepared to recognize the value of the various vernaculars in whatever primary education they supported. Nor was there the same dominance of the resulting empire from a central headquarters: London was not Paris. Local arrangements and compromises were possible. The English language was highly privileged, to be sure, but other roads to salvation were also available: you could remain Muslim, Hindu, Malay, or Chinese and use your native language and not necessarily feel pressured to be somehow British if you wanted to prosper in the colonial possessions themselves. In fact, the British did not want their colonial peoples to feel 'British'; it was enough that the British Empire should work and that the subject peoples should remain loyal to it. In the French Empire, however, you had to be prepared to assimilate to French ideals and culture through the medium of the French language if you wanted to prosper. But there was a key difference: once 'civilized' or 'evolved', you could prosper in France as well. Military conquest achieved different results in the two empires so far as language was concerned and much of the present-day spread of European languages in the continent of Africa can be explained as the lasting effects there of military conquest.

Military conquest is, of course, reversible and even when it appears not to be reversible there can be resistance that can last for centuries. Resistance is still apparent in such long-established political entities as the United Kingdom and France. English was spread throughout the British Isles to bring about a certain kind of cultural and national unity in the wake of military conquest and unification; in the same way French was spread deliberately within France. English and French were used to promote a national identity for those who found themselves within the areas ruled from London and Paris respectively. However, within both the United Kingdom and France we can see continued resistance to languages' being used to promote a feeling of national identity which is to supplant some other identity. For example, in Wales, Brittany, and Occitania, to cite just a few instances, there is considerable resistance to any further spread of the majority and dominant language of the country; many people still do not want to be 'included' with the majority, and for them the surviving minority language remains as a last, often somewhat token, defence against final, complete conquest.

Political control is the most direct result of military conquest. Language is an instrument of politics, and the state wields its influence through the choices that it makes in the language, or languages, of administration, law, the military, education, and so on. Benefits and inducements can be held out. In the Roman Empire a knowledge of Latin could lead to social and political preferment, to material rewards, and even to full citizenship with all the attendant rights and privileges. In the Greek Empire the great inducement to learn Greek was the opportunity such learning brought to enjoy the advantages of life in the flourishing business, social, and cultural Greek colonies of the Mediterranean. Undoubtedly in this process of hellenization the business advantages were a stronger factor than the cultural advantages for those who sought them: the latter probably followed the former for the few who also found such advantages attractive. Today, political ideas cross national boundaries even without the benefit of the kinds of imperial motives characteristic of previous eras. Contemporary neo-imperialism is of a different kind, as ideologies compete with one another and languages find themselves used as weapons of considerable importance in the world-wide competition for minds and power.

Religious factors can also be important in the spread and decline of a language: they can either help or hinder. For example, the spread of Islam has been an important factor in the spread of Arabic. As they spread their religion, the Arabs were able to absorb many different cultural characteristics and make them their own. However, concurrently, they spread Arabic as the unifying holy language, the key to their holy book, the Koran, and entry into Paradise. In like manner, the English and French languages were associated with the spread of Christianity, although once again perhaps not so strongly in the case of English as in the case of French. The English were much more willing than the French to use the vernacular languages they found for the saving of souls. Religion is also an important factor in the spread of Swahili in East Africa. It is also a factor that restricts to some extent any further spread of English in that continent: in sub-Saharan Africa, for example, the association of English with Christianity leads Muslims to resist English and encourages them to prefer either Arabic or Swahili. Likewise, the spread of Amharic has met with resistance in Ethiopia among the minority Muslim population, who regard it as an agency of Coptic Christianity. In the Roman Empire Greek was preserved well into the fourth century as a language of culture but a growing Christian Church came to oppose the 'paganism' of Greek and that opposition, along with the breakdown in the learning system caused by invasion and insurrection, led to the abandonment of that language. Sometimes the spread of language and the spread of religion are largely independent: when the Spanish colonized the Philippines they left their religion behind rather than their language, but with the French in the Maghreb it was their language rather than their religion that remained on their departure.

One aspect of language spread that has been frequently noted is the relationship between the spread of religions and the scripts in which various languages are written. Christianity has resulted in the use of romanized scripts for many disparate languages and the spread of the Islamic faith was accompanied by the spread of the Arabic script. The Hebrew script has been used not only for Hebrew but also for Yiddish and even at times for Spanish, Arabic, and Persian. The spread of religion can also bring about the adoption of different scripts for what is really the same language, e.g., for Serbian and Croatian, and for Hindi, Urdu, and Punjabi. Serbs and Croats understand each other's spoken words just as speakers of Hindi, Urdu, and Punjabi understand one another; however, each has a different script which reinforces the sense of using a different 'language'.

Historic factors are not unimportant. Languages can have historical and cultural prestige. They can even be endowed, sometimes retrospectively, with such characteristics during the process of an attempt at 'revival'. The classical varieties of Latin and Greek still have prestige in the Western world. Arabic is a language of prestige in many parts of the world because of its strong religious affiliation and its undoubted past glories. English and French are both languages of prestige almost everywhere, but the French often worry that English appears to have eclipsed their language and constantly seek ways to preserve what influence it still has in the world. Minorities who see their languages threatened tend to claim what they regard as historic rights to their tongues and often point to past glories in justification.

However, the prestige, historical or contemporary, local, national, or international, that a particular language or variety of a language enjoys cannot account for its spread in all instances. There are too many counter-examples, whether they are the persistence of local varieties of French, e.g., of Joual in Quebec or of Creole in Haiti, or of nonstandard vernaculars throughout the English-speaking and French-speaking worlds, but particularly where the languages are most 'native', i.e., in the British Isles and in France. Prestige is an important factor in the spread of standard languages such as English and French, but on occasion other factors prove to be more influential in determining what exactly happens to this or that language or variety. Swahili has considerably less prestige than English in East Africa but it seems currently to possess possibilities for expansion there that English lacks.

Economic factors are obviously very important in influencing how languages come to relate to one another. The internal economic development of a country may well involve shifts in the internal linguistic balance so that one or more languages are advantaged at the expense of others. Likewise, the economic arrangements of empires, of trading blocks such as preference systems and common markets, and of countries or areas that prefer 'to go it alone', will have linguistic consequences. Currently the English language is associated with an economic system and patterns of trade, banking, and finance that have spread throughout vast areas of the world. In comparison, French has a much more limited use in the world's economy. We can also observe that the language of a very strong trading nation like Japan spreads minimally beyond the boundaries of Japan, so economic power alone does not appear to provide sufficient leverage to spread a language. The Japanese are forced to learn other languages in order to trade with the rest of the world: they speak Arabic when they deal in the Middle East and they speak Spanish in South America, or they speak English, the growing lingua franca of international trade, just as they do in their trade dealings with the anglophone world.

Among the many factors that must be considered in accounting for the spread of languages one usually gets very little mention: Are some languages inherently more suited to spread than others? Are some at more risk than others because they are easily superseded linguistically if a 'better' language comes along to compete? Linguists are in general agreement that all languages are equally serviceable for all purposes and that no language is inherently 'better' or 'worse' than any other language. They would argue that whether or not a particular language 'lives' or 'dies' has nothing to do with its inherent viability. Only in the final stages of dying does a language cease to be a viable medium but these stages are reached for reasons that are not linguistic in nature. It is such factors as those mentioned above that operate in determining what is to be the ultimate fate of a language. If Bahasa Indonesia eventually spreads throughout Indonesia and its principal victim is Javanese, Javanese will not have been superseded because it is inherently an inadequate language for the affairs of a modernizing state, even with its complex levels of styles and honorifics. It will have been superseded because of the promotion of Bahasa Indonesia and the opportunities that accrue from learning the new national language rather than the language of what is still the major ethnic group in the country. This fact that all languages are equally capable of being developed to meet any needs for which they might be required is a painful one to confront for those who find their languages being forced to give way to others. They know that what is happening is that opportunities are being denied them to use their languages in every sphere of activity and, as these opportunities continue to be denied, the languages become more and more precarious and less and less viable. Nor is it very long before a point of no return is reached and the task of revival really becomes quite hopeless.

A factor that is gaining more and more attention because of its relation to the spread of not only languages but also the influence and dependency that goes along with the choice of a particular language is that of neo-colonialism: the persistence of old colonial ties and dependencies long after the dissolution of the empires that created them. Many nations are still tied to their old colonial masters. Most attention has been devoted to the arrangements that superseded the collapse of the British and French Empires but other countries too find themselves in similar arrangements with former dependencies or new ones – countries as different as Portugal, the United States, and the Soviet Union. Neo-colonial ties lead to the continuation of certain kinds of linguistic influence and to new pressures.

Languages such as English and French are now supported in former colonial possessions by élites who have been schooled in those languages. These élites have often become quite westernized during that schooling and many individuals have come to accept what they have been taught about the 'superiority' of European languages. The old colonial languages often still dominate the educational systems of these states, systems themselves that are often quite inappropriate to their real needs. The state bureaucracies also often continue to use the languages to the extent that they often seem to be quite remote from the people they are supposed to serve. There is as well a dependence on the old colonial languages in science and technology, in banking and trade, and so on. The results are quite predictable: the old colonial languages remain the languages of prestige and power, of mobility and opportunity, and of privilege. Much of the indigenous book publication in anglophone and francophone Africa is still in English and French respectively even though only small minorities may be literate in either language. A like situation prevails in India where, although only about two per cent of the population is literate in English, half the books published there are published in that language. Moreover, the old colonial masters continue to promote and encourage this situation: an estimated 80 per cent of the United Kingdom's foreign aid goes to former dependencies and

France's proportion of 90 per cent exceeds even that.

Africa is the key continent so far as neo-colonialism is concerned and the situation in which the colonial powers left Africa is likely to have profound consequences for how languages will arrange themselves there. Most modern African states lack coherent boundaries: with very few exceptions they are usually neither historical states, nor states with natural geographic frontiers, nor states defined by a common ethnicity, religion, language, or culture. Nearly all are considerably mixed so far as these last factors are concerned and each to some extent shares common characteristics with one or more others: one or more colonial languages, common ethnic groups, religions, indigenous languages, cultures, and so on. African states are almost never nation-states so the factors affecting how languages are to relate to one another in Africa, both within particular states and among various states, are likely to be quite different from those that operate in certain other parts of the world where language and nation or state are much more closely equated and where linguistic unity and national identity are regarded as primary symbols of statehood.

When leaders of African states seek to intervene in linguistic matters, they find themselves confronted with very serious choices. Should they maintain the precarious status quo with all the drawbacks to internal equity that such a decision, or failure to find an alternative solution, has as its consequences? Or is there a language of historic importance in the state that can be modernized and spread? Or should one or more of the indigenous languages be developed and given some preferred status? Or should preference be accorded to a widespread second language, one possibly used in trade, but not necessarily a European language, although possibly a pidgin or creole derived from a such a language? These are some of the possible choices that are available. Each choice has its own attendant problems and no choice is likely to be uncontroversial, being sure to advantage some in the state and disadvantage others. Each choice too will affect the future of the various languages that are found in the state.

Lieberson (1982) has made an important observation about language spread: he claims that the factors that cause a language to spread initially are not necessarily those that maintain the way the language continues to spread. Military conquest can be responsible for the first spread of a language but that language may continue to win converts long after the days of military domination have come to an end. We can easily see how such is the case with English: one important factor in the spread of English in the nineteenth century was the rapid expansion of the British Empire. But the twentieth century saw an even more rapid change of that Empire into a Commonwealth. British domination ceased so far as political matters were concerned. But by the time political domination ceased English had become the language of another superpower, the United States, and international trade and finance and much scientific and technological development had become heavily dependent on the English language. Consequently, the need for English shifted from a need to use it for the affairs of empire to uses in international trade and relationships and in scientific and technological endeavours. Likewise, the influences of languages such as Greek and Latin remained long after the circumstances that brought about their initial spread – Greek, for example, lasting for centuries within the Roman Empire as a language of culture.

It is possible to make much of the fact that a language such as English spreads because of its vast vocabulary and its widespread use in science and technology. However, this may be but a temporary advantage, for in principle any other language is quite capable of the same development: Arabic was once a language of science just as French was once the language of international diplomacy. It is conceivable that some language other than English could take on functions which would, for a while perhaps, seem in some way to be universally desirable so hastening its spread and resulting in the decline of English. However, such a possibility would appear in the late twentieth century to require some kind of political or natural catastrophe to bring it about.

One factor that is apparently very important in accounting for why one language spreads in certain circumstances whereas another does not in similar circumstances has to do with the attitudes of the speakers of the two languages: how they perceive others as potential speakers of their languages. The French are very possessive of their language. They do not approve of its being spoken in any but its most 'correct' form, the form it takes in metropolitan France, and even speakers of French from Quebec are likely to find themselves patronized for the way they speak the language when they have occasion to visit France. Speakers of English are much more accepting of differences in the ways in which English is spoken and used in the world. They are not as possessive of their language as the French. Of course, part of this different attitude has resulted from the profound shift over the past two centuries in where the main groups of English speakers are located as the centre of the English-speaking world has moved dramatically westward across the Atlantic. But it is also the consequence of a much weaker equation in the English-speaking world of language to culture. For the French the equation of language to culture is an important cornerstone of language policy. However, such a policy is not without its dangers and may contain within it the seeds of its own destruction: a refusal to accept one may lead to a refusal to accept the other. We can contrast this situation with English: since no cultural requirements are tied to the learning of English, you can learn it and use it without having to subscribe to another set of values. English, therefore, seems more 'open' to the acquisition of new speakers than French.

The 'openness' of languages to expansion has at least one further dimension. Very localized languages like Basque or Icelandic seem to be quite without the means of expansion. Basque is actually severely threatened through Icelandic is fairly secure in its isolation, at least for the foreseeable future. But even a language like Japanese, in spite of the recent industrial success of Japan, has shown little tendency to diffuse and little or no 'openness' to the world. Arabic, a major world language, is closely connected with Islam but its further diffusion would seem to depend largely on a new surge of that faith. English is the least localized of all the languages in the world today. Spoken almost everywhere in the world to some degree, and tied to no particular social, political, economic, or religious system, nor to a specific racial or cultural group, English belongs to everyone or to no one, or it at least is quite often regarded as having this property.

In its openness English today somewhat resembles Latin in the Ancient and Medieval World. Latin persisted for a long time because it became everyone's language, that is, every educated person's language, and its influence lasted long after that of the Roman Empire itself. Latin was associated with learning, with Christianity, with a system of laws, and with its ability to adapt to the conditions with which it was faced. It ceased for these uses only when people began to put local needs ahead of more universal ones. Then the very openness of Latin had to be resisted.

Because a language is 'open', it becomes more readily available to potential speakers than a language that does not have this characteristic. But there are other kinds of availability too. As Lieberson has pointed out (1982), an important factor in any competition between languages to gain new speakers is the position taken by 'third parties'. In the nineteenth century and early twentieth century, French was the favoured language of international diplomacy, but English kept on gaining in head-to-head competition. However, third parties whose languages were neither English nor French continued to favour French: hence its continued use in peace treaties, e.g., the Treaty of Versailles of 1919, although on this occasion, largely because of the presence of the United States at the peace table, only as one of two equal languages, the other being English. Third-party nations also preferred to employ French in such agencies as the League of Nations, in internationally distributed documents, such as census reporting, and at international conferences. It was not until World War II that French experienced a profound decline in such functions. Third parties shifted their linguistic choices as the geopolitical nature of the world shifted. English became the predominant third-party choice as the language of trade, of science and technology, and of international banking and finance. It was not until the French colonies achieved independence that French regained some of the influence it had lost, in the United Nations for example.

The ability to capture speakers as a language of wider communication is important for many languages: it is important for Swahili and for Bahasa Indonesia, and the future of India could depend on Hindi's success or failure in this regard. Conversely, it is why the spread of Russian often meets with resistance in the Soviet Union and why almost everywhere those who are concerned with the maintenance of minority languages regard bilingualism in a minority language and the advancing majority language as a threat to the ultimate survival of that minority language.

Trying to account for the rise and fall of a particular language is a complicated matter. Attempting to predict the future may also be equally foolhardy. It is simply not possible to devise some kind of mechanical formula that takes into account all the factors affecting how languages prosper and decline and use it to predict trends. We do not know precisely why Aramaic spread as widely as it did in ancient times nor do we understand all the factors in the spread of Ancient Greek or Celtic or even Latin: each started to spread and then seemed to continue under its own momentum. But we can say the same of both Arabic and English: they too seem almost to have taken on lives of their own in their spread. It sometimes seems almost as though certain languages acquire speakers rather than that certain speakers acquire languages – quite the opposite of the conventional wisdom in the matter!

Most language spread is unplanned and this may still be largely the case even when states directly involve themselves in language matters, for example, in language-planning activities. Many of the factors affecting what happens to this language or that may be well beyond the control of all but the most wealthy and/or autocratic governments. Laws may be passed, sanctions may be employed, and various agencies and reinforcing systems may be established. However, as just indicated, a spreading language seems to have a dynamic all of its own and many such moves may do little or nothing to alter that dynamic. For example, it is a matter of considerable controversy in Canada just what effect nearly two decades of federal government policy and direct intervention have had in stemming the decline of French outside Quebec. Just how far it is possible for a state to 'plan' the spread of one language rather than another, maintain the linguistic status quo, or reverse the fortunes of a declining language are important issues. They are also issues that emotion and ideology soon cloud, and therefore do not lend themselves easily to rational discussion.

PERSONAL NEEDS AND USES

Languages exist to meet the needs of humans to communicate with one another. A new language is acquired to meet new needs just as an old language is lost because it appears to have lost any real usefulness. Usually the new needs are instrumental: the language offers those who would acquire it certain advantages of some kind: political, social, cultural, educational, religious, etc. A language flourishes when it appears to convey advantages on those who learn it; it decays when it seems to offer only disadvantages. The language policy of a state can obviously be directed to increasing advantages or decreasing disadvantages for individuals and/or groups but in the long run it is each individual who must decide for himself or herself what to do. Furthermore, such decisions are likely to be affected by factors other than particular state decrees concerning language policy, artificial reward systems, or even certain kinds of sanctions.

When speakers of different languages come into contact with one another, there is always the likelihood that one language will spread at the expense of others. Indeed, it is possible to argue that this is more than a likelihood, that it is a certainty. Multilingual situations may be inherently unstable. If this is so, and if language contact is the inevitable consequence of a world filled with different languages, then there will be an ebb and flow in the fortunes of individual languages. When language contact is minimal because a language boundary is supported by some other strong boundary, e.g., a territorial, religious, ethnic, political, or even functional boundary, as in a diglossic situation (i.e., when two languages coexist within a group but each serves quite different functions), there may be little pressure from one language on the other or others. However, when such boundaries are weak, the languages will not only be in contact they will also be in competition. As one gains territory, speakers, or functions, all others lose. Bilingualism may not be a real choice in such circumstances; it may be no more than a temporary expedient, a somewhat marginal phenomenon, because when one language encroaches on another, bilingualism may prove to be only a temporary waystage to unilingualism in the encroaching language as the latter assumes more and more functions and is acquired as the sole language by greater numbers of speakers. English has spread as rapidly as it has in the world because in the final analysis individuals in a wide variety of places and circumstances find some advantage in learning some English and have the opportunity to do so. This principle also accounts for the learning of certain other languages, e.g., Swahili in East Africa and Pidgin English in West Africa.

The social needs of speakers for particular languages are especially important. According to Lewis (1982), there are four types of social factors that tend to have consequences for language spread. The first is the attitudes that people adopt to both the threatened and the threatening languages. The second concerns the relationships among the speakers of the various languages: their geographical relationship, their historical relationship, and the consequences that seem to follow from these. The third is a cluster of factors subsumed under the concept of 'modernization': economic, demographic, educational, mobility, and so on. The fourth is entirely ideological, factors having to do with cultural, political, and religious beliefs, and how these affect the languages that come into contact with one another. Singly and in combination these types of factors considerably influence why individuals will choose to give up one language in preference to another, or resist 'to the death' a new language, or try to effect some kind of accommodation.

When a language does spread, it spreads either horizontally in a society or vertically. When it spreads horizontally only a certain segment of the society uses it: for example, French in Imperial Russia among the upper classes; Swahili among traders and merchants in East Africa; and English or French as the languages of élites in former imperial possessions. Vertical spread apparently requires considerable social integration so that the language can spread throughout the whole society. Vertical spread is also absolutely essential if all segments of society are to be unified under a single language. English and French are now vertically spread in countries like the United Kingdom and France in contrast to Kenya and Haiti. Insofar as educational systems are made to serve all segments of society they become powerful agencies of vertical language spread. They are also effective to the extent that educational policies reinforce social realities: if learning the promoted language really provides access to opportunities that would otherwise be denied, then such learning is reinforced, e.g., the learning of English in Singapore; if, on the other hand, such learning leads nowhere, the results of education are likely to be meagre, e.g., the teaching of French in Haiti. Most African countries face serious problems in the vertical integration of their societies and some of the difficulties arise from the roles that English and French fill in their educational systems, roles that sometimes block social integration.

Languages acquire new users not only through natural population increase or the drastic language shifts that occur when people choose to abandon one language in favour of another but also through speakers using a language for either a new function (e.g., literacy, religion, or scholarship) or replacing one language with another for a specific function (e.g., trade and commerce). In the history of the English language within Britain we can see a gradual spread of the language into law and religion where it replaced French and Latin. Today, while English is undoubtedly the principal language of science and technology in the world, at the same time it is being replaced – or at least serious attempts at replacement are being made – for scientific use in countries as diverse as Malaysia, India, the USSR, and Israel.

LANGUAGE DECLINE

While some languages prosper, others experience decline and fall. The signs of such decline and fall are many. Edwards (1985, pp. 71–2) has listed a number to which a few more may be added. A declining language loses its territorial base and is spoken by fewer and fewer monolinguals. Those who speak it become bilingual, finding that they must acquire the language that is beginning to dominate. That bilingual population also becomes increasingly an aging population. The dominant language intrudes into more and more domains of life and assumes more and more functions. The dominated language is less and less used and is finally threatened as the language of the home itself. Diglossia may prevail for a time with each language having clearly marked domains of usage but, unless that diglossia is stable, the dominant language will continue its advance.

A declining language is also likely to have a rural base only and to lack strength in towns and cities. It may be associated with emigration and other forms of population dispersion. It is also likely to have strong associations with older, uneducated, and rural speakers and lack those of progress and modernity. Men and women may have different uses for a declining language: it is not uncommon to find that women have less use for such a language than men and so have less favourable attitudes toward its preservation. However, this phenomenon is by no means universal and may indeed be associated with the kinds of opportunities that are available to young people in different societies.

A society experiencing a linguistic decline is also likely to be experiencing a concurrent decline in other areas, e,g., social, political, and economic. It may not be able to focus its attention on linguistic matters alone: in fact, it is likely that other matters will seem to be more urgent, at least to the majority. Cultural activities are much more likely to survive than linguistic ones. Again, the language of various cultural activities may be replaced by the dominant language so that even folk festivals may come to be organized and conducted in an alien idiom. Language traditions will be lost and writing and literacy will be abandoned.

There may be an increase for a while in the numbers of 'secondary bilinguals', those who deliberately seek to preserve or revive the language. Linguistic and cultural entrepreneurs are likely to try to make a public case for changes they believe to be necessary if the threatened language is to regain its past glories. However, there is likely to be only minority support for their views within the affected group and the majority will be largely indifferent. In all of this latter activity the various media may play a somewhat ambivalent role.

Finally, there are clear linguistic signs that a language is in serious trouble. It is spoken 'badly', i.e., the people who use it know they have an unsure grasp of the language and lack confidence in their abilities because they have no strong sense of what is right and wrong in their usage. Such linguistic insecurity among speakers is a strong indicator that a language is in sharp decline. Extensive borrowing from the encroaching language may also be evident, borrowing into various parts of the language – into the phonology, morphology, vocabulary, and syntax. In ultimate decline only a kind of pidginized version of the language may survive for a while, speakers being able to remember only a few words or phrases here and there but without having any sense about where or when a particular utterance is appropriate.

Ultimately, a language may be lost but such loss does not mean inevitably that the group that used it has lost its identity although such loss of identity often does follow. There is little doubt that the Irish have lost their language but no one would maintain that Irish people have lost their sense of Irishness. The Welsh too are losing their language but they are still quite clearly not English. Basques, the majority of whom no longer speak Basque, are definitely not Spaniards much to the regret of the Spanish state. And Jews are Jews no matter what language they speak. It is not therefore inevitable that identity is lost when language is lost, but many people believe that some part of their identity does disappear in such circumstances. That is why it is sometimes possible to organize them to resist a language that for one reason or another is assuming a dominant position over the language they speak so that they might preserve this aspect of their heritage.

FURTHER READING

General discussions of some of the issues treated in this book: Edwards 1985, Fasold 1984, Leclerc, 1986, Weinstein 1983; language spread and conflict: Cooper 1982, Deutsch 1975, Haugen 1966; languages in contact: Weinreich 1966; multilingual states: Beer and Jacob 1985, Fishman 1972a, 1978, Fishman et al. 1968, Laponce 1984, Savard and Vigneault 1975, Touret 1973; language and colonialism: Calvet 1974, Hechter 1975; vehicular languages: Calvet 1981; language decline: Dorian 1981, Kahane and Kahane 1979; language planning: Cobarrubias and Fishman 1983, Eastman 1983, Fishman 1974, Fishman et al. 1968, Kennedy 1983, Rubin and Jernudd 1971, 1979, Rubin et al. 1977, Rubin and Shuy 1973.

2

Language Diversity

A fundamental problem that exists in the modern world is the imbalance between the number of languages that are spoken and the number of autonomous states. There are difficulties in defining what constitutes a language but, as we indicated in the previous chapter, even the most conservative estimate would put the number of different languages spoken in the world at over 4,000. Counting states is much easier although areas of disagreement undoubtedly exist. (Is the United States one state or fifty states?) However, the number is not likely to range very far beyond the 160 or so represented in the United Nations. Languages are also much more fluid entities than states. The boundaries of states tend to remain fixed until they are upset through strife, but today even strife does not tend to change state boundaries, modern states apparently being reluctant to support or approve boundary changes proposed elsewhere that arise from either conquest or a desire for separate status based on linguistic or cultural differences. It is as though they fear the possible consequences of recognizing such a principle so far as their own well-being and internal stability are concerned. When we look at the internal linguistic composition of the vast majority of states, such a fear is not surprising, for it is the exception rather than the rule in the world to find a state in which language does not have some potential for disrupting whatever internal harmony that exists.

INTERNAL DIVERSITY

The modern state is involved extensively in such matters as the economy, education, security, planning, employment, government services, culture, etc. Consequently, it is not surprising that language matters often become important too and end up 'politicized' when they might not have become so in 'simpler' times. Most states are linguistically diverse and find it difficult to achieve linguistic harmony. If such harmony is once ever achieved, it must also be constantly protected. Languages are also not fixed entities so far as their distribution in society is concerned and the arrangements that have been made for them. As Lieberson (1981, p. 11) has indicated, they are constantly expanding or contracting in relation to one another because of the 'constant flux and shift in such relevant conditions as the birth rate, immigration and emigration, the economy, the areal distribution and concentration of populations, technology, changes in the needs of the labor force, and levels of educational achievement'. Many states have been unable to achieve internal linguistic harmony and have experienced very serious internal linguistic tensions, some to the extent that observers question from time to time their long-term viability as states if no better solutions are found than those that currently exist.

States in which more than 90 per cent of the population speak the sole official language are very few indeed: they include both East and West Germany, Bangladesh, the Dominican Republic, Portugal, Iceland, Japan, North and South Korea, Tunisia, and Austria. Such states as the United Kingdom, the United States, China, and France may also be included in this category; however, many people might contest this inclusion. They would argue that 90 per cent of the population of each of these states can be said to speak the language only if some violence is done either to the definition of language, as in China, or to the language preferences of many people, as in the other cases cited. There are many states in which far fewer than half the people speak the official state language or one of the official languages, e.g., Ghana, Haiti, Indonesia, Nigeria, Tanzania, Uganda, Senegal, and India. Most states fall in the middle somewhere, e.g., the Soviet Union, Spain, Vietnam, Morocco, Yugoslavia, and Malaysia.

In Africa, in particular, it is unusual to find a state in which the vast majority of the people can communicate using a single language. Somalia and Burundi are almost completely homogeneous linguistically and therefore notable exceptions to the general rule. However, in choosing a language to promote, the governments of these two countries have made quite different types of choices. The Somalis have chosen to promote Somali, a highly standardized language, and one for which there is a tradition of use in education. Consequently, Somali is used almost universally in primary and secondary education, and it is only at the highest levels that English, and, to some extent, Italian are used. Burundi, equally homogeneous, with Kirundi the mother tongue of 95 per cent of the population, has chosen French as the official language of administration and education because Kirundi is not standardized nor does it appear to offer the advantages that French seems to offer those who are prepared to learn French. Both French and Kirundi are official languages but it is Kirundi that everyone speaks. In neither country is there a significant linguistic minority but there is the potential in Burundi of a split, possibly along class lines, between those who become proficient in French and those who do not; and therefore there is the potential for creating a 'linguistic minority', although which group will comprise this minority – those who speak French or those who do not – may be an arguable point.

Rustow (1975) estimates that only two-thirds of the states currently recognized in the world have a language common to the majority of their population. It is also rarely the case that there is an identity of language and state, i.e., that the vast majority of those who speak a particular language also find themselves living together in one state which contains insignificant numbers of speakers of another language or other languages. Rustow cites only seven examples: Hungary, Iceland, Japan, Malagasy, Malta, Thailand, and Turkey. Nationalist feelings are therefore likely to be thwarted in many different parts of the world and language used as a symbol of such feelings because of its potency. Language is often regarded as a key component in national identity, and, if, as the Italian patriot Mazzini proclaimed, 'Nationalities are sacred and providentially constituted', language will almost certainly be pushed to the fore in a minority group's struggle against the majority.

Some states have tried to accommodate to the fact that two or more languages are widely used within their borders by declaring themselves to be officially bilingual or even multilingual. Such declarations have different degrees of force so far as actual language use is concerned. Are all government services provided in both, or all, languages? Which language or languages are used at the highest levels of government, e.g., at cabinet meetings? What is the language used on passports and postage stamps? The answers will be various, and it will be rare indeed to find a state in which bilingualism is not only policy but also actual practice so that the languages are indeed equal in all respects. One or more linguistic groups in such states are likely to consider themselves to be discriminated against. Even the very complex arrangements that states such as Switzerland and Yugoslavia have made to eliminate or reduce such feelings are likely to appear to be inadequate from time to time. Belgium and Canada are even more obvious examples.

The above discussion introduced the notion of various percentages of a population speaking this or that language. While it is a fact that quite often certain people who live within a particular state cannot or do not communicate with one another because language gets in the way, it may not be at all easy to discover what precisely is the language problem or determine its extent. Whether or not people feel that they speak the same language as certain others may have very little to do with whether there is some degree of mutual intelligibility. Hindi, Urdu, and Punjabi are mutually intelligible just as are Serbian and Croatian, Czech and Slovak, Russian and Ukrainian, and Norwegian, Danish, and Swedish. However, depending on the person asked and the context of the asking, you may receive an opinion on one or more of the above which runs contrary to the facts just stated. At the opposite extreme almost all Chinese will insist that Cantonese and Mandarin are just two 'dialects' of Chinese even though they will readily admit that Cantonese monolinguals and Mandarin monolinguals cannot converse with one another. As we will see, claims about language rights will be based repeatedly on this issue of the 'separate' nature of the speech of a particular group, but others may well deny those same claims.

Statistics on language use within particular countries are also often not very reliable even when they are available. Some countries, such as Belgium and Pakistan, prefer not to collect statistics on language use through the usual census instruments: language issues are just too controversial in both cases. In countries like France and Spain there is similar neglect, for in each the central authority has long assumed the state to be unilingual. The figures produced from time to time also depend on the kinds of questions that are asked and the ways in which the responses are recorded. The Soviet Academy of Sciences, for example, identifies people as being speakers of Karelian, Moldavian, or Tadzhik rather than of Finnish, Romanian, or Persian. The Swiss census allows for only a single response to the 'mother tongue' question – you cannot claim both German and Romansch as mother tongues but must choose one only. The question concerning knowledge of Irish on the Irish census, with its failure to distinguish between knowledge gained as a native speaker and knowledge gained through compulsory schooling, is so loose that up to 20 per cent of the population claim knowledge of Irish; however, there is good reason to believe that far fewer than 3 per cent of the population actually use Irish in daily life. The figures from India for those who speak Hindi have varied according to the ways in which particular censuses have been conducted and the concurrent linguistic controversies in the country as a whole. Even a country such as Canada with its long history of asking about languages in its decennial censuses has had problems with the questions asked about languages spoken, known, etc. and the interpretations given to the answers. Most recently, Canadians have been asked about their 'bilingualism' in the two official languages, English and French, but no guidance has been given as to what constitutes 'bilingualism'. It may not be surprising therefore that recent figures seem to show some increase in such self-declared bilingualism in an era in which 'being bilingual' has become a desirable self-categorization.

It is for reasons such as those just given that we often find wide discrepancies in the numbers of people who are said to be speakers of this or that minority language. How many people speak Breton in France? Is it less than half a million or more than a million? And what about Occitan? Fewer than a million or many millions? Even when good census data are available, as in Wales or Canada, there will be disageement about what particular figures mean. However, what we can be sure of is that in just about every dispute one party to it will have an interest in minimizing the number of people who speak the minority language and the other party will try to do the opposite, or that numbers will be involved in some other way, for example to show a decline in the minority language or, much more rarely, a revival.

INTERNAL DISCONTENT

It is usually around the issue of ethnonationalism that a minority unites over its language. Throughout the world the late twentieth century has witnessed state after state being attacked from within by minorities who seek some redistribution of the powers of the state or, in some cases, complete separation from the state. *Ethnonationalism* is but one of the terms that have been used to describe this phenomenon; others are the *ethnic revival* and the *new tribalism*. As Shiels (1984, p. 1) has written, 'Secession and autonomy movements are rife, respect for linguistic and educational local control demanded; bombs are being hurled at government officials and state offices barricaded.' What is particularly puzzling is that the phenomenon has occurred so universally. It is not associated only with 'developing nations' or with people who are obviously severely disadvantaged in any one of a variety of ways that are easy to understand, e.g., politically, economically, socially, or religiously. On the contrary, it is a phenomenon that finds some of its strongest manifestations on both sides of the North Atlantic, possibly the richest and most modernized part of the world. Modernization and development themselves may indeed have promoted the feeling as they brought people into contact with one another and differences that had been unobserved for centuries gradually revealed themselves and took on significance.

It is certainly not the case that economic disadvantage alone is the cause of ethnic discontent. The Basques and Catalans of Spain are economically better off than the Castilians, and the Croats of Yugoslavia are better off than the Serbs. Moreover, there is plenty of evidence from such places as Wales, the Soviet Union, and Brittany that moves to increase economic well-being may be resisted by the potential beneficiaries themselves if the price appears to be a further dilution of linguistic ability and ethnic identity among a minority. We must admit too that in some cases language itself is not as strong a factor as it might be in the struggle of a minority group to challenge the existing status quo: the Scots, Welsh, and Basques exhibit different degrees of indifference on this matter.

However, a challenge, successful or not, by a group in one place encourages a group somewhere else to make a similar challenge. As Connor (1977, p. 30) has observed, 'Each claim to national self-determination has tended to trigger still others.' Connor calls this the 'demonstration effect'. He adds that in any relationship between a majority group and a minority group, the intensity of that effect will be felt to vary according to such factors as the time involved, the proximity of the groups to one another, the comparability of size of population and territorial extent, the myths involving ancestral relationships, and whether or not the two groups were once ruled from the same capital. As an example he cites the relevance of Irish independence to the Scots and Welsh: the latter may feel that they have just as good a case for independence as the former.

Claims to the right of self-determination are strongly resisted by the world of nations: they are just too threatening. While the Charter of the United Nations recognizes such a right, it does little or nothing to allow for its exercise. That this is the case is easily seen in the way in which the various African states became members of the United Nations. Heterogeneous colonial entities became 'nations' overnight without regard to their ethnic or linguistic composition and the few attempts to change boundaries through secession were resisted. The earlier League of Nations took a different view of its role toward ethnic and national groups: it was their protector. However, in that role also lay some of the seeds of the League's eventual destruction.

One interesting consequence of the way states view linguistic and ethnic conflicts within state boundaries is that they usually do not allow such internal conflicts to become major sources of conflict among states themselves. This is not to say that internal conflicts are not carried beyond the boundaries of states. They certainly are, as when Greeks and Turks quarrel over Cypriot affairs, or the Lebanese conflict spills over into the outside world, or Sikhs protest against Indian actions in the streets of Vancouver. However, such spill-overs are usually carefully contained. What does *not* happen is that the United Nations gets involved or even individual states in any formal way. Any involvement is likely to be indirect – a state offering refuge to malcontents from another state or some kind of outpost from which to pursue activities that would be illegal in the home state – or to emanate from sympathizers within the state, particularly ethnic kin.

ASSIMILATION AND PLURALISM

The majority of states pursue a policy of linguistic and cultural assimilation of minorities within their borders while observing the convention that one state should not interfere in the internal affairs of others, at least not directly. The result is conflict of another kind. Such conflict arises from two opposing trends in the modern world: the trend toward larger organizations, cooperation, and assimilation and the trend toward separatism, competition, and differentiation. Consequently, in Europe we can observe the development of the European Economic Community (EEC) and the rise of Basque violence; in the world in general there is the issue of free trade versus protectionism; and in countries like the United Kingdom, the United States, Australia, and Canada there is serious discussion of the linguistic and cultural policies that should prevail for those who speak languages other than English.

Among the terms used above one in particular, *assimilation*, arouses considerable feeling whenever minority languages are discussed and such feeling is almost always entirely negative. To those who seek to preserve minority lanuages there can be nothing of value in policies that tend to bring about any kind of assimilation. They insist that assimilation must be resisted and propose instead policies which fall under another term, *pluralism*. For them it is quite simply 'Pluralism good, assimilation bad', and there can be no argument.

Pluralism is part of a general movement in the world against many of the characteristics of modern society that do not seem to benefit individuals or groups seeking to be different in some way. The homogenization and drive to uniformity that are so characteristic of the modern state are regarded as threats to personal and group identity. The result is that people often experience a sense of depersonalization sometimes accompanied by a feeling of uprootedness, and all the state appears to offer is coercion to its authority in the name of loyalty together with a very doubtful security.

In the struggle against the state, language can become an important defence against assimilative pressures. The 'health' of a language can also be used as some kind of gauge of the assimilation of those who use it. This is why it is so important to know how a minority language is faring at any time and what measures are being taken to keep it alive. Assimilation is almost certainly an irreversible process just as is language loss. When one group merges into another, it has lost its identity forever, and when one language is given up for another, it is lost to those who might have spoken it in following generations. Minority groups are therefore interested in such matters as who speaks what languages, the extent of bilingualism, the rights enjoyed by the speakers of the various languages, the amount of government support given to the teaching of languages, and the attitudes toward languages of the various interested parties.

A pair of examples will show how important are such factors. In the late nineteenth century the Hungarian part of the Austro-Hungarian Empire pursed a policy of magyarization, a policy designed to reduce the influence of German and increase that of Hungarian. Budapest was the key city. If we look at the census figures for the period between 1857 and 1920 we can see how successful that policy was. Between 1857 and 1920 the German-speaking linguistic group in Budapest fell from 56.0 per cent to 6.5 per cent and the Hungarian-speaking group rose from 36.0 per cent to 90.2 per cent. The figures for bilingualism also clearly reveal the process that was at work: German speakers became more and more bilingual in German and Hungarian, the percentage rising from 40.6 per cent in 1880 to 70.7 per cent in 1900, whereas Hungarian speakers became less so, the percentage falling from 71.7 per cent in 1880 to 53.1 per cent in 1900. Bilingualism serves as a clear indicator of assimilation in both cases.

The second example concerns Brussels. Although this city is located in what is historically the Dutch-speaking part of Belgium, its unilingual Dutch population had fallen to 7.2 per cent by 1947 whereas its unilingual French population had risen to 40 per cent in the same year. Moreover, the bilinguals of the city of Dutch origin were switching more and more to French in their daily lives. Their children were also becoming speakers of French and abandoning Dutch. Since the Dutch are actually a numerical majority in Belgium, it should not be surprising that language is such a potent issue in the country and that Brussels has become the focal point of linguistic disputes there. Here again we can see a direct confrontation between what appear to be strong assimilative forces and the efforts of those who resist these forces in the name of preserving a particular personal identity, or a piece of territory, or another way of life, and definitely a threatened language.

MINORITY LANGUAGES

It is this notion that a particular language is threatened that is basic to its categorization as a *minority language* and its speakers as a *linguistic minority*, two terms which have been used to this point but which now deserve fuller attention. Languages emerge and disappear as part of larger historical processes. Some disappear without struggle. It is those for whom their speakers struggle against the odds that we might want to call minority languages. In this sense minority languages come into existence when their speakers use them to express their identity as a group, an identity which may be tied concurrently to feelings about a shared racial origin or to a desire to attach themselves to a particular place, religion, or way of life. There must also be a recognition that there is some other group – or other groups – that the speakers of the language want to unite against if they are not to be submerged, possibly numerically, culturally, politically, and so on, but most certainly linguistically.

In discussing minority languages, Price (1979, p. 1) maintains that one should distinguish between 'those languages which, though characteristic of a minority in one country, are a majority language elsewhere, and those languages, on the other hand, which are nowhere the dominant language in the state'. He includes in the first category such languages as French in Switzerland and Dutch in a small area of northern France. In the second category are languages like Welsh, Breton, Irish and Scottish Gaelic, Basque, Catalan, Occitan, Romansch, Frisian, Faroese, and Sardinian, all from Western Europe. Not all the languages in the second category have the same status. Irish Gaelic is in a very precarious position even with the weight of a state behind it. On the other hand, Faroese is a good example of a language spoken by a very few people – 40,000 or so – who live on a group of islands well isolated from, but belonging to, Denmark. Standard Faroese is universally spoken in the Faroe Islands; it is also the language of education; and there is a literature in Faroese. In the islands the language has actually replaced Danish, which has become a second language, the one learned at school rather than in the home. While Danish remains the language of higher education, it is no longer the language the Faroese turn to when they seek to borrow words, Icelandic being preferred. Hence the gap increases between the two languages. So Faroese is a minority language within Denmark as a whole but very much the majority language where it is actually spoken and apparently unthreatened there.

Stephens (1976, p. xiii) offers a different definition of *linguistic minority*: the term refers to 'indigenous and, in some cases, to autochthonous populations, or to communities so well established that they can properly be regarded as the historic occupants of the territories in which they live'. He therefore excludes all refugees, expatriates, and immigrants. He adds that there are two types of linguistic minority in Western Europe today. 'The first comprises those communities whose language, whether it is accorded a certain status or none at all, is certainly not the official language of any State'. These minorities are, in Héraud's terms (1963), '*les ethnies sans état*' or, in the views of many writers on the subject, 'internal colonies'. In this category are such groups as the Bretons, the Frisians in the Netherlands, the Basques, and the Welsh. The Faroese and the Catalans also fall into this category but since these languages are majority languages where they are actually spoken, the term *minority language* is not without its difficulties in such cases. According to Stephens (p. xiv), the second type of minority language 'consists of communities which, while in a numerical minority within the States of which they are citizens, speak languages which are official, State languages elsewhere'. He cites as examples French-speakers in the Aosta Valley of northwest Italy and the Danish-speakers of Schleswig-Holstein in West Germany.

For Allardt (1984, p. 196) the key issue in determining the minority status of a language is whether or not those who use it feel they are in a subordinate status to those who use another language: 'A minority language is always subordinated in some sense but it is apparent that there are many different kinds of subordination.' Allardt cites the subordination of being either less powerful or numerically smaller as a group, but he affirms that 'the decisive factor [in determining minority status] is the social organisation related to patterns of subordination and maintained by processes of categorisation and self-categorisation.' It is for this reason that both groups in Belgium, the Flemings (Dutch) and the Walloons (French), are sometimes listed as minorities: each group categorizes itself as a minority and behaves accordingly. By this criterion Guaraní would have to be considered a minority language in Paraguay even though it is spoken by about 95 per cent of the population and the majority language, Spanish, is spoken by no more than 60 per cent. On the other hand, in Switzerland the French as a whole in spite of their numerical weakness do not consider themselves to be in a minority vis-à-vis the Germans; however, the French speakers of the Jura, when they lived in the German-speaking canton of Bern, were very much concerned with their minority status.

Allardt adds that size alone is not crucial. He points out that there are some very small but very tenacious linguistic minorities, citing as examples the 800 or so speakers of German in the parish of Sauris in northeast Italy and 900 Islamic Tatars in Finland. He adds (p. 198) that 'the decisive factor in making them linguistic minorities is not the size but rather the social organisation and their place in society.' This is even the case when certain people seek to revive an extinct language, e.g., Cornish or Manx, because of the way in which any such attempt at revival is tied to the 'social organisation of the society'. It is also the case when only a small proportion of the population speak the language they are rallying around. One of the most militant minorities in Western Europe are the Basques of Spain, but only a minority of those claiming Basque ethnicity actually speak the language. The Irish also rally around Irish: that very few ever learn enough of the language to carry on the simplest of conversations is irrelevant to the place that Irish holds in Irish consciousness.

Allardt recognizes too that majority populations can sometimes be listed as language minorities, citing both the Faroe Islands and Greenland as examples. He also adds the case of Luxembourg where the majority language is Letzebuergesch but where French and German are the two languages that are used in many vital sectors in society. Local pride though has led to significant advances in the use of Letzebuergesch, for example, in internal administration. However, sometimes such a local majority has no reason to seek the label of a national minority. Allardt points out that this is the case for the Piedmontese spoken by about 5 million people in the area centred on Turin, the former capital of Savoy. He says (p. 199) : 'Regionalist sentiments in Piemonte exist, but they have not been focussed on claims for the status of a linguistic minority. A contributing fact is perhaps that Torino and its rulers played a crucial role in the unifying of Italy in the 1850's and 1860's.'

The four criteria that Allardt regards as crucial in determining whether a language is truly a minority language are self-categorization, common descent, distinctive linguistic, cultural, or historical traits related to language, and the social organization of the interaction of the language groups in such a fashion that one group becomes placed in a minority position. He adds that sociolinguists like Fishman have usually accounted for the first three criteria in their analyses of language and ethnicity. On the other hand, social anthropologists like Barth usually look at the social structures and organizations which govern the interactions of groups.

Allardt finds this last criterion the most interesting one. He says (p. 203) that: 'In all ethnic and all linguistic groups there is a set of rules regulating interaction and contacts with other ethnic groups. In other words, all ethnic groups have some form of *social organisation for inter-ethnic interaction.*' It is the prevailing social organization that turns some language groups into minorities, specifically the patterns of subordination that exist. He adds: 'The patterns of subordination can be based on very different factors, such as military might, political power, economic domination, or sheer numbers. At any rate, the pattern of subordination reveals itself in social life in such a fashion that the minority language in a number of important societal realms is subordinate to the majority language.' It is also possible to speak of some languages and groups as being in more of a minority position than others: *Ils sont plus minorisés.*

A state may even refuse to acknowledge the existence of a minority. The Kurds in Turkey and the Macedonians in Greece find their very existence denied by the authorities of the two states. They are therefore much worse off than the Bretons of France or the Basques of Spain whose existence is at least acknowledged. But the latter suffer in comparison with the Faroese or the Romansch.

However difficult it may be to define what constitutes a linguistic minority – and many have been the attempts – there is considerable agreement on the lists that emerge. Most investigators of minority languages in Western Europe agree that there are approximately 50 such languages associated with territorial claims of one kind or another. Excluding such petty polities as Monaco, Andorra, the Vatican, etc., the only states in Western Europe without a linguistic minority of one sort or another are Iceland and Portugal. (The Jews and the Rom are spread everywhere but since they have no historical claims to territories in Western Europe, they are generally ignored in studies of linguistic minorities there.) In the rest of the world the figure runs into many hundreds, for, as we indicated earlier, the phenomenon of language discontent is a widespread one that is not associated with any particular social, political, economic, or religious system. Rather, it is a fact of modern life just about everywhere in the world today.

INDICATORS OF MINORITY STATUS

Simpson (1981, pp. 235–7) says that a minority language exhibits a number of characteristics. It is not the language of all areas of activity indulged in by its speakers. It may live in the shadow of a culturally dominant language, that dominance arising from political, educational, social, or religious factors. There may be people committed to its extirpation and some of these may even come from the ranks of those who speak it. Speakers of the language may borrow extensively from another language or languages, particularly from the language that most threatens their language. Bilingualism will also be a characteristic of many, even all, speakers. The language itself may not be standardized. It may lack norms and be limited in its internal resources. There may also be some reluctance to pass on the language to new learners, even to the next generation. Opponents of the language may well point out the 'deficiencies' they see as existing in the language at risk. On the other hand, proponents of the minority language may take up its cause for ends that sometimes do it little good or, on occasion, considerable harm. Attempts may be made to plan for certain uses of the language or to purify it. There will certainly be educational issues to be addressed, and there may also be traditions either to respect or to accommodate concerning older forms of the language or how the language should be written. Simpson adds (p. 237):

whether or not a language is a minority one has nothing to do with the language, but everything to do with the situation in which it finds itself: Danish is the threatening language for Faroese but is itself a minority language in Germany, German in turn is a minority language in Italy, while Italian is a minority language in France and Yugoslavia.

One claim for some minority languages that Simpson rightly dismisses (pp. 237–8) as 'curious' is that they are 'old', and therefore deserve preservation on that account alone if on no other. To say that one language is 'older' than another is to make a meaningless linguistic observation, for there is no sense in which French, English, or Basque can be said to be older than Cree, Tagalog, or Tiv. The 'oldness' of languages is a quite arbitrary matter having to do mainly with who writes history and the sources that are available to those who do that writing: it seems to have little or no place in discussions concerning the viability of a particular language, either majority or minority.

When people realize that they are in a minority and come to believe that they are being systematically discriminated against, there is likely to be conflict of one kind or another. There may well be an overt struggle for power to see who is to control the state itself and the various resources the state has at its disposal. There will certainly be some form of ideological conflict over the appropriate roles for each of the parties in the various disputes that will arise. In that conflict different resolutions may be proposed and solutions tried ranging from strong coercive measures to successful separation. Specific issues will also loom large in the disputes that will erupt: who gets to use what language where and for what purposes. The outcome of the conflict will, of course, determine how the state reproduces itself and therefore the eventual 'winners' and 'losers'.

Most states recognize that they must deal with such conflicts since successful dealing is crucially important to their well-being. They must become involved in language-planning activities of one kind or another. Such linguistic engineering can be a costly and controversial matter even in states where the problems are relatively minor. However, in states where linguistic minorities are vocal, where language issues may be related very directly to other issues, and where the leadership of the disaffected is strong, the controversies may have the potential for tearing apart the very fabric of the state, as, for example, in Belgium, Canada, Spain, and Sri Lanka.

A NEW DIVERSITY

There are also significant linguistic minorities of another kind in the modern world: these are the minorities that have arisen through the process of migration. The causes of migration are many: the population of new lands; the desire to escape from some kind of hardship, whether it be political, economic, religious, or otherwise, in order to find a better life; the importation of 'guestworkers' to fill certain kinds of jobs that otherwise would not be filled; or the growth of a world-wide system of trade and communications which makes the movement of peoples easier in many parts of the world and difficult to control or regulate. These new minorities have to be considered along with the 'historical' language minorities, for they often interact with them in very important ways.

As we will see, the resulting situations may be very different from one another. Countries like Australia, Canada, and the United States were created through immigration. However, the recent ethnic upsurge has had very different consequences for each of these countries. Australia, which once had not only an 'English-only' policy but also a 'whites-only' policy has had to become 'multicultural' and recognize the linguistic needs of its post-World War II immigrants. Canada has had to try to accommodate a wide spectrum of immigrant peoples and languages within its basic, but not necessarily very equitable, bilingual structure, and the resulting policy of 'multiculturalism within a bilingual framework' is still not without its considerable controversies. The United States has 'rediscovered' ethnicity and certain cherished beliefs are under attack, particularly the idea that it is 'one nation' if that idea requires also that there be but one language.

In Western Europe the problems that France experiences with its territorial minorities are exacerbated by the millions who have flocked to France from its former imperial possessions with their very different languages and cultures. Some French see their very way of life being threatened and have reacted in outbursts of xenophobia. The situation is not far different over the Channel where the United Kingdom now has a significant minority population in which languages other than English are spoken and many traditional English values seem to be unobserved. The United Kingdom, of course, does not have the so-called 'guestworkers' of many of the other affluent Western European countries, having preferred instead to import 'cheap' immigrant labour from its former imperial possessions. Such guestworkers, immigrants, and their families now number many millions in Western Europe as a whole and more and more have become permanent residents who are either unwilling or unable to return to ancestral homes. They sometimes have few rights in the countries in which they now find themselves, but they are more and more inclined to mobilize to protect themselves. Language issues are often some of the first to be pressed when such mobilization occurs.

Most immigrants find it difficult to maintain the langages they bring to their new countries of residence. How successful they are is related to a variety of factors. Among these we can mention such matters as the degree to which immigrants are isolated geographically and socially. The familiarity that individual immigrant groups have with problems of language maintenance and language loyalty may also be very important to what happens to its members: some groups, e.g., the overseas Chinese, have a strong tradition of maintaining their language but others, e.g., Germans in North America, seem to lose their language very quickly. The prevailing 'linguistic climate' of the 'host' society is also important: Is it supportive of differences that immigrants bring believing that they enrich the receiving society or does it preach conformity to major values? What are the educational opportunities that exist and how are career choices influenced by, or depend on, certain linguistic abilities? How are linguistic factors related to other factors such as sex and age differences, religious background, racial origin, and so on? These are but some of the factors that influence what happens to various immigrant languages and account for why one seems to be able to survive for a while whereas another disappears very quickly.

A major issue turns out to be just what language rights immigrants have. Do they abandon all rights by reason of their migration no matter what the circumstances of that migration? Or do they still have certain rights, particularly if their numbers are considerable and they can maintain their linguistic viability but perhaps only with help from the state? Does the state have any duty or responsibility to help? Or do immigrants themselves have a duty to adopt the language – and possibly even the ways – of the state in which they find themselves? Should territorial minorities try to organize or even exploit the issues that can be raised, i.e., try to co-opt immigrants in their own struggles for language rights in the hope that all will benefit from the cooperation that results? Or should the issues be kept quite separate in case the state tries to use them to 'divide and rule'? What is the relationship, if any, between the language needs and rights of Algerians and Vietnamese in France and those of Bretons and Alsatians there? And of West Indians,

Greeks, and Punjabis in the United Kingdom and those of the Welsh and of the remaining few speakers of Gaelic in Scotland?

MANAGING CONFLICT

Managing linguistic conflict of one kind or another has become a regular part of the agenda of many states. But then conflict itself is a necessary part of political and social life. The real test is how it is managed. States cannot exist without internal conflict: they are just too complex to be confict free. What they must do is develop mechanisms for defining and handling conflict and they must try to contain such conflicts to manageable issues.

Some states have tried to manage conflict along ethnic and language lines (particularly when the groups are weak and likely to be competitive rather than cooperative) rather than along class or economic lines, but there is a danger in such management, in playing off groups one against the other. The demands made are likely to escalate and competition increase. Not all demands can possibly be met and there is a considerable risk that feelings of dissatisfaction may actually increase rather than diminish. Glazer (1983, p. 336) has commented on such a situation as follows:

When every group insists it must match every other group in economic resources, occupational status, and political representation, and that public power be used to attain these ends – and to maintain the existence of the group as a separate group, to boot – we have a sure recipe for conflict. We will have to do better, and one way of doing so is to explore whether the much maligned goal of assimilation does not still have much to teach us.

Assimilation is, of course, the imposition of the will of the majority on that of a minority. Yet it is easy to see why it may appear to be an attractive solution. The majority may well become disaffected with what they regard as misdirected policies of appeasement which seem to increase levels of conflict. Repression may even follow in some circumstances. The result is a classic 'no-win' situation.

Marxists take another approach to these issues. They say that minority groups of the kind to which we have referred should put aside many of their concerns in favour of seeking to redress their grievances through social and economic reorganization. Marxists declare that many states deliberately use the aspirations of minority groups to keep them weak and powerless. Groups can be played off against one another because the kinds of conflicts they indulge in can be managed relatively easily. The costs to the state of any 'concessions' it makes are not really very high. Marxists believe that minority groups would gain more if they were to organize along class lines, set aside their narrow ethnic or linguistic goals, and insist on a redistribution of power. However, there is little evidence that groups are willing to forgo support for those characteristics around which they presently unite in order to pursue the dubious rewards that might be gained from waging class war.

Linguistic diversity and the resulting potential for conflict are facts of life in many polities. It is possible to look at either or both from a variety of perspectives. McRae (1983, pp. 28–33) has suggested four possible dimensions in which the the various languages that exist in particular states may be studied. The first dimension is the institutional one: the arrangements given the sanction of law and/or practice. The second dimension is structural: the characteristics of the language groups and how the languages they use relate to various social characteristics, e.g., religious, economic, social class, etc. The third is the historical dimension: the history of relations among the groups and each group's view of those relations. Finally, there is the attitudinal dimension: the view each group has of its place in the state and of the places of other groups, and the means through which such views are given political expression. In the latter part of this book we will look at a variety of countries and language situations in order to see how important these dimensions are. The situations differ widely as different languages are involved in different ways. We will also see that the sources of conflict also differ widely and that the kinds of solutions that have been proposed and attempted do not lead one to believe that some ready-made universal solution is available or even possible.

FURTHER READING

Useful Western European survey: Stephens 1976; minorities in general: George 1984; various issues, including education: Corner 1984, Edwards 1984, Grosjean 1982, Haugen et al. 1981, Megarry et al. 1981.

3

Ethnic Group, Nation,
and State

One potentially destabilizing factor common to many modern states is the ethnic and linguistic composition of the state itself. World War II did little to solve many of the issues that the Treaty of Versailles, which ended World War I, failed to resolve. At Versailles President Wilson of the USA led the way in a general willingness to experiment with the principle of self-determination in an effort to solve the problems that existed in the Balkans and Central Europe. That the same principle might also have had some application in other parts of the world, even in parts the USA itself controlled at that time, seems not to have occurred to those who wrote the terms of peace in Europe. The treaty did try to constitute the boundaries of many states along ethnic or linguistic lines but did so with only partial success.

While the principle of the self-determination of peoples is an important part of the Charter of the United Nations, in practice it seems to mean only that the emergent ex-colonial states become instant 'nations' and that whatever 'nations' that emerged from either the treaties that ended World War II or the collapse of the old empires of countries such as the United Kingdom, France, and Portugal are 'self-determined peoples'. States are also not supposed to involve themselves in the internal affairs of other states; attempts at secession are to be resisted, by force if necessary; and there is almost no possible way of resolving lingering international disputes such as those between Yugoslavia and Italy over Trieste and Austria and Italy over the South Tyrol. Since the vast majority of the states in the United Nations are multinational in composition, it is really not at all surprising that they would be unsympathetic to attempts to alter boundaries to accommodate emergent 'nations'. The reality of the modern world is that most 'states' are not 'nations'. Most are merely 'states; some are 'state-nations'; a very few are actually 'nation-states'.

Most states contain within themselves groups which for one reason or another do not readily identify themselves with the particular state in which they find themselves and who would prefer either a different internal status, an entirely separate status, or a transfer to another state. However, as Héraud (1963, p. 22) has observed, most states try to maintain silence on such matters: *'rien ne vient rompre la conspiration du silence, ni contester l'affirmation tranchante de l'État posant que chez lui 'il n'y a pas de minorités'. C'est ainsi qu'il n'y avait pas de 'problème colonial' au beau temps de la colonialisation.'* ('nothing occurs to break the conspiracy of silence nor dispute the bold declaration of the State claiming that within it "there are no minorities". In the same way there was no "colonial problem" in the heyday of colonialism.')

This conspiracy of silence has not proved to be entirely effective. Events in the last twenty years or so have clearly shown that there is widespread discontent with the modern state as an organizational unit. Not only have states had little success in evolving suprastate or international organizations in which particular state interests would be submerged for the benefit of all, but individual states have found it difficult at times to manage conflicts of various kinds arising internally from a resurgent ethnonationalism. Such conflicts have sometimes been quite violent, as in Sri Lanka, Malaysia, Spain, Nigeria, India, Pakistan, Cyprus, Lebanon, Indonesia, and Uganda to cite but a few examples. Violence may have been less in other states but the conflict has still been considerable on occasion, e.g., in Belgium, Canada, France, the United Kingdom, and the United States. It is also apparent even in Marxist-oriented states in which, according to Marxist-Leninist philosophy, it should not be found at all, for even the Soviet Union, China, Vietnam, and Yugoslavia have experienced its effects.

ETHNONATIONALISM

Ethnonationalism is a force that threatens to tear apart the fabric of many modern states just as it tore apart the fabric of nineteenth-century Europe. However, it is not a force which is easy to account for in the modern world, which is, after all, a well-organized world of autonomous states, of international trade and arrangements, of strong assimilative forces, of mobility for many individuals, and of very powerful communication networks. What accounts for ethnicity being such a potent force in that world and for its expression through demands for language and other 'rights'? Yinger (1981) says that scholars have answered this question by reference to three sets of forces.

The first set arises from 'the continuing power of primordial attachments'. People who cannot attach themselves to the state because it does not express their sense of 'nationality' or who see inequities and injustices within the state may prefer to seek identity with those for whom there appears to be an historical attachment. While this revival of a felt historical identity can account for many cases, it runs into difficulty in explaining how an ethnic identity may be recovered after long periods of assimilation, e.g., Manx or Cornish identity, or how particular ethnic identities are chosen, e.g., Ukrainian rather than Russian or Polish, or how on some occasions entirely new identities are manufactured, e.g., Amerindian rather than Sioux, or Hispano-American rather than either Spanish, American, or Mexican.

The second set arises from the very conditions of life in large, heterogeneous, changing, modernizing societies, conditions which stress social conformity and the impersonal treatment of individuals. Ethnic consciousness is a by-product of this life. It results from the sense of alienation that such conditions produce. As Yinger says (p. 258), 'An ethnic attachment ... helps one to preserve some sense of community, to know who one is, to overcome the feeling of being a "cipher" in an anonymous world.' Writing in the same vein, Fishman (1977, p. 36) says: 'The more "modern" society is open to strangers (resident foreigners, migrants, immigrants, seasonal labourers), the more ethnicity must become one of the operational bases for the negotiations of these strangers with "society at large", particularly if their social and economic assimilation is blocked and other forms of social action are controlled.' Much of the discontent we see in modern life may be accounted for in this way. Modern life does force people and groups into contact without necessarily making them come to like one another. In fact, the opposite may well be true in many cases: such contacts may well lead to self-consciousness and the awareness of differences and inequities. The consequence is that individuals may unite on some issue to promote their interests and compete with others in order to reduce the feelings of alienation they have.

Banton (1983) has argued that competition itself is the crucial process in shaping patterns of racial and ethnic relationships, but its intensity and form depend on the nature of the units that compete and on the issues on which the competition focuses. He says (p. 12): 'When members of groups encounter one another in new situations the boundaries between them will be dissolved if they compete as one individual with another; the boundaries between them will be strengthened if they compete as one group with another. In competition, people seek to realize the values of their groups.' Cohen (1976, p. 96) shares this view, arguing: 'Ethnicity in modern society is the outcome of intensive *interaction* between different culture groups, and not the result of a tendency to separatism.' He adds (p.97): 'Ethnicity is fundamentally a political phenomenon, as the symbols of traditional culture are used as mechanisms for the articulation of political alignments.'

Although ethnic competition may arise from feelings of economic disadvantage or even from the 'pains' sometimes said to be inherent in the process of modernization, there are exceptions. On occasion ethnic disaffection within the state can arise among the economically advantaged, as it has in Spain among the Basques and Catalans, or in states which appear to be fairly well integrated and modernized, as in France. Ethnicity as a weapon to be used to resist discrimination or as the last gasp of traditionalism in the face of modernity does not work as an explanation in such cases. Ethnic conflict has occurred in a variety of economic circumstances and both with and without modernization. So there must be some other factor or factors still to be taken into account if one is to attempt to offer a full explanation of the rise of ethnonationalism in the modern world.

Yinger's third set of factors relates to 'the usefulness of ethnicity in the struggle for power, status, and income'. In other words, ethnic identification is a tool available to those who see its usefulness for winning concessions of various kinds in the struggles for power that are characteristic of social organizations. It can be used as a political resource against the state if people can be organized around appropriate issues and it is most effective when the state is weak or lacks the structural resources necessary to deal with the issues that it raises. A very disadvantaged group can unite to win concessions but so can an advantaged group in order to increase certain advantages it already possesses.

Concessions are also likely to lead to demands for more concessions to the same group or to demands from other groups for similar concessions. In this way we can see how ethnic demands need not necessarily be confined to states of particular social, racial, political, or economic composition. If, in addition, we recognize the demonstration effect – that gains achieved by one group will encourage groups elsewhere to make similar demands – we can see how ethnic consciousness can become an important factor in the internal politics of any state. According to Cohen (1969, p. 15), ethnic groups: 'manipulate values, myths, rituals and ceremonials from   their cultural tradition to solve their basic organisational problems. To the casual observer ethnicity is taken as a manifestation of conservatism, separatism and stagnation, when on careful analysis we discover that it is a dynamic organisational mechanism involving intensive interaction with other groups. Ethnicity is ... essentially a political phenomenon.' And, of course, if it is necessary to revive or restructure an ethnicity to achieve certain desired goals, then one is free to do so.

Yinger adds that these three sets of forces do not really offer competing explanations of the phenomenon of ethnicity: rather they are complementary. The various factors reinforce one another. However, in Yinger's view (1981, p. 260), 'the "interest group" interpretation of ethnic group strength is generally ... the most powerful.' People can be persuaded to rally around ethnicity just as they can be persuaded to rally around religion and sometimes patriotism, but only very infrequently around social class. As we will see too, language often becomes the key symbol of ethnic identity and the focal issue in such rallies.

ETHNIC GROUPS

People can band together or be banded together because of real or perceived similarities of many kinds: language, religion, caste, race, occupation, sex, age, social class, life style, sexual preference, and so on. Ethnic identity also figures in this list. At different times one or other characteristic, or some particular grouping of characteristics, becomes important. Today, ethnicity is important, particularly when it is allied to one or more of the other characteristics, especially language, race, or religion.

So far we have used terms such as *ethnicity* and *ethnic identity* without offering definitions. However, in this respect we are not very different from most who use such terms, certainly in their various everyday uses. The meanings of such terms seem intuitively obvious and it may appear somewhat pedantic to insist that they should be defined. Scholars who have devoted considerable attention to the phenomenon of ethnicity have found the underlying concept not at all easy to deal with; they have found both of the above terms difficult to define so as to cover all the purported instances.

Fishman has long been a student of the phenomenon of ethnicity. He maintains (1977, p. 17):

The notion of ethnicity requires a central experiential concept or chord around which all others can be clustered. This central experience is here termed paternity, and deals with the recognition of putative biological origins and, therefore, with the hereditary or descent-related 'blood', 'bones', essence', 'mentality', 'genius', 'sensitivity', proclivity' derived from the original putative ancestors of a collectivity and passed on from generation to generation in a bio-kinship sense.

He admits that this 'bio-kinship' may be real, mythical, or fictive but whatever it is, it is the key feature. This bio-kinship also manifests itself in a variety of ways: physical traits, qualities of 'mind', and, of course, through culture and language. Other commentators have similar views. De Vos (1975, p. 9) states:

An ethnic group is a self-perceived group of people who hold in common a set of traditions not shared by the others with whom they are in contact. Such traditions typically include 'folk' religious beliefs and practices, language, a sense of historical continuity, and common ancestry or place of origin. The group's actual history often trails off into legend or mythology, which includes some concept of an unbroken biological–genetic generational continuity, sometimes regarded as giving special characteristics to the group. Endogamy is usual, although various patterns for initiating outsiders into the ethnic group are developed in such a way that they do not disrupt the sense of generational continuity.

For Schermerhorn (1978, p.12) an ethnic group is:

a collectivity within a larger society having real or putative common ancestry, memories of a shared historical past, and a cultural focus on one or more symbolic elements defined as the epitome of their peoplehood. Examples of such symbolic elements are: kinship patterns, physical contiguity (as in localism or sectionalism), religious affiliation, language or dialect forms, tribal affiliation, nationality, phenotypical features, or any combination of these. A necessary accompaniment is some consciousness of kind among members of the group.

In this view ethnicity is an involuntary characteristic, being one that individuals are born with. In Isajiw's words (1980, p. 24), ethnicity refers to 'an involuntary group of people who share the same culture or ... descendants of such people who identify themselves and/or are identified by others as belonging to the same involuntary group'.

It is easy to find instances of this appeal to real or putative ancestry. Romanians sometimes see themselves as the direct descendants of the Romans who brought Christianity and civilization to the Balkans; in this way they can distance themselves from other Slavs. Irish leaders often appeal to pre-Roman times when a Celtic culture flourished in Western Europe so as to demonstrate the legitimacy of things that are 'Irish' against those that are not or to justify attempts to revive or restore a language that has all but disappeared. Both Welsh and Breton separatists look back many centuries to times when the lands of their forefathers were not parts of the United Kingdom and France respectively but were more or less independent political entities.

Many ethnonational movements have some version of an 'ideal past' and a myth of some kind of return to that past. Such a past is a fiction, an intellectual, ideological creation. It is quite often a past that never existed. History can be neither re-created nor undone; it can only be conjectured about and come to terms with. Even the history of any particular language is not well understood nor can much be done about its present state if one seeks to recapture its past 'glories'. Attempts too to change or revive a language will surely set it off in entirely new directions, a lesson that Israelis have learned from their experience with Modern Hebrew, some to their dismay.

In this view of ethnicity ethnic groups are defined above all by the characteristics of their members. Ethnicity is primordial, part of one's descent and one shares one's descent with others and may rightly seek to unite with those others. The ethnic group itself not only has a sense of its historical continuity, but it also has traditions, beliefs, and practices which have been handed down, and among these none is usually more important than the language of the group.

An alternative view of ethnicity is that ethnic groups are best defined by patterns of boundary-maintaining behaviour. It is not the characterisics of the group that are important or the particular myths its members have about their ancestry. What is important is how the group is organized to distinguish itself from other competing groups in society, how strong its boundaries are, and how its members are able to use their collective group strength in managing intergroup conflict. As De Vos (1975, p. 6) has observed, the 'boundaries are basically psychological in nature, not territorial. These boundaries are maintained by ascription from within as well as from external sources which designate membership according to evaluative characteristics which differ in content depending on the history of contact of the groups involved. The resulting collective sense of separateness may lead to continual accommodation or conflict.' This approach, which stresses boundary-maintaining behavior, is particularly useful if one believes that a conflict model is the most appropriate model for understanding how groups must accommodate to one another in any society – and even states themselves in the international society. Groups continually strive for power and rewards against other groups and, if individuals are to achieve what they see as their legitimate rewards, they must unite with like-minded individuals against those whom they regard as different. In this view ethnicity is just one of the possible groupings that is available to individuals. It is also often very readily accessible because some of the key symbols that can be used, particularly language, are so easily recognizable. Unilingualism provides for very strong boundary-maintenance; bilingualism weakens those same boundaries and makes crossing them a real possibility.

Ethnicity has both objective and subjective attributes. The objective ones are such matters as language, religion, cultural characteristics, perhaps certain institutional arrangements, and almost inevitably an historical tradition. The subjective ones have to do with feelings about identity and shared interests. The particular characteristics and details may shift over time, just as the boundaries between ethnic groups and the boundary-maintaining behaviour may also vary. Ethnic identity may also be lost and it can even be created. Colonial policies sometimes created ethnic groups when no such previous group consciousness existed, e.g., Malays in Malaysia, Kikuyu in Kenya, Ibo in Nigeria, through the systems of local administration that were developed, systems which categorized and controlled people in such a way as to build a common supralocal identity. A particularly telling example is the creation of a Swahili identity in East Africa.

Ethnicity itself can be put to work. An ethnic group may believe that its grievances lie within the political system as a whole or in relation to some other ethnic group. If it occupies a particular territory that it can exert some control over, it may find itself with considerable power in the resulting conflict. If it does not, it may not make many, or any, gains at all. It is for this reason that territorially based ethnic groups within modern states have received most attention in recent years. Those ethnic groups without territories and, of course, those that arise in states through migration have received somewhat less attention and often a lot less sympathy, even from groups of the first kind.

An ethnic group is not necessarily a minority group. It can be a majority group. Indeed, the terms *minority* and *majority* may not be the most useful terms for discussing many of the issues that arise when ethnic groups must interact. If everyone must belong to an ethnic group, then we can have states which range from almost monoethnic composition to those which are extremely multiethnic. An ethnic group becomes a minority group when it finds itself in conflict with one or more dominant groups. It will usually be smaller in numbers than the dominant group, but this is not an absolute requirement: the black people of South Africa are in a numerical majority but it would be hard to deny them a minority label, and both the Walloons and the Flemish behave like minorities in Belgium. What makes a group a minority group is the feeling that the members of the group have that the way in which society is structured to distribute rewards does not allow them to receive their just entitlement because of that membership. All kinds of groups can become minority groups, recent examples being blacks in North America, guestworkers in Western Europe, women's groups, and homosexuals. Ethnic grouping is just one available type of grouping, but because of its special characteristics, particularly its relationship to territory, it is possibly the most potent so far as conflict is concerned.

ETHNIC RESURGENCE

Ethnicity is a potential force awaiting use: it can remain dormant for centuries; it can be revived; and it can even be created. The idea that the people of the United States have an 'American' ethnicity derived from their relationship to the particular 'nation' that is the United States is an interesting example of such a creation. 'American' ethnicity in this sense is far different from French, German, Japanese, or Chinese ethnicity. It is a new ethnicity in the world, and it is not one to be discounted. However, it may stand in the way of many who proclaim it in their attempts to understand ethnic conflicts elsewhere. American impatience with the Old World and its ways derives in large measure and from a blindness to certain facts about the New World they inhabit, one fact in particular, that it too is built on an ideology which is no more tolerant of certain kinds of minority views than most other ideologies. Minorities that have questioned the dominant ideology in the New World have not had the easiest of times there.

An ethnic minority may choose not to make use of any force it might muster and not enter the fray at all. In such a case the likelihood of its weakening in both numbers and strength is quite considerable. A good example is shown in the behaviour of the Arvanites of Greece. Arvanitika is an Albanian dialect spoken in the villages of Attica and Biotia in Greece. As Trudgill and Tzavaras (1977) show, the Arvanites of Greece are quite proud of their ethnic origin, although by now they are almost entirely culturally assimilated to the Greeks. Very few young Arvanites any longer wish to see their language preserved, although about 140,000 of them still continue to speak Arvanitika. Although many Arvanites seem to think that their ethnic identity can be preserved if the language disappears, Trudgill and Tzavaras regard such a view as unrealistic since language is now the sole differentiating characteristic that distinguishes Arvanites from Greeks. They found that children are adopting Greek identity, a tendency reinforced by the Greek policy of disregarding minority languages, by the growing attractions of urbanization, and by the Arvanites themselves' being completely cut off from Albania, the most isolated of all European states. What kind of future can the Arvanites look forward to? Will it be one in which they assume a Greek ethnicity and melt completely into the wider Greek society? Or will it be one in which a strong ethnic consciousness resurfaces, perhaps as a result of education revealing to the Arvanites that a stress on differences may bring them greater rewards than the assimilation that is presently occurring, particularly if Greek life itself becomes more diversified? However, at the moment the residents of the villages are content to be

Arvanites without feeling that that they are particularly disadvantaged by their ethnicity or have much to gain by asserting it.

Tha Arvanites are somewhat unusual in that they have not asserted their ethnicity in order to improve their lot in society. But they are a small group and an isolated one. What the world has seen in recent years is a resurgence of ethnic feeling among ethnic groups which have found themselves in similar minority situations. When World War II ended few observers would have predicted such a resurgence; in fact, the opposite prediction was usually made, that old loyalties would be put aside and a new world freed of ethnic particularism would dawn. But such was not to be the case. In the two decades following the end of the war there were militant movements almost everywhere of peoples who wanted some other arrangement than the one that existed between themselves and the states in which they found themselves. Ethnicity has resurfaced as a potent force in modern political life, in some cases even coming to threaten the arrangement of states that had been worked out so painfully over the previous half century.

Esman (1977b, p. 388) has enumerated five conditions which he regards as being important in trying to explain the resurgence of the kind of national sentiment, based on ethnicity, that has arisen in Scotland, but which he admits 'can be generalized to explain and predict the politicization of ethnic solidarities elsewhere in the First World'. The first of these is group identity based on objective properties such as a distinctive language or history and the concomitant solidarity associated with these properties. The second is a set of grievances based on perceived political, economic, or cultural deprivations or discrimination within the overall system in which the minority finds itself. The third is 'rising expectations resulting from credible prospects that the existing situation can be improved'. Grievances are therefore necessary but they are not sufficient if there is no expectation that anything can be done about them. The fourth condition is that there should be declining authority and effectiveness at the political centre of the state so that the centre's claim on peripheral and marginal groups is weakened. The final condition is that there be some kind of 'political organization to articulate ethnoregional goals and group interests, to mobilize support and participation, to contest elections, and to seek political power'. At the present time the Arvanites mentioned above meet only the first of these conditions so it is not surprising that they are a silent minority.

Giles, Bourhis, and Taylor (1977) have proposed a more comprehensive set of factors to account for the vitality of ethnic groups. An ethnolinguistic group with little or no vitality would eventually cease to exist as a group and the more vitality a group has the greater its chances of survival. They have identified three clusters of factors that they regard as important in accounting for such vitality. They call these status, demographic, and institutional-support factors. The first have to do with the prestige the group has in the intergroup context. The second relate to the sheer numbers of people that are involved, their territorial distribution, and the demographic trends. Finally, institutional support is the matter of how the various agencies within society support or do not support the group's efforts, both formally and informally.

The status factor covers such matters as the economic status of the group: how far it is in charge of its own economic well-being. The social status of the group is also important, particularly the degree of esteem the group has in the wider society and its members' self-esteem. Sociohistorical status is also important: the history of the group and how that history can be used to further the ends of the group. Finally, language status must be taken into account. Is the language an international language, a language with connections to other parts of the world, or one associated with a prestigious religious or cultural system? Or is it not yet standardized, downgraded as a 'dialect' or 'patois', and perhaps not held in any great esteem even by those who use it?

The demographic factor covers such matters as the territorial distribution of the group, particularly its relationship to 'ancestral' territory and its ability to monopolize that territory. A minority that is weakened in its own territory by the in-migration of others will be less vital than one that has preserved its territory virtually intact and certainly more vital than a minority that has been widely dispersed and perhaps no longer holds any territory for itself. Absolute numbers will be of concern, just as will be how these numbers are affected by such matters as the birth rates of various groups, mixed marriages, and patterns of migration. Statistics to do with all of these are used quite freely in most disputes because of the trends they are said to indicate. All such figures should be treated with caution, however, because even though there is a sense in which figures do not lie, certain figures which are compared may not be directly comparable and those who use figures may have other motives than letting the figures speak for themselves, even though this may be their claim.

'Institutional support refers to the degree of formal and informal support a language receives in the various institutions of a nation, region or community.' That support may be informal, as when members of a group have developed pressure groups to pursue their goals. More formal support requires that the language and those who speak it are represented in the various institutions in society. They find their way into the media and the institutions of the state; their language and cultural needs are satisfied through policies and practices that allow them to use their language and to hand it on to their children in schools which they control; and they can live and work freely in the language of their choice. Ethnic groups obviously vary widely in the kinds of institutional support they receive; there are the kinds of bilingualism we find today in countries such as Switzerland, Belgium, and Canada, and there are also the situations that existed in Franco's Spain and for a long time in countries such as the United Kingdom, France, and the United States in which only the majority language was readily tolerated and all other languages were either proscribed or ignored.

One factor that is not included in the above lists is the factor of leadership. Groups need leaders and there is a remarkable similarity among the leaders of the various ethnic groups that have sought either recognition or a redistribution of power in recent decades. As Esman (1977b, p. 376) has indicated, 'a substantial component of the ethnoregional movements consists of relatively well educated persons, including teachers and technicians, whose economic rewards, social recognition, or opportunities for the exercise of power and influence fall short of their expectations.' These people provide the leadership initially and often become a new élite to rival the élite of the majority group. However, the members of the minority élite are likely fairly soon to disagree among themselves about the right course of action to be pursued. The major élites may also try to forestall demands through deliberate policies of co-option, a kind of 'buying off' of the rival leadership by giving in to some of its demands but requiring as the price that the new status quo be supported.

Young (1976) has called such leaders 'cultural entrepreneurs'. He points out that the kind of group with which we are concerned needs an ideology if it is to be successful. A statement of that ideology must address itself to the uniqueness, historical virtues, and future destiny of the group. He says (p. 45):

The ideologization of identity depends upon the emergence of cultural entrepreneurs, almost always associated with the rise of a professional middle class and intelligentsia; although the basis for historical mystique may exist in rich measure in the reservoir of folk tradition and myths of origin, the move from the oral repository of the traditional elders to the written page multiplies the potential mobilization of identity. This cultural educated class has many tasks to absorb its energies: the language must be standardized and a literature of verse and prose accumulated; history must be recorded and a vision of the future defined.

Young is unequivocal about the place of language in this scheme of things: it is the major resource available to those who would be cultural entrepreneurs. He points out that the cultural entrepreneur necessarily works with the political broker. While it is the function of the cultural entrepreneur to enlarge the resources of the community, it is the function of the political broker – or cultural politician – to mobilize ethnicity in particular situations in an attempt to bring about social and political change.

We can see the importance of such leadership in the events that led to the break-up of the Austro-Hungarian Empire. Young explains (p. 25) what happened as follows:

The rise of professional and commercial middle classes to challenge the dominance of the landed nobility in the outlying lands of the Hapsburg domain ... was a critical development. From this group emerged the cultural leaders who unified the languages, provided them with grammars, dictionaries, and literature and invested the cultural heritage with a historical sanction. Nationality armed with ideology then acquired the potential to slowly percolate into the submerged rural peasantry.

The new leadership was eventually successful. For example, the empire was split in two and the Hungarian minority gained substantial autonomy. But once this minority became a majority, it acted like one and quite disregarded the claims of other potentially emergent peoples such as the Croats, Romanians, and Slovaks, who found that they had merely exchanged one form of unsympathetic rule for another.

Fishman (1972b, p. 15) prefers protoélites as a term to describe the leadership of such groups. Protoélites are the crucial catalysts. It is they who, according to Fishman, are, or feel themselves to be, 'excluded from the power and influence they covet and who possess the personal gifts or material resources to move symbols and masses toward desired sociopolitical regroupings'. Fishman points out that one of the obstacles to the spread of nationalistic sentiments in Western Europe, particularly in France, was the failure to enlarge the sense of national identity. It was only in the early twentieth century that many peasants in France really achieved any sense of French identity (Weber, 1976). Prior to that time they had no reason to regard themselves as sharing any kind of common identity with people in other parts of the country. As Fishman says (1972b, pp. 15–16):

The spread of nationalism is, therefore, marked not by its existence in the upper reaches of society, but by its successful communication to and activation of the urban (and ultimately also the rural) lower middle and lower classes. Such spread frequently involved a new intellectual and economic protoélite just as much as it involved a new class of respondents.

Protoélites serve as catalysts and facilitators and without them movements are unlikely to go anywhere if they can exist at all.

Protoélites, however, may not be at all representative of those for whom they claim to speak. They are likely to consist mainly of intellectuals who may have goals that are very different from the masses they strive to mobilize. As Breuilly (1982, p. 332) says, leaders whom,

we might loosely call intellectuals have certain skills which can be employed in the formulation of political ideas and the organisation of political movements. These skills are of particular relevance to nationalist movements in which ideology plays a prominent role and from which members of the leading social classes usually remain aloof. However, this leadership by intellectuals is subject to all sorts of constraints from its bases of support.

Such leaders may well have nationalist aspirations for the groups they claim to lead. Breuilly points out (p. 19):

nationalism is usually a minority movement pursued against the indifference and, frequently, hostility of the majority of the members of the 'nation' in whose name the nationalists act. Nationalists can cope with these difficulties to their own satisfaction by arguing that the nation has 'forgotten' itself (such forgetfulness extending back over most of its history) and it is their task to bring it back to its true self.

In his example of such a case from Wales, Lewis (1982, p. 257) shows what can happen when a language goes into a steep decline and 'activists' try to resist:

we are faced with fewer people, many with only a mediocre command of the language, having the option to use it for more purposes, some of them the most prestigious. It is an ominous situation, suggesting the creation of an increasingly militant, declining minority disproportionately reflecting the views of and led by ministers of religion, university and school teachers, and 'intellectual' professional interests, as well as small but highly 'activist' University student groups.

However they are formed, protoélites do exist and do learn from one another. They spread ideas, they point to successes elsewhere, and they encourage the kinds of feelings that need to exist if movements are to be successful. They also give these movements a sense of authenticity by appealing to the past, creating the myths and symbols that are so necessary, and even on occasion reviving or attempting to revive a language that is no longer in use. Language can be a particularly important component in ethnic resurgence; those who claim to lead may sometimes even have to learn a language in order to validate their very claims to leadership, as Bandaranaike had to learn Sinhala in Sri Lanka to lead his people there in 1956 or, more recently, Rajiv Gandhi in India has had to improve his knowledge of Hindi. As Horowitz (1985, p. 222) says: 'Language is ... a potent symbolic issue [in ethnic conflict] because it accomplishes a double linkage. It links political claims to ownership with psychological demands for the affirmation of group worth, and it ties this aggregate matter of group status to outright careerism, thereby binding élite material interest to mass concerns.'

NATIONALISM

The leadership of an ethnic group, no matter how we define ethnicity or how narrow or wide ranging the support that leadership has, is likely to have a very clear idea that the ethnic group should somehow control its own destiny. As Breuilly says (1982, p. 382), 'an effective nationalism develops when it makes political sense for an opposition to the government to claim to represent the nation against the present state.' The principal way in which an ethnic group controls its own destiny is by having a territory in which it can govern itself. That is, the ethnic group achieves recognition as a separate nation. Or, if that is not possible, the state in which the group finds itself becomes pluralistic in nature so that no one group can dominate others, no group is particularly advantaged or disadvantaged by reason of its ethnic composition, and all groups share equally in the governance of the whole.

One of the first difficulties we confront if we accept such a view as being valid is that it would lead to a reordering of the world which would be drastically different from the one that currently exists. The world is presently comprised of states rather than nations. The terms *state* and *nation* are not synonymous and the name *United Nations* is actually a misnomer. Fewer than 10 per cent of the states of the world are also nations if we insist that a nation be virtually monoethnic in composition. Some such states are Portugal, Greece, Iceland, Malta, Norway, South and North Korea, and Japan. Another 20 per cent or so contain significant minorities but have majorities of over 90 per cent belonging to a single ethnic group. Another 20 per cent contain a nation or potential nation accounting for between 75 per cent and 89 per cent of the total population. Almost a quarter of existing states have the largest ethnic group containing between half and three-quarters of the total population with the rest of the population belonging to one or more other groups. Finally, in the remaining states the largest ethnic group comprises less than half the total population.

The idea that ethnic groups are entitled to 'nation' status, that nation-states are more legitimate than states based on some other principle, and that there is something natural and right about 'nationalism' as an organizing principle for political entities is a relatively new one in the history of the world. It is an important outcome of the Romantic movement of the late seventeenth and early eighteenth centuries. Its principal exponents were the Germans Herder, Fichte, and Humboldt and the French Jacobins. One of the first and most influential statements equating language with nationhood was an essay by Herder (1744–1803) entitled *Über den Ursprung der Sprache* (*On the Origin of Speech*) published in 1772 after being the prize essay of the Berlin Academy of Sciences two years before. He argued there and in other writings that national feeling should be based on language: 'Has a nationality anything dearer than the speech of its fathers? In its speech resides its whole thought domain, its tradition, history, religion and basis of life, all its heart and soul. To deprive a people of its speech is to deprive it of its one eternal good. . . . With language is created the heart of a people.' In his *Address to the German Nation* of 1807, Fichte (1762–1814) also praised German and deprecated other languages. In his view, German, unlike French, was a superior, unpolluted language and this made German people superior too. Von Humboldt (1767–1835) also equated language with national sovereignty in his concept of *Heimat* (native land).

Such views are much stronger than those of the earlier views of someone like Dante (1265–1321). Dante was disillusioned with the Italian city-state and also unhappy with Church policy and he rejected both the city state and the Catholic Church as satisfactory bases for political unity. He saw such unity being achieved through language. In his essay entitled 'On Vernacular Language' he tried to outline what an Italian language would be like. He recognized that there were Slavic, Germanic, and Romance language groups and also localized dialects, particularly the various dialects of Italy. An Italian language would have to be located at some point between the Romance group and these dialects. He then proposed what such a language would be like and used that proposal to define an Italian identity. He maintained that writers had a particular obligation to use that language to promote Italian identity and he did this himself in his *Divine Comedy*. He believed that those who recognized themselves as similar by reason of speaking a common language would join together to form a political unit but did not hold that this should be an autonomous unit, as his German successors were to maintain.

At the time of the French Revolution the Jacobins insisted that the French nation must be united around the French language with such unification to be at the expense of any other languages or varieties that had survived in what they considered to be the proper bounds of France. This Jacobinian view has ever since influenced French thought about the relationship between language and the state. It has been modified from time to time. For example, Renan (1823–92) argued that nationalism is based on something beyond language, religion, common interests, geography, or race. It is based on something spiritual – a common memory and a desire to live together. It is also not immutable but can change with time. Whether or not Renan's view is correct, it is fairly easy to show from how they behave in language matters that the French are still really Jacobins at heart.

In England an important philosopher like John Stuart Mill (1806–73) also identified language with nation, declaring in his essay on 'Representative Government' (1861) that: 'Free institutions are next to impossible in a country made up of different nationalities. . . . the boundaries of governments should coincide in the main with those of nationalities.' There were dissidents, of course, even contemporaries in his own country. Lord Acton (1834–1902), for example, insisted that it was a requirement of civilized life that different nations should learn to live together within the bounds of a common state, a pluralist or federalist rather than a nationalist point of view. In his essay on 'Nationality' (1862) he declared that: 'A State which is incompetent to satisfy different races condemns itself: a State which labours to neutralise, to absorb, or to expel them, destoys its own vitality; a State which does not include them is destitute of the chief basis of self-government.' Acton saw nationalism as leading ultimately to the loss of individual freedom because the individual must become submerged in the group and he deplored this erosion of personal liberty. Later, Marxists were also to oppose nationalism since they claimed that it diverted the attention of people away from class struggle and internationalism and was therefore no more than a 'tool of the bourgeoisie'.

Nationalism has, however, had a wide appeal in the world and nowhere more so than in Europe. Everywhere there people have accepted it as a kind of natural phenomenon and assumed that its legitimate realization is the nation-state. For example, Breton (1981) concludes his book *Les Ethnies* by declaring that each *ethnie* ('national group') should be recognized to have certain rights: to a collective existence; to its historic territory; to self-determination; to its language; to its culture; to the natural resources of its territory and to the use of those resources; to the regulation of its own population; and to the control of all the decisions that affect its well-being. Moreover, there is a widespread belief that language is one of the cornerstones of national identity, because language is one of the clearest indicators of ethnic difference. Language could be used to make claims of others and to lay claims on others. As long ago as the seventeenth century, Henry IV of France could say to deputies elected from his newly acquired provinces: 'As you speak the French language by nature, it is reasonable that you should be the subject of the King of France. I quite agree that the Spanish language should belong to the Spaniard and the German to the

German. But the whole region of the French language must be mine.'

Language is certainly a powerful tool in the hands of nationalists, although it is not the only one. As Philip (1980, p. 5) has remarked:

It is an accepted wisdom that nationalism needs to be buttressed by certain key factors which distinguish one nation from another. Among these factors are counted a common territory, a common language, a common culture, a common history, and a common religion. Not all these factors are present in every national movement but no nationalism worthy of the name can thrive if they are all absent.

Williams (1984, p. 186) argues that the 'orthodox' explanation for why language is so closely linked to nationalistic aspirations is perhaps too facile. Instead of the position that since 'language is a natural barrier separating cultural groups, language conflict is both inevitable and peculiarly unamenable to compromise', he argues (p. 187) that 'it is more profitable to treat language as a political resource which can be used as a grievance factor to mobilize mass support for the separatist cause.' Whichever view is correct it remains inescapable that in the last two centuries a special relationship has come to exist between 'language' and 'nation', whatever the two are or however that relationship is defined. Moreover, there is no sign at all that this relationship will not persist into the future.

STATE-MAKING

We have just noted the existence of a common belief that ethnic groups have some kind of natural right to autonomous national status. As evidence for this, the cases of the 'historic' nations of Western Europe are often cited, nations such as the United Kingdom, France, Spain, Portugal, Holland, Denmark, and Sweden. (Conspicuously missing from the list, of course, are Belgium and Switzerland, the two embarrassing counter-examples.) At the end of the nineteenth century these did appear to be rather good examples to which one could add those of a united Germany and a united Italy as additional evidence. A twentieth-century view of some of these countries would be a little different because the absorption of minorities that seemed to be nearing completion in the late nineteenth century did not occur, as the recent activities of groups such as the Welsh, Bretons, Basques, and Catalans have most clearly demonstrated. Nationalism has not been triumphant in the twentieth century, at least in the way predicted; on the contrary, it has brought about movements that have threatened to break up some of those same historic nations. There is now reason to believe that in these cases states became nations rather than nations became states, and the evidence for this alternative view is particularly strong in the two cases that are most frequently cited, those of the United Kingdom and France.

Seton-Watson has observed (1981, p. 4) 'that national consciousness grew and spread together with the rise of the state. The two most conspicuous examples were France and England.' Weber (1976) has provided plenty of evidence of this fact so far as France is concerned; he clearly shows how French identity was a concept unknown to the rural masses of the south of France quite late in the nineteenth century. Young points out (1976, pp. 23–4) that in states such as England and France we can see how the kings gradually extended their power and influence over the territories they controlled and tried to homogenize and standardize the various parts. The king was the state and his influence was to be spread and felt everywhere. Even revolution did not change the one essential fact that the force of those at the centre of the state, in this case the revolutionaries, should be felt everywhere within the state, the Jacobin ideal. In such a case the state could be declared to be a nation. As Young observes (p. 24): 'The kingdom became the state; the state became the nation. The nation-state provided the ideological model for the sweeping reconstruction of the political map of Europe.' But perhaps a more accurate term would be *state-nation*. Even in the United States, that new 'one nation under God', nationality followed rather than preceded independence – the new nation was founded as an act of political will; it did not produce that will.

There are other views concerning how such states as the United Kingdom, France, and Spain developed. However, any view has to deal with the fact that eventually the centre of the state has come to dominate the periphery, e.g., London and the Home Counties to dominate the United Kingdom, the Île-de-France to dominate France, and Castile to dominate Spain. One widely held view is that a diffusion model best accounts for the facts. In this view the influence of the centre of the state spreads out to the peripheries, and from the conflicts and the adjustments that must be made a homogeneous state arises and eventually perhaps a nation is formed. Local differences will disappear as will regional inequalities and all groups and individuals will come to benefit equally from the process once it has worked through to completion. In Hechter's opinion (1975, p. 8), this view 'is decidedly optimistic: it does not seem to square with much that is happening in the world today. It contrasts in many respects with the expectations of another model, which I will call *internal colonialism*.' In this latter model the centre dominates and exploits the periphery. Those on the periphery may come to tolerate, even welcome, this fact, but there also exists the strong possibility that they will resist such colonialism because, as Khleif (1985, p.184) observes, 'the colonized become *possessions* of the conqueror; they are *administered from the outside* by representatives of the dominant group who are imported from the metropolis; their culture is systematically destroyed; they are the object of an ideology of racism; they are systematically excluded from the higher rewards of the occupational structure; their dignity is constantly assailed.' Consequently, a peripheral group may seek to assert itself against the centre and insist on better treatment than it has had, or make special cultural demands, or go so far as to demand a 'separate' status.

In considering centre-periphery relationships today it is important to realize that in both the United Kingdom and France the economies are highly centralized – with that of France probably the more so of the two. In each country most of the important businesses, the largest firms, and the major banks are located in the capital cities of London and Paris. In contrast, Italy is much less dependent on its commercial centre, Milan, and the Milan-Rome axis is a countervailing force to any strong centripedal tendency. The United Kingdom and France may be examples of states that have not quite succeeded in becoming nations because of the inherent flaw in the strategy that has been pursued, that flaw being that colonial systems often create among the colonized a strong opposition to the colonizers.

In the late nineteenth and early twentieth centuries the fact that a number of important states had become nations rather than those same nations had become states was widely ignored. The prevailing philosophy was that an ethnolinguistic group had a right to national sovereignty, and it was this philosophy that guided those who were responsible for the reordering of Europe at the end of World War I. However, many of the new states that resulted in the peace that followed that war were probably too small to become truly independent political and economic entities, so it is not perhaps surprising that many were swallowed up once again in new 'empires' created after World War II. This state-into-nation process is, however, the one that must be applied in many of the new states that emerged from the break-up of the European empires in the mid-twentieth century, particularly in Africa and Asia. 'Nationalism' in such a context has generally meant freedom from European rule, but those proclaiming it have been most insistent that the states that emerged be left as they were at independence regardless of the anomalies that are obvious to even the most casual observer. As Friedrich says (1966, p. 32), 'Nation building in the contemporary world ... is a matter of building group cohesion and group loyalty for purposes of international representation and domestic planning.' Nations must be built; they do not necessarily exist just waiting to be recognized. Indeed some that exist may have to be discouraged from pressing their claims if the political ordering of the world is not to be put at serious risk.

Nowhere then is this process of nation-building more necessary today than in those states that were until so recently the colonies of European powers. Often such states lack a common language (except a European one veneered onto certain prestige institutions), are multiethnic, may be split along religious lines, can make little or no appeal to a unifying history (except the recent colonial one), and are extremely poor. The creation of a superethnic identity, agreement on language issues, the forming of a common culture, and the development of a national ideology are therefore likely to be formidable, possibly even insuperable, tasks. We must remember too that states with much longer histories, states like the United Kingdom, France, and the Soviet Union (if we include its history as Russia), have still not completed all such tasks in circumstances that have been much more promising of success.

These post-colonial states are faced with the issue of assimilating divergent groups if they are eventually to become nations. Yinger (1981, p. 249) says that 'assimilation is a process of boundary reduction that can occur when members of two or more societies or of smaller cultural groups meet. Seen as a completed process, it is the blending into one of formerly distinguishable socio-cultural groups.' In this view the extent of assimilation in a given setting is a function of the strength of four interdependent processes, those of biological amalgamation, psychological identification, social acculturation, and structural integration. These processes can occur in various combinations and sequences and each is also reversible. Furthermore, other factors can be involved. Yinger adds (pp. 256–7) a number of these: comparative group size; the nature of the initial contacts between the groups; the recency of those contacts; the geographical concentration or dispersion of the various groups; the degree of cultural similarity or dissimilarity, especially in language and religion; the degree of racial similarity or dissimilarity; the state of the economy; the legal and political status of the groups; the levels of discrimination and prejudice; and the conditions in, and the nature of the contact with, ancestral homelands. He also maintains that: 'these historical, cultural, demographic, institutional, and attitudinal factors are highly interdependent. It is only when several combine that rapid assimilation occurs or, under opposite conditions, is blocked or reversed.'

When a considerable amount of assimilation has occurred, those who seek to reverse it must adopt somewhat extreme measures to 'purify' the group and its language, history, culture, and so on. They must be seen to be unequivocally in opposition to the dominant culture, even to the extent of 'over-reacting'. In some cases the leaders themselves may come from the most assimilated among the minority; they, therefore, may find themselves compelled to become extremely dogmatic in their 'orthodoxy' in order to assert their leadership.

The so-called ethnic revival is also a clear indication that assimilation is still not complete in certain states. In still others it threatens even the very existence of the state itself. It also reminds us of Lord Acton's words and raises the possibilty that it may be unrealistic to assume that all states can be made into nations. Perhaps alternative models of the state must be considered, models that not only allow linguistic and cultural diversity but actually encourage it, if many existing states are eventually to achieve domestic harmony.

The ethnic revival as a mainspring of nationalism has been criticized on many grounds. It is said to be romantic, unrealistic, reactionary, and little more than an attack on modernity. Those who lead are said to be confused and they are often seen to be pursuing conflicting goals. Leaders are sometimes accused of being self-serving rather than altruistic in their motives. As an organizing principle in society, ethnicity is said to be divisive in that it insists on group loyalties and undermines individual rights and responsibilities, it assigns people to particular positions and roles in society and stifles the possibility of the distribution of rewards by merit alone, and it gives individuals privileges by reason of group membership, privileges that may be undeserved and sometimes not available to members of other groups. Ethnicity is sometimes even attacked on the basis that it assumes the equality of all cultures and that premise would not be a very happy one on which to conduct affairs among various cultures. Finally, Marxists regard ethnicity as a distraction put forward by those in power to divert the attention of the masses away from the class struggle on which they would be better advised to focus their concerns, and from international cooperation. The *Great Soviet Encyclopedia*, for example, says of nationalism that it is 'a bourgeois and petit bourgeois ideology and policy' which is incompatible with communism.

On the whole, while such criticisms of minority-group aspirations are frequently voiced – and public opinion polls in those societies which use this device often show considerable support for them – most governments recognize that public policy dictates that there must be some accommodation to the wishes of ethnic minority groups. Of course, the amount of accommodation varies immensely. Many states are also faced with the new minorities that they have created for themselves, e.g., those states which owe their existence to the migration of people from the Old World to the New but which now are receiving people from new sources, and those Old World states whose governments decided to import 'foreign' labour to solve certain 'temporary' economic problems but which have found themselves with a new kind of 'permanent' population.

PROBLEMS AND SOLUTIONS

States face formidable problems in trying to maintain their stability while satisfying the demands of their various component elements, and, when there is strong linguistic, ethnic, or religious cleavage, that task may appear at times to be almost impossible. In general, those in power will want to retain power and, in order to do so, they may find themselves engaging in any one of several courses of action. They may designate a dissident group as one to be protected in some way. Such protection may actually in some cases lead to the group being excluded completely from the affairs of the state, and it will usually be futile for such an excluded group to try to appeal to outside states or international bodies. States do not meddle overtly in such affairs in other states and even agencies such as the United Nations prefer to concern themselves with 'individual' rights rather than 'group' rights. The powers that be may, of course, grant such a group certain special rights, quotas, etc. to allow it 'to catch up'. An alternative policy is to stress that the state treats all individuals equally and just simply refuse to acknowledge that groups, as opposed to individuals, can have grievances. Even if they do, then such grievances are best dealt with by ensuring that everyone benefits from the equal protection of the law.

Very rarely will still another course of action be pursued: the development of the state as a consociational entity. In this kind of arrangement the state institutionalizes proportional ethnic representation within a complex, negotiated system of compromises and balances, and treats all ethnic groups as equal partners in the state. Consociational theorists see possibilities for accommodation and compromise when ethnic conflict occurs. According to Lijphart (1977), the solution to such conflicts lies in forming a 'grand coalition' of the ethnic groups, granting mutual veto powers in decision making, allocating certain offices and opportunities proportionately by ethnicity, and promoting ethnic autonomy, particularly through federalism. He admits that Anglo-American adversarial institutions are not very well suited for consociationalist solutions.

The paradigm cases of consociationalism are said to be Belgium, Austria, the Netherlands, and Switzerland. However, only Switzerland can be regarded as a thoroughly stable pluralistic state. It is also not possible to be sure what is cause and what is effect, i.e., whether the consociational arrangements have produced whatever harmony there is or whether that harmony has expressed itself through adopting consociational arrangements. Another less optimistic view is that of van den Berghe (1981, p. 349): 'consociation is in fact often a fragile, unstable sytem, workable only under very special and rarely realized conditions. Consociation boils down in practice to a conservative cartel of ethnic élites sharing power by giving priority to their class over their ethnic interests. The success stories are few; the problems are many; and the democracy is largely a fiction.'

All kinds of states exist in the world but not all are equally viable. In a discussion which focuses on non-European, mainly African and Asian states, Young (1976, pp. 92–5) lists eight types. There are states with historically arbitrary boundaries created through immigration from Europe, e.g., Australia, Brazil, Canada, and the United States. There are states created through colonization but in which there has been a transfer of power, e.g., many West Indian states and Singapore. There are two states which are homelands for diasporas, Liberia and Israel, that is, states in which people 'went home again'. There are the arbitrary colonial creations, states resulting from the dissolution of the old European empires, e.g., many African states, Indonesia, and the Philippines. A fifth kind also arises from colonialism but in this case the states have a clearly defined cultural identity, e.g., Algeria, India, Syria, and Iraq. Young places Sri Lanka in this category but recent events there suggest it may be misplaced. The sixth kind were also colonial states but they had a pre-colonial identity; now they also have a post-colonial one, e.g., Burma, Tunisia, Egypt, and Vietnam. A seventh type is a group of historic states which either escaped colonization or experienced little of it, e.g., Ethiopia, Thailand, and Japan. The final kind are states established out of the wreckage of colonialism by cultural self-definition, with Pakistan the prime example. According to Young, the historical genesis of the state is likely to be an extremely important factor in determining its internal policies and external relationships.

Those policies and relationships are also likely to be affected by the internal cultural composition of the state. Young also defines (pp. 95–7) six types of state on the basis of internal cultural composition. There are a very few culturally homogeneous societies, e.g., Uruguay, Costa Rica, Barbados, Japan, and the two Koreas. There are states in which one cultural group is massively dominant, e.g., Algeria, Cuba, and Jamaica. A third group of states has a preponderant core culture because all other groups are very much peripheral to that dominant core, e.g., Bolivia, Guatemala, Thailand, Burma, and Vietnam. A fourth group has a 'single, bipolar cultural division', which can often be explosive, e.g., Cyprus, Malaysia, and Guyana. In the fifth type there is the same sharp cultural cleavage but more than two groups are involved so that ethnicity and culture are forced to become neutral issues if the state is to survive. This is the situation in much of sub-Saharan Africa. In the final group there is cultural diversity along a number of axes. States such as India, Indonesia, Nigeria, and Uganda are split by religion, ethnicity, language, and so on; they therefore must strive hard to minimize differences and find unifying modes of action.

When we turn to look at what has happened in a wide variety of states, we will find that many different arrangements have been made to deal with language issues. We will also see that a great number of issues remain to be resolved. It is also probably true that there is no universally 'right' solution. The problems of each state are different from those of any other. There are also often strong ideological disagreements that must be resolved, with the fundamental cleavage between assimilationists and pluralists. It is also too simplistic to say that one ideology is right and the other wrong. Neither is without its weaknesses and either can bring benefits if the circumstances are right. We will look at a number of situations to discover what policies are being pursued and the effects these appear to be having. It is unlikely, however, that we will come to decide that there should be only one solution that applies in all cases.

FURTHER READING

Ethnicity: Barth 1969, Breton 1981, Royce 1982, Smith, A. D. 1981, Thernstrom 1980; ethnic groups in Europe: Héraud 1963; ethnic relations and conflict: Banton 1983, Esman 1977a, Giles 1977, Horowitz 1985, Schermerhorn 1978, Shiels 1984; nationalism: Breuilly 1982, Chabot 1986, Connor 1978, Fishman 1972b, Foster 1980, Gellner 1983, Mayo 1974, Seton-Watson 1981, Tiryakian and Rogowski 1985; pluralism: Lijphart 1977, Young 1976.

4

Great Britain

The present language situation in the British Isles provides a good example of how one language has come to dominate various other languages. English has been spread throughout the various islands to the extent that only a very small 'Celtic fringe' remains to remind us of the linguistic diversity that once existed. English itself for a while was forced into competition with Anglo-Norman (or Norman French) but eventually triumphed. Today, one of the basic issues that has arisen in the British Isles is what future is possible for the languages that have managed to survive until now. As we will see too, in the final chapter, a new factor must now be considered: with the post-World War II influx of immigrants to Britain the hegemony of English itself is being challenged from an entirely new direction.

THE RISE OF ENGLISH

We do not know who the earliest inhabitants of Britain were. The earliest people for whom we have written evidence are the Celts. Celtic is an Indo-European language, which today survives in two distinct varieties, Q-Celtic and P-Celtic. The Q-Celtic (or Goidelic or Gaelic) languages are Irish, Scottish Gaelic, and Manx; they retain a labialized voiceless velar stop from Indo-European. The P-Celtic (or Brittonic or Brythonic) languages are Welsh, Cornish, and Breton; in these languages the original labialized voiceless velar stop has become a voiceless bilabial stop. This is why Irish has *ceathir* and *ceann* for 'four' and 'head' respectively and Welsh has *pedwar* and *pen*.

There is some controversy about exactly when the Celts arrived in Britain. It is known that they did migrate from the southeast of Europe westward to France and Spain, and then eventually to the British Isles. Today, there is general agreement that the Celts arrived in Britain no later than the sixth or seventh centuries before Christ, undoubtedly coming in successive waves. There is also some uncertainty concerning whether or not Ireland was colonized by Celts from England or directly from Gaul. Even the timing of the Q-Celtic–P-Celtic split is uncertain, that is, whether it occurred before or after the colonization of the British Isles. In early Roman times the basic split was between the Q-Celtic Irish and the P-Celtic Welsh, with each group having its own island domain. The Irish did manage to extend their influence into the Isle of Man and Scotland and they also made incursions into Cornwall and Wales. However, P-Celtic Wales and Cornwall were not seriously threatened.

The Romans invaded a Celtic Britain but, even though they were to colonize much of England for several centuries, this colonization did little to weaken the hold that Celtic had as the language of the people. During the Roman occupation Latin did become the 'official language', i.e., the language of military and civil administration, of justice, and of what education that existed. Considerable controversy exists, however, over the degree to which Latin became a common language in England. It undoubtedly became the language of the élite and one or other varieties may have been in widespread use as a lingua franca in the towns, but it is highly unlikely that a majority of the population acquired more than a smattering of the language. Bilingualism also does not appear to have been widespread. After the Romans left at the beginning of the fifth century, Latin did hang on for at least another hundred years or so but only as a 'high' and somewhat artificial language with no real roots in the people the Romans left behind. When they departed the Romans took their language with them so far as any everyday use was concerned.

The Romans were superseded by the Anglo-Saxons. Again, who the Anglo-Saxons were is not at all clear. Tradition has it that the invaders were the Angles, Saxons, and Jutes, but the historical evidence does little to support this tradition. What does seem clear is that successive waves of Germanic invaders crossed the North Sea from an area corresponding to modern Friesland, the Frisian Islands, and Saxony in northwest Germany. The first Anglo-Saxon incursions date from sporadic raids in the third century, and from the fifth century on there were both Anglo-Saxon invasions and settlements. The new settlers gradually worked their way north and west so that by the late sixth century they had separated the Cornish from the Welsh. Later, possibly in the late seventh century, they cut off the Welsh from the Celts of Scotland, and the splitting up of the Celtic inhabitants of the British Isles was begun in earnest.

These invaders undoubtedly influenced the Romans to leave. There is some evidence too that the romanized people who were left behind may have tried to accommodate to the invaders rather than suffer continual defeat. Some of the Celts were anglicized, others fled, and undoubtedly there were those who resisted. Place-name evidence suggests, however, that Celtic enclaves were few and that Anglo-Saxon domination was soon complete. We know that even as early as the time of the coming of St Augustine to Britain in 597, the Anglo-Saxons controlled extensive areas of England in both the southeast and northeast. The Celts had been pushed back to Wales and Cornwall and some of them had even left for what was to become Brittany. However, Ireland, the Isle of Man, and the Highlands of Scotland remained unaffected, being too remote from the lands on which the invaders preferred to settle. The Celtic languages were to survive there for many more centuries, although, except in the cases of Irish and the Gaelic of Scotland, with little sense of a common linguistic identity until the eighteenth century.

Latin did return to England along with the Christian religion that St Augustine brought with him in 597. The Latin the Romans had brought with them had long gone by then, but with St Augustine's coming Latin once again became the language of wisdom and scholarship, even though for a while its status was threatened by the Danish invasions of the late eighth and ninth centuries and the disruptions that attended them. King Alfred even found it necessary to have several books translated into English (e.g., Gregory's *Pastoral Care* and *Dialogues* and Boethius' *Consolation of Philosophy*) because of the temporary decline in the knowledge of Latin. However, Latin continued to be the preferred language of scholarship and of the Church for many centuries.

The Danish invasions, which began in earnest with the destruction of the monasteries of Jarrow and Lindisfarne in 793–4, were a threat to the English language but one that it survived. King Alfred successfully rallied the Anglo-Saxons and made peace with the invaders, a peace that confined them to the north and east of the country, to the Danelaw east of the old Roman road Watling Street running from London to Chester. Large numbers of settlers intermingled with the English who remained there. Eventually though, the influence of the south came to be felt throughout the north, and the late ninth and early tenth centuries saw the kingdom of Wessex gradually extend its control over the whole of what is today called England and even into the Scottish Lowlands.

By this time Gaelic had supplanted Pictish in the very north and west of Scotland; the Picts seem to have given up their language by the seventh century. Later the Celts had to share their lands with the invading Norse, who took control of the Shetland and Orkney Islands, settled on some of the better mainland coasts, and even ventured as far south down the west coast of Scotland as Ireland and the Isle of Man. By the eleventh century, however, this Norse advance had been repulsed and the Norse and their language found themselves confined to the northern periphery of the country, where, as we will see, the language hung on into the eighteenth century.

In England the English and the Danes succeeded in blending together as one people, even to the extent that it was the Danes who provided the kings in the period 1016 to 1042. It was the English language though which was triumphant in the union. There is evidence in the English language itself of a period of close contact between the English and Norse peoples: a myriad of place names, borrowings like *sky* and *plough*, pairs like *shirt* and *skirt* and *shrub* and *scrub* – the second in each case being Norse in origin – and even the introduction into English from Norse of the pronouns *they, them,* and *their.* By the tenth century the two peoples had clearly been unified and had established in England what was for that era a fairly strongly centralized state. This state was also able to collect a tax, the Danegeld, to help it resist further incursions and those who ruled did so through a common language that had spread to the far reaches of the state.

There is no evidence that prior to the Norman invasion of 1066 any deliberate effort was made to promote English in any official way. The English had triumphed over the Celts and the English language had replaced Celtic because speakers of English had simply displaced speakers of Celtic and driven them to the borders of the state or had confined them there. The Danish invasions had only a limited effect on English since the languages of the two groups, the invaded and the invaders, were very closely related. Certainly there was no attempt made to prescribe or proscribe who should speak what, and local varieties prevailed for purposes of commerce, administration, and even literature. Only if some permanent record were required or in the case of overseas dissemination would there be a resort to a language that all agreed gave the appropriate mark of permanence or was required if others were to be properly informed; and that language was Latin. The Norman invasion changed all such *laisser faire* attitudes and changed them permanently.

The French influence on England actually predates the Norman Conquest. Edward the Confessor, who came to the throne in 1042 after a period of Danish rule, had spent most of his life in Normandy and on his ascension to the throne he surrounded himself with Normans. He even appointed one, Robert of Jumièges, as Archbishop of Canterbury. However, the invasion of 1066 did more than bring a few Normans into positions of power at the very top of the administration. Normans occupied all the important posts and a deliberate policy of colonization was pursued. The Norman variety of French, Anglo-Norman, came for a while at least to be a serious competitor to the indigenous English and Celtic languages.

By the late eleventh century the 1.5 million or so inhabitants of Britain were dominated by a small minority, estimated at between 10,000 and 20,000, of speakers of Norman French. French was the language of the court and of the new aristocracy, of the Church (except for the liturgy where Latin continued in use), and of the law, administration, and of what literature there was. While there is some evidence of bilingualism, the vast majority of the people apparently remained unilingually anglophone. A classic case of diglossia appears to have resulted with each language used exclusively in certain domains. Bilingual ability was necessary for both anglophones and francophones only in those areas in which the two groups came into contact. Latin also persisted as the language of scholarship and legal writings. Eventually this situation led to the erosion of French, not English, when the Normans found themselves cut off from France.

In the twelfth century a kind of balance prevailed among the languages. French was more and more the language only of the court and of the legal system. Latin was the language of the liturgy, of works of scholarship, and of official record-keeping. English was the language of the mass of the population, but a language deemed unsuitable for writing anything other than the most casual matters.

The year 1204 marks a decisive turning point in the relationship between English and French and the beginning of the sharp decline of the latter. In that year King John lost Normandy to the King of France and the Normans in England had either to return to France to claim what possessions they had there or to abandon them and cast their lot to live cut off in England. In 1215 the English barons forced King John to sign the Magna Carta, a move which effectively consolidated a new aristocracy for England and a new relationship between it and the monarch. In 1258 English was used officially, for the first time since the Conquest, to summon a parliament from all parts of England. This was at the time when Henry III (1216–72), an ardent francophile, was seeking to people his court and the higher administration of the country with his friends from his lands in Poitou and the south of France. By the Provisions of Oxford of 1258, the barons forced the king to abandon any claims he felt he had in France and send back the supporters he had welcomed to England. It is also of interest that the Provisions themselves were promulgated in English not French. Henry's successor Edward I, who died in 1307, further reversed these francophone tendencies; he was also the first king to speak English after 1066.

But French still persisted at court: in Robert of Gloucester's words: 'Unless a man know French he is little thought of'. French was an important cultural language in the thirteenth century rivaling Latin itself, and was used in law and theology, and throughout Europe. The universities also made use of French in their teaching, it being the medium through which Latin, the language of scholarship, was acquired. The English language was in addition borrowing vocabulary from French in great quantities. However, the influence of French was weakening rapidly in the thirteenth century too. England had been separated from France, the clergy were preaching in English, manuals were being produced to teach good French, and an English literature was developing as certain types of popular romances and religious works were produced in the language.

The result was that by the mid-fourteenth century English had spread just about everywhere. In 1356 the proceedings of the sheriff's courts in London and Middlesex were required to be in English. French did persist as the legal language of the land, having replaced Latin for government records and for such matters as writs, petitions, and charters. But English was encroaching fast. For example, in 1362 during Edward III's reign, an Act of Parliament, the Statute of Pleadings, was passed requiring English to be the language of the courts but leaving Latin as the language of legal record. The Act itself, however, was written in French. Of particular interest is the preamble to the Act which explains why such a measure is necessary. In that preamble we are told that French has become virtually unknown in the realm and that 'great mischiefs' have arisen when people have had to observe laws written in a language they could not understand. Hence there was a need to use English in all court pleadings. As it happened, the legal system proved particularly resistant to changes that had gone on elsewhere. It was not until the eighteenth century that the English language prevailed everywhere in the English legal system as the language of the law, an act of 1731 specifying that all proceedings in courts in Great Britain had to be 'in the English tongue and language only, and not in Latin or French, or any other tongue or language whatsoever'. Today, we can still see the relics of Latin and legal French in those legal systems that have evolved from the English common law.

The Hundred Years War, which began in 1337, did nothing to improve Anglo-French relationships, and the Black Death, which began in 1348, had its effects too, ultimately killing off about a third of francophones and anglophones alike, with the actual cost to the francophone population much greater in view of its small numbers. The plague drastically eroded the unilingual French-speaking population that existed at the time and strengthened the process of the complete anglicization of bilinguals. There are actually those who claim that by the time of the Black Death there were very few, if any, unilingual francophones left in England and that French was little more than an affectation for many of those who claimed to speak it. There may well

be merit in such a case, for contemporary literature contains references
to some of the pretences associated with the French of the time, which
had also by then distanced itself considerably from that of the continent.
French had become so foreign that manuals began to appear offering
instruction to those who might want to learn French but who could not
easily find suitable instruction.

Although French could still be found in use in England at the end of
the fourteenth century, it is quite clear that by then English had reasserted
itself as the language of England. The French language was to leave its
mark on English, mainly on the vocabulary, and in later centuries the
English were to exhibit mixed feelings toward the French language and
the people who spoke it and their culture. But in less than three centuries
England had turned its back on the opportunity to become francophone
if indeed that opportunity had ever really existed. Instead of the English
learning the language of their invaders, the invaders gave up their
language for English. In giving up their language for that of the people
they had conquered, the Normans joined other conquerors elsewhere;
among them other Norsemen in the south of Italy and in Russia; Franks
in France; Bolgars, a non-Slavic people, in Bulgaria; Dalmatians in
Ragusa; and Mongols in Western Asia.

Whereas before the Norman Conquest the language of the court was
the Wessex dialect of English but both the Midlands and the Northern
dialects flourished for literary purposes, after English reestablished itself
it was the Midlands dialect which came to be preferred. It was also
from this dialect that Standard English eventually arose. There is some
dispute as to whether the particular Midlands dialect was an East
Midlands variety or a Central Midlands one. Those who favour the first
stress the importance of the influence of the university cities of Oxford
and Cambridge and the administrative centre of Westminster. Those
who favour the second emphasize the importance of the spread of a
literary standard through the wide dissemination of Chancery English.
In this latter view the estimated 120 or so civil servants in Chancery
were responsible for introducing a variety of English which was to set
the standard for the administrative language of the country by the mid-
fifteenth century. It was this standard that the printers adopted and
which both Wycliffe and Caxton followed, the first in his translation
of the Bible and the second when he introduced printing into England
in 1476. After the Midlands dialect came into such favour there was a
precipitous decline in the use of the Southern dialect for literary purposes
so that there are almost no literary works in this dialect after the
fourteenth century. The Northern dialect was more fortunate and writers
continued to employ it for many years; we may even see its continuation
in the poetry of Burns and in other more recent Scots writers.

After the fifteenth century the major concern about English was its possible inadequacy. It existed in different dialects, there was a very low level of literacy, and the language lacked the prestigious associations that Latin had and French still retained in some circles. In spite of the glories of Shakespeare's plays, the King James Bible, and the *Book of Common Prayer*, there were still numerous complaints about the inadequacies of the language. Suggestions as to how to improve the language were also numerous. One suggestion often repeated was to establish some kind of academy to help in the task of developing the language. Other countries had established such academies for this purpose. Nothing resulted from this suggestion, and in England today there is no institution equivalent to the Académie Française. However, there is little doubt that in the seventeenth century for example the proclaimed virtues of Latin and a feeling among many of the educated that the language of the court at Westminster should be emulated had a considerable influence on how the language developed elsewhere in the country and on attitudes toward any other variety of the language.

Only the Northern dialect, with its separate existence and legitimacy assured by the existence of an independent Scotland, remained somewhat immune from such pressures. But even the Scots were not entirely unaffected, using as they did English translations of the Bible and noting the prestige that the new written English of the south was acquiring. The variety of the language that the Scots spoke was less affected, but the result was the creation of a break between the two varieties, the written and the spoken. As we will see, this break would later seriously undermine any case that Scots might have to be a separate language of the British Isles rather than just another variety of English.

By the mid-eighteenth century English was quite secure in England. Parliament finally resolved the status of English, French, and Latin in the legal system. It prohibited French and Latin and made English the exclusive language of legal record. One consequence, of course, was that the same law also banned Cornish, Welsh, and Gaelic for such purposes since it forbade the use of 'any other tongue or language whatsoever' in legal matters. English was finally to prevail but now at the expense of indigenous languages as well as those that had been brought through post-Anglo-Saxon invasion or by missionaries and scholars.

The eighteenth century was also a century in which a new middle class emerged and in which there was a marked increase in literacy. It was an era too that prized the classical tradition and showed a concern with standards and improving on nature. Although in the Preface to his *Dictionary* of 1755 Johnson had warned against the futility of trying to 'fix' the language for all time, much attention was still given to attempts to 'purify' the language and linguistic propriety became a serious matter. There was much discussion of such matters during the course of the century and gradually the earlier rather free-wheeling acceptance of differences gave way to authoritarianism. This authoritarianism continued into the nineteenth century and found its way eventually into the schools as mass education developed. It was in the late nineteenth century that a particular variety of pronunciation of English, the variety called *Received Pronunciation* (or RP), achieved whatever prestige it had and still has. We should note that this authoritarianism, this concern for 'standards', and its allied feeling so often proclaimed that the language is 'declining' through neglect and indifference, is one we can still see today, particularly in North America.

By the eighteenth century too Scots, the only language that might have competed seriously with English in Great Britain, was rapidly becoming moribund. Scots is now generally regarded as just another regional dialect of English. That it is the direct descendant of the Northern dialect of the Anglo-Saxons is ignored and that it was also the language of an independent country carries little weight to those who hold no regrets about the union of England and Scotland.

Michael Canmore (1059–93) was the last king of Scotland whose native tongue was Gaelic. Since he had spent some of his life in exile in England and had married a princess from Wessex, English customs prevailed in his court and his descendants became anglicized or were subject to some Anglo-Norman influence after 1066. That influence was not particularly strong – it was hardly more than a brief flirtation – because the Scottish court became a haven to survivors of the Norman invasion of the country to the south and the English language and customs came to be preferred in Scotland. As Celtic influences were also rejected, particularly by David I (1124–53), who pushed the Celts and their influence back into the Highlands, the area that came under the domination of the Northern dialect eventually extended to all the south and east of the country.

In this Lowland area the kings established English-speaking towns and installed English-speaking masters in lands that had previously been dominated by Celts. The English language and English ways came to dominate life in the area in contrast to the Anglo-Norman domination of England itself. The variety of English that was spoken, at first known as *Inglis*, also came to be called *Scots* to distinguish it from the variety that predominated in the capital to the south. This language also became an important literary language and for a time in the fifteenth and sixteenth centuries a true national language.

Scotland enjoyed a considerable independence from England in the four centuries that preceded the Union of 1707. During much of that time it enjoyed a relationship with France and developed its own system of government, education, and law. There was also a flourishing literature in literary Scots. In the last of these centuries, following the union of the crowns of England and Scotland in 1603, this independence was severely eroded. That erosion had actually begun at least a generation before when in 1579 a law was passed requiring every Scottish householder with 300 marks to possess an English bible. The use of Tudor versions of the Bible and later of the King James authorized version and of the *Book of Common Prayer* also encouraged literacy in English rather than Scots and helped to hasten the anglicization of Scotland, particularly in the eighteenth century. The court at Westminster and its ways also proved to be extremely attractive to the Scottish nobility who sought to intermingle with their English counterparts. Consequently, under the centralizing pressure exerted from the south and from its own élites, Scotland was deprived of much of its special identity. In the mid-eighteenth century certain middle-class Scots including schoolmasters also actively began to promote the elimination of those distinctions that differentiated Scots from English. There were to be dissidents like Burns and Scott but even they spoke English no matter how much their writing encouraged the continuation of a literary Scots. Scots became a literary language rather than a spoken one, a tradition carried into the twentieth century by the well-known writer Hugh MacDiarmid (1892–1978).

Scots suffered less noticeably in its struggle with English than did Gaelic, which was, after all, a completely different language. Scots came to be regarded as just another dialect of English at a time when people were concerned with standardizing the language and eliminating as much variation as possible. It became like varieties spoken in Yorkshire in the north of England and Somerset in the west, varieties perhaps suitable for study by antiquaries but not to be taken seriously by modern progressive scholars. That there was resistance to such views was to be expected but that very little has resulted from this resistance is not surprising. The nearest parallel example to the situation in Scotland is perhaps the two varieties of Norwegian that exist in Norway today. The Norwegians have succeeded in creating for their language an indigenous variety, *Nynorsk*, to rival the dominant variety, *Bokmål*; however, Nynorsk still does not enjoy the widespread acceptance of Bokmål. The current situation with regard to Scots and English in Scotland also raises but a small measure of the passion that is aroused in Norway over the language competition there.

Whatever Scots was and in spite of attempts to continue the literary tradition into modern times and to study and promote it as a bona fide language, it seems that today more and more Scots themselves regard the language – also known as *Lallans* – as no more than one of the regional dialects of English. There are those who readily give it up for a standard variety of English, there are those who try to promote it at every opportunity, but the vast majority of Scots are apparently unconcerned either way, going on speaking in a distinctly Scottish manner but choosing to write Standard English.

Most Scots see no real need for a separate language for Scotland. Indeed most seem to find the present political arrangement with England quite acceptable. Scottish affairs do tend to bring together Scots of various political persuasions both in Westminster and elsewhere but the current system does meet certain Scottish needs. Home Rule for Scotland got nowhere in the 1880s and the recent move for devolution foundered in the referendum of 1979. The Scottish National Party has also lost considerable support since the election of October, 1974 when it captured 30.4 per cent of the vote. Not even North Sea oil has made Scots want to renegotiate the union. Whatever problems Scotland has – and like many other parts of the United Kingdom it does have problems – Scots do not see the solution to lie in autonomy for Scotland and language issues seem to have little more than a sentimental appeal and only to a very small minority.

Although English has been the majority language of the British Isles ever since the days when the invading Anglo-Saxons pushed the Celts to the northern and western extremities, it still had a considerable struggle to become accepted as a language suitable for every function. But that struggle was won eventually. English was also deliberately promoted in the British Isles. Although never made the official language anywhere in the British Isles, English was actively promoted through its use in the various agencies of government, in religious institutions, and later in mass public education. Other languages were neglected and on occasion prohibited entirely. Even property rights could be lost if one did not know English, and certainly without a knowledge of the language many avenues to preferment remained closed. The result was the marked decline of all other languages than English in the British Isles, a decline that continues to this day. In the view of many observers this decline is also by now virtually irreversible and may well lead to the British Isles becoming completely unilingual in English in the not too distant future.

EXTINCT LANGUAGES

Certain languages have disappeared entirely from the British Isles or are in their death throes. In this category we can place Shetland Norn, Manx, Cornish, and Channel Islands French. There are still those who claim to speak either Manx or Cornish but not one of these speakers speaks the language natively. There are no speakers of Shetland Norn, and there is every reason to believe that soon there will be no surviving speakers of Channel Islands French.

Shetland Norn descended from the language that the Danish invaders brought with them, with the first settlements beginning near the end of the eighth century. These invaders penetrated as far as Ireland and the Isle of Man and even today the system of government in Man owes something to the invaders. Norn existed as a spoken language in the Orkney and Shetland Islands until the eighteenth century. It is also believed to have been the first language of the natives of the Orkneys until the end of the sixteenth century and of the Shetlands until well into the seventeenth century. Norn suffered from the migration of Lowlanders to the islands and from a shift in trading patterns which led to an increase in trade with the Scottish mainland to the south and a decrease in trade with Norway. The growth of literacy and the spread of what little education that was available may also have contributed to the decline of Norn. What is clear is that increasingly in the sixteenth and seventeenth centuries the population of the islands became bilingual in Norn and Scots so that monolingual Norn speakers were few by the late seventeenth century. In the eighteenth century there is evidence that Norn survived mainly through massive borrowings into the Scots that was spoken. However, by the end of the nineteenth century there was such a large reduction in such borrowing that the natives of the islands could be said to speak Scots with a colouring of Norn vocabulary. Today, apparently only minuscule traces of Norn remain and the language has effectively disappeared.

Manx, the Celtic language of the Isle of Man, a possession of the English Crown since 1765, has also disappeared, its last native speaker, Ned Maddrell, dying in 1974 at the age of 97. Gaelic came originally to the Isle of Man from Ireland in the fourth century. The language survived a period of Norse domination between the ninth and thirteenth centuries but then became subject to Scottish influence, particularly that of the Scottish variety of Celtic. For several centuries the island was held as a private fiefdom, but, when it came more and more under the control of the English Crown, Manx began to weaken. By 1871, for example, out of a total population of 50,000 less than a quarter spoke

Manx and these were mainly old people living in isolated areas. By 1901 only 8 per cent of the population spoke Manx, by 1931 only about 500 people did, and this number had dropped to one by 1974. Even these last survivors who spoke Manx acknowledged their Manx to be poor in quality; the language had completely lost its vitality in the late nineteenth century and existed in a largely bastardized form.

Although Man enjoys a certain amount of autonomy from Westminster, being like the Channel Islands a largely self-governing Crown possession rather than part of the United Kingdom itself, there is apparently little desire to try to revive Manx in order to further the little independence that exists. The island has been thoroughly anglicized so that even ardent Manx nationalists regard the task of language revival as hopeless and the learning of Manx as nothing more than a hobby, and it is as a hobby that any Manx that is spoken today is spoken – by about 300 speakers according to the 1971 Census.

In Cornwall, we can see a situation that largely parallels that of the Isle of Man. Cornwall too was once an independent entity but it no longer enjoys that status and is now no less anglicized. Cornish was, or is, like Welsh, a P-Celtic language brought to the part of the world with which it is associated well before the birth of Christ. Cornwall apparently came under Roman domination during the Roman occupation of England but that occupation seems to have left almost no traces at all on the life of the people. The Romans took some minerals and left the Celtic people to continue their rural ways. There was a little Irish settlement in the fifth and sixth centuries, but the greatest influence on Cornish life was to come from the Anglo-Saxons. When the Anglo-Saxons did invade England some of the Cornish fled to Brittany, the ancestors of the present Bretons there. The rest remained to fight the invaders. From the beginning of the eighth century the Anglo-Saxons began their advance into Cornwall and it was not until the tenth century that the last independent King of Cornwall, Hywel, was defeated and Cornwall became part of the English kingdom. Place-name and other evidence from the *Domesday Book* of 1086 shows that by the mid-tenth century there was considerable Anglo-Saxon settlement in Cornwall, particularly in the east.

Although the Normans claimed Cornwall after their invasion of England, they made little or no attempt to promote French in the new domain, their numbers there being too thin. Ironically, too, among the opponents of the spread of French in England was John Trevisa, a Cornishman. Cornish became a victim in the struggle between English and French, its uses being confined almost entirely to the most mundane of matters. Even when many Cornish and Welsh helped Henry Tudor to overthrow Richard III on Bosworth Field in 1485 and some were rewarded for that help, they adopted English as their language in their new positions of power. Later fifteenth-century insurrections, particularly that led by Perkin Warbeck in 1497, were unsuccessful and merely served to confirm a growing belief that any separate status for Cornwall on account of its language would be a mistake for a kingdom bent on centralizing power in Westminster. Cornwall was also becoming increasingly important for its tin, and the towns and seaports which the Tudors developed were important to the country's defences.

A particularly crucial blow to Cornish as a language was the Act of Uniformity of 1549. This act required the use of English in church services in which use of the new *Book of Common Prayer* was also required. The Cornish objected, demanding that they should be allowed to continue to use Latin, which at least was a neutral language, but one with the weight of custom attached to it and none of the burden of the alien English language. A translation of the *Book of Common Prayer* into Cornish was also proposed as a possibility. However, Cornish protests, once again backed by arms, were to no avail and the anglicization of Cornwall proceeded at an even faster pace from that date. Whereas the Welsh were allowed to use their language for religious purposes and religious materials were made available in Welsh, the Cornish were not so fortunate. The Reformation had not spread to Cornwall and the Cornish had remained largely Catholic; state policy did not allow them to be treated generously.

It appears that in the fifteenth and sixteenth centuries Cornish was the prevailing language west of the River Tamar but from that period it declined with an astounding rapidity. English was the language of the rulers, of administration, and of the towns and seaports. On the other hand, Cornish was completely cut off from its religious sources and from its natural contacts in Brittany. The language itself began to show the considerable influence of English and fewer and fewer people were able to speak it well and then to speak it at all. At the beginning of the eighteenth century only small pockets of Cornish speech, with probably no monoglots left, could be found along the coastline near Land's End, and the last recorded native speaker, Dolly Pentreath of Mousehole, died in 1777. English had just simply overtaken Cornish. One interesting consequence of the persistence of Cornish until the eighteenth century is that the variety of English that is now spoken in West Cornwall is less 'dialectal' than that of East Cornwall. East Cornwall English shows regional similarities to the dialects of neighboring Devon and Somerset, but West Cornwall speech more closely approximates Standard English, the result possibly of the greater influence of education in the promotion of English there.

A few hundred people claim to be able to speak and read Cornish today. There are also societies that exist to encourage use of the language, e.g., Cowethas Kelto-Kernuak (Celtic-Cornish Society) founded in 1901, and a small literature. The revived Cornish is a somewhat piecemeal and quite artificial creation of antiquaries, and some Celtic scholars have been quite critical of it. But it is this variety that is used whenever 'Cornish' is used today and it is on this variety that those who see a future for the language and possibly too for a Cornish nation have pinned their hopes. The Cornish that exists today is really to be found only among those who seek to bring about a revival of the language along with a revival of a Celtic ethnic consciousness.

The Channel Islands (in decreasing order of size Jersey, Guernsey, Alderney, and Sark) came into the orbit of the English Crown as a result of the Norman Conquest. They were part of the Norman lands before 1066 but it was not until 1154 that they were actually united to the Normans' new possessions in England under Henry II, who on his succession to the throne was also Duke of Normandy, and not until 1204 that they were finally severed from France. It was in that year that Philippe of France forced the Normans lords to choose between him and the King of England and the Channel Islands went to England along with the new allegiance.

The French of the Channel Islands derives from the French of the Normans; it is not the French of Paris, although it is the latter variety of French which now serves as the 'official' variety when one is called for on rare occasions, e.g., property conveyancing in Jersey. Norman French has survived to this day but the current situation is far from healthy. The language is spoken in several dialects and there is no standard form and almost nothing exists in writing for speakers to read. Channel Islands French is actually now extinct on Alderney and it is in a precarious situation on Sark. Both islands saw a considerable influx of English-speaking workers in the nineteenth century and bilingualism became common. This bilingualism led to the loss of French over very few generations. Similar anglicization is now apparent on Guernsey and Jersey. It has been helped by such factors as the spread of education, the arrival of people from the mainland to settle, the temporary evacuation of children to England during World War II, the influence of the mass media, and the sheer attraction of English as a world language.

Like the Isle of Man the Channel Islands have a unique status vis-à-vis Westminster and one might expect to see that status reflected in language in some way. But English has become the language of government in the Islands, of the courts, and of the records that are kept. The mid-twentieth century was the time in which French was finally abandoned for such purposes. The decline in French, both of the local spoken variety and the standard written variety, has been precipitous in the twentieth century. It was only in 1900 that the right to address the legislative assembly of the States of Jersey in English was recognized. By 1946 the official language of the States had become English with French reserved for formal and official occasions and for keeping official records. But this provision did not last beyond 1966. The Channel Islands seem well on their way to being completely anglophone within the very near future.

WALES AND WELSH

The Celtic languages still survive in the British Isles in spite of centuries of oppression and neglect. How much longer they will survive is an issue that concerns many who still speak them. As we have seen, Manx and Cornish have effectively disappeared. Only Welsh, Gaelic, and Irish survive as living languages and there are very few, if any, monolingual speakers of these today. These languages are also spoken only in the peripheral areas of the British Isles, along remote coastlines or in rural pockets. Those who do speak them will generally also be literate in English; they may not be literate in the Celtic language they happen to speak. They are also likely to be older than those of similar background who do not speak the language. Consequently, the Celtic languages in the British Isles are often associated with older people and with rural, traditional ways of life at a time when urbanization and modernity attract the young.

The history of the Celtic languages is one of retreat ever since the coming of the Anglo-Saxons, a retreat that shows no sign of stopping. Today, the speakers of the remaining Celtic languages have rather different attitudes toward them and the place each language should have in the national consciousness of those who speak it. For the Welsh, language figures prominently as an issue. For the Scots, Gaelic is of relatively little importance since Scottish nationalism has never tied itself to language. For the Irish, language is no more than a symbolic issue, independence having come long after the Irish masses had surrendered their language to English.

The Anglo-Saxons had driven the Welsh into Wales, *Welsh* itself actually being an Anglo-Saxon word meaning 'foreign'. They could be left to their own devices there. The loss of Celtic control of Wales began in the period immediately following the Norman Conquest. In the late eleventh and early twelfth centuries various Norman barons decided to extend their power into Wales by subduing the Celtic chiefs who lived in the border regions. These conquerors became known as the Lords of the Marches. The lands they conquered were outside the king's control and each lord ruled as he pleased collecting what taxes he wanted and dispensing justice as he wished. The Crown eventually came to regard this system as a threat just as it regarded the residual Celtic areas as a threat to its centralizing plans for a united kingdom. Consequently, in the fifteenth century a succession of moves was made against the Welsh and the Lords of the Marches in order to extend the royal prerogative to Wales, moves that regulated who could hold land, the use of language, and the place of the two ethnic groups in Welsh society. In 1534 Henry VIII converted the Lord Marcherships into English shires and extended the English system of law and administration into Wales. Finally, in 1536 the Act of Union effectively annexed Wales to England, although at no time previous to then had Wales been a truly independent, unified country.

The Act of Union established the authority of the King of England and the Parliament of England over Wales; it enabled England to protect its western border; it ended the continual problems that the Marcher Lords had created for the king; and it promoted a centralized English-dominated state. English law and religion were imposed. London became the focal point of administrative activity and the new aristocracy and leadership that emerged looked to English as the language of preferment. Welsh was not actually proscribed but a knowledge of English was necessary for success. The Act of Union itself specified that: 'from hensforth no personne or personnes that use the Welsshe speche or langage shall have or enjoy any maner office or fees within the Realme of Onglonde Wales or other the Kinges dominions upon peyn of forfaiting the same offices or fees onles he or they use and exercise the speche or langage of Englisshe.' Apparently though, in spite of the requirement that English was to be the sole language of the courts of Wales, Welsh continued in use where necessary and this practice has never ceased. However, by the end of the sixteenth century English was clearly in ascendancy over Welsh in law, administration, education, and commercial activities. Only religion was left to the Welsh language.

In 1561 the English passed an Act of Parliament that was to be of immense importance to the Welsh and their language. In that year an Act for the Translation of the Bible and the Divine Service into the Welsh Tongue was passed so as to ensure the spread of Protestantism into Wales. The work of translation was completed by 1588 and the Welsh language found itself buttressed with a powerful literary document. The Welsh were able to use their native language for worship even if they were forbidden to put it to certain other uses. Since religion was a strong force in Welsh life, the language gained a significant protection from this official blessing, and, still later, when the Welsh turned to

Nonconformism, the link between language and religion remained firm. The new Bible also reinforced Welsh as a literary language. If the Bible could exist in Welsh, then so could other works. Furthermore, the Bible established a standard for written Welsh, one that could serve those who sought to write in the language. As a result, in the four centuries or so since the Bible first appeared in Welsh there have been approximately 20,000 books published, not a large literary output to be sure but a continuous one, and one that has had an important impact on both the language and the people. Other minority languages of Europe, e.g., Breton, Basque, and Occitan, did not experience this same early development of a standardized written form and have had to pay dearly for their lack.

The Welsh have been much less lucky so far as education is concerned. A prevalent attitude has been that the Welsh language has been a barrier to progress in Wales. In 1846 a Blue Book produced following an investigation of Welsh education by three English commissioners – the *Report of the Commission of Enquiry into the State of Education in Wales*, otherwise known as the 'Treason of the Blue Books' – observed among other things that: 'the Welsh language is a vast drawback to Wales and a manifold barrier to the moral progress and commercial prosperity of the people', and that 'because of their language, the mass of the Welsh people are inferior to the English in every branch of practical knowledge and skill.' The report was in many respects biased or factually incorrect, e.g., in its reporting on the rates of illegitimacy in Wales, but the Welsh people responded to it as the commission had hoped and began to learn English. English was to be the language of education in Wales. Welsh could be used in the classroom as a means to the end of teaching English; it could not be an end in itself. The Education Act of 1870, which laid the foundation of public school education in England and Wales, provided for education in English alone. Shortly afterwards, indeed as early as 1875, some provision was made for teaching Welsh but really only to support the teaching of English. A Welsh Language Society (Cymdeithas yr Iaith Gymraeg) was also founded in 1885, with its full title being, The Society for the Utilization of the Welsh Language in Education for the Purpose of Serving a Better and More Intelligent Knowledge of English; its goal was to promote bilingual education in the hope that Welsh would also be taught, but its organizers also knew that by this time the Welsh would not accept Welsh-only education.

A century ago no one would have predicted that there would be so few monolingual speakers of Welsh so soon. In 1891 Professor John Morris-Jones concluded an article in the second edition of the *Welsh Encyclopedia* by stressing how vital Welsh was as a language and rejecting the idea that the next century would see its extinction. He could well be optimistic since at that time Welsh vitality appeared to be as strong as it had been for a considerable time A majority of the Welsh population spoke Welsh although many of these, perhaps a half, also spoke English. But there were a number of danger signals on the horizon. The process of urbanization that was to produce drastic shifts in the Welsh population had begun as Wales began to industrialize. One immediate result was the beginning of rural depopulation. Another was that workers from England began to move into Wales. There is some disagreement as to the significance of such factors. Industrialization in Wales may have been a mixed blessing. While it brought into Wales many thousands of English-speaking immigrants, it also led to internal migration and kept the Welsh at home. Unlike the Irish, who left their country as rural Ireland was depopulated, the Welsh were just as inclined to move into the industrializing parts of Wales as to leave for distant parts. In this way the language was kept alive in the urban concentrations in which Welsh could continue to be used for a while at least. Welsh migration may actually have boosted Welsh-speaking ability temporarily in the new industrial areas.

By the middle of the nineteenth century the labour needs of Monmouth and Glamorgan could no longer be met from the Welsh countryside and neighbouring English counties and long-distance English immigration began. It seems that after about 1850 an English immigrant to the industrial Wales of coal and iron no longer needed to learn Welsh to get by. English also became the language of promotion and opportunity in the area and Welsh began its hasty retreat. The result was that whereas in 1825 it is estimated that 70 per cent of the population of Wales could speak Welsh, with half of these monolingual, by the 1891 census, which was the first census to ask questions about language, the proportion had fallen to 51 per cent, with only 29 per cent of these monolingual. By that time too the economy of Wales was completely geared to that of England. When the Welsh economy eventually collapsed during the 1920s and 1930s the consequences were drastic; people had to leave Wales but by that time they had become very thoroughly anglicized to the extent that most were unable to take their language with them if they left or find solace in their language if they stayed.

In 1901 about half the population of Wales could still speak Welsh, some 930,000 people. By 1931 the proportion had declined to 37 per cent, some 909,000, and by 1981 to 19 per cent, some 508,000. Today the monolingual Welsh-speaking population has dropped to about 21,500 or about one per cent. The current statistics indicate that if present trends continue Welsh will disappear at some point not too far into the next century. More and more Welsh people have forgotten

Welsh or have never learned the language, 81 per cent in the 1981 Census, and those who do know Welsh are likely to be older people. Young people are overwhelmingly monolingual anglophones. In those rural areas where there is still a considerable amount of Welsh spoken Welsh is now the language of either the very young or the very old.

The geographical distribution of those who speak Welsh is also not very promising. The majority of those who speak Welsh live in urban and industrial areas where English predominates , e.g., Glamorgan with its 12 per cent of Welsh speakers. Even Cardiff, the capital of Wales, had a Welsh-speaking population of less than 5 per cent in 1971. In urban areas there is still actually a lot of Welsh spoken but alongside even more English. In such areas Welsh still retains a symbolic value for many but for others it is not very useful, and the many English monolinguals are indifferent to the language, seeing no threat in Welsh but also no real need to support its preservation. Places in which Welsh speakers find themselves in a majority, e.g., Anglesey with its 66 per cent Welsh speakers, are mainly rural enclaves. Each census shows Welsh to be retreating and these enclaves to be getting smaller. The Welsh-speaking areas are increasingly isolated from one another: they are rural, interior areas. Moreover, there is a great anglophone wedge between those of the north and those that are left in the south. In the northwest the Welsh heartland is in what is now the county of Gwynedd; in the southwest it is in the county of Dyfed. The strength of the Gwynedd heartland showed little decline between the 1971 and 1981 censuses; however, there was considerable shrinkage and fragmentation in the Dyfed heartland during the same period. Maps superimposed on one another show Welsh to be drying up like a lake with pools left here and there and these evaporating until they eventually disappear.

Welsh is disappearing because Wales has been in decline economically and because English penetration has been massive. The railways, for example, tied the various parts of Wales to places in the outside world rather than to one another. The English have migrated to Wales to work and more recently to buy up property, particularly for vacation homes. The Welsh have also tended to abandon their own countryside in pursuit of better prospects elsewhere. The English language has been spread through the mass media, through education, and through the economic and administrative integration of Wales into the United Kingdom. Finally, the traditional bulwark of the Welsh language, its connection with religion, no longer works because of the massive decline in religious observance.

There has been a revival in the use of Welsh in education in Wales; now there is a recognition that Welsh has a place in the educational system of the country. Such recognition has been grudgingly, for

numerous have been the stories of the punishments and humiliations
suffered by those who were caught speaking Welsh at school when
English-only policies prevailed. We have to remember though that the
Welsh themselves often deliberately sought out opportunities to learn
English. They often had mixed feelings about the value of Welsh,
particularly for their children; they did not want them necessarily to
abandon Welsh but they certainly did want them to acquire English as
well. As Durkacz (1983, p. 225) says: 'There can be no doubt, therefore,
that throughout the Celtic periphery of the British Isles the people were
keen to learn English. The schools ... pandered to this demand. The net
result was ... to reinforce the trend to bilingualism in the Celtic fringe.'

By the beginning of the twentieth century there was no prohibition
of the teaching of Welsh in the schools of Wales; in fact, numerous
reports and regulations were aimed at encouraging Welsh as both a
subject and a language of instruction. But the response was slow as was
the development of the necessary resources. It was not until the mid-
twentieth century that the first really effective measures were taken. The
first Welsh medium primary school was established in Aberystwyth in
1939. Now there are over 60 such schools and also 14 designated
bilingual secondary schools located mostly in predominantly English-
speaking areas. In 1984 the Welsh Office of the Department of Education
and Science reported that Welsh was the sole medium of instruction in
18.8 per cent of all primary schools and was used as a medium of
instruction in a further 14.2 per cent of such schools. The language was
taught as a second language in another 43.4 per cent of the schools and
not used or taught at all in the remaining 23.6 per cent. Welsh was also
used extensively in secondary schools, but in these it is usually given no
greater emphasis than being the first 'foreign' language that students
choose, alongside languages such as French and German.

It is now government policy to provide every child in Wales with the
opportunity to learn Welsh and in some cases to learn through the
medium of Welsh. However, a lack of either resources or commitment
has left this policy unfulfilled, for still today 23.6 per cent of primary
schools and 13.4 per cent of secondary schools make no provision for
Welsh. Even though there is quite clearly far more provision for Welsh
in education than there has ever been, Welsh children still opt to study
in English, much as they always have. For some people the growth of
bilingual education in Wales suggests that the decline of the Welsh
language can be arrested even though it may not be reversed. Others
are less optimistic, being unsure of genuine Welsh commitment to
preserve their language through the educational opportunity that now
seems to exist. The attractions of English are still very strong indeed,
particularly for the young.

The Welsh do, however, still value their language. Books are still written in Welsh. The Eisteddfod, revived in 1880, still plays an important part in the cultural life of the nation. Organizations such as the new Welsh Language Society (Cymdeithas yr Iaith Gymraeg), founded in 1962, and Plaid Cymru (Party of Wales), founded in 1925, have promoted language as an important unifying symbol for Welsh identity. There have been victories too. In 1942 the Welsh Courts Act declared that 'the Welsh language may be used in any court in Wales by any party or witness who considers that he would otherwise be at a disadvantage by reason of his natural language of communication being Welsh'; however, in practice it has been left to the courts themselves to make such a decision, not to the party or witness, and English prevails almost exclusively still as the language of the law in Wales. In 1967 the Welsh Language Act extended the uses of Welsh in Wales and in 1982 the long-awaited fourth television channel S4C (Sianel 4 Cymru) telecasting in Welsh came into existence with its 22 hours of Welsh-language programmes in peak hours covering the whole range of usual television programming and with its potential audience of three million people. The provision of the channel was won only after a period of confrontation with the government. It is still too early to predict what effect the new television channel will have on preserving Welsh language and culture, particularly as there is clear indication that the initial enthusiasm for it has considerably diminished.

It would be false to say that Welsh is not today in serious jeopardy. The majority of the population are fairly apathetic about the future of the language. There is a middle-class-led movement to strengthen its position and to resist any further encroachment by English. Plaid Cymru has been the longtime leader, stating as long ago as 1930 in one of its pamphlets that: 'The cornerstone of the Welsh National Party's language policy is that the Welsh language should, within its own territory, have the advantage over all other languages.' A recurring slogan is *Cenedl heb iaith, cenedl heb galon* (A nation without a language is a nation without a heart). The Welsh Language Society, founded after Saunders Lewis's famous broadcast of 13 February 1962 on 'The Fate of the Language', has provided another kind of leadership, its members having participated in such activities as the painting over of road signs written in English, attacks on English television facilities, and, in 1969, opposition to the investiture of the Prince of Wales. But it has captured remarkably little popular support for such activities.

Welsh leadership seeks to expand the opportunities for Welsh in education and daily living. The general direction is cultural separatism not political dissociation, Wales being characterized by a fairly strong cultural but a very weak political nationalism. In March 1979, only 11 per cent of the voters in Wales (actuallly one-fifth of those who voted) voted for a form of political devolution when the issue was put to the Welsh people. Even the Welsh-speaking areas were against the small measure of autonomy that the Wales Act would have allowed. Writing of the way the Welsh voted at the time, Morgan (1981, p. 405) says: 'However powerful their sense of cultural and historic identity, the Welsh were, in political and economic terms, strictly unionist.'

Many Welsh people still hope to see their language preserved. The government-sponsored Council for the Welsh Language, which existed from 1973 to 1981, issued a report in 1978 entitled *A Future for the Welsh Language.* The report called for establishing a permanent language commission to turn Wales into a thoroughly bilingual nation, but little has been done to implement its recommendations and the Council itself has ceased to exist. Some observers have been heartened by the census figures of 1971 and 1981, interpreting them to indicate that Welsh has now at last achieved a period of stability as a result of the various measures that have been taken. Others are less sanguine: even though the decline of the language was very small between 1971 and 1981, they see a continuity in the historical process which would indicate that Welsh will be extinct well before the middle of the next century. Betts (1976), guided by the experience with Irish, argues that the only viable solution is to devise a heartland for Welsh and protect it there. A very general view is that the Welsh themselves are really quite indifferent, perhaps even cheerfully so, to the fate of their language; it may be a 'good thing' to preserve but not something that they are willing to make great personal efforts to do. It would appear that for the vast majority of the two and a half million, by-now thoroughly anglicized people of Wales the tie with England is a permanent one, and that although a small still influential minority believes that much can be gained in the battle to stay the race of the Welsh language toward the oblivion it seems headed for in the next century, the majority remain almost totally indifferent.

SCOTLAND AND GAELIC

Gaelic lost its social dominance in the 'civilized' Lowlands of Scotland as early as the thirteenth century when it was superseded there by English. In the fourteenth century Gaelic in Scotland was clearly identified with the Highlands, occupied by a 'wild and savage' people, the 'wild Scots'. From that time on it was apparent to the Lowlanders that the Highlands would have to be 'civilized' and that a major obstacle to be overcome was the Gaelic language. Apparently James IV

(1488–1513) was the last Scottish king to speak Gaelic but even during his reign the language had ceased to have any claims to be Scotland's national language.

Until the Reformation there was considerable contact between Scotland and Ireland because of a common Catholic orientation. However, the Reformation saw the Lowland area of Scotland shift to Protestantism with the Highland Gaelic area retaining its Roman Catholic religion. A further reason was created for the suppression of the Highlanders and their language. The crowns of England and Scotland were united in 1603, and the seventeenth century saw the first moves against both the religion and the language of the Highlanders. For example, the Statutes of Iona of 1616 restricted certain of the Highlanders' rights. During the seventeenth century the English lived in constant fear that the Scots would pursue a strong independent course of action, particularly fearing that they would unite with France against England. Since France had remained Catholic there was the additional danger that there would be especially strong support for such an alliance among the Highland Gaels.

England negotiated a Union of the Parliaments of the two countries in 1707 and Scotland ceased to have a separate political identity. However, the union did allow Scotland to retain a considerable cultural identity. The Scots were allowed to retain their own legal system together with their system of local government. They were also allowed to retain their separate Presbyterian Church. Consequently, from the very beginning of the union there was a recognition that affairs could be ordered somewhat differently in Scotland than they were in England.

Within Scotland the Lowland speakers of English, or Scots as it came to be called, continued to assert themselves against those who spoke either Norn or Gaelic. The Norn were easily swamped and the language eventually died out in the Shetland and Orkney Islands. The speakers of Gaelic found themselves increasingly confined to the high lands in the north and west and to the western isles. They grew more and more isolated from power and influence and they lost contact with other Celtic peoples. In the eighteenth century, for example, the Jacobite Rebellions led to a succession of very oppressive measures against the Catholic Highlanders and deliberate measures to cut them off from Catholic sympathizers in Ireland. After the union, the English pursued a deliberate policy of pacification of the Gaels.

In the late eighteenth and early nineteenth centuries still further erosion of the Celts and their Gaelic language resulted from the policy of clearing the Highlands for grazing. This policy of Highland clearances forced the Celts into even more isolated areas or to abandon Scotland altogether and seek new homes across the oceans. Scots emigrated in large numbers from the Highlands during this period. The clearances turned out to be a double disaster: they ruined the land, often turning good farmland into moors suitable for nothing else but breeding grounds for certain types of wildfowl, and they hastened the decline of the Gaelic language.

In the last century or so the decline of Gaelic has been rapid. Its use was opposed by the authorities, and it found little or no place in administration, education, and commerce. Only in religion did it persevere but here too it has weakened in recent decades. Rural depopulation and mass emigration have also had disastrous consequences.

The educational system that was imposed on the Highlands must bear much resposibility for what has happened to Gaelic there. In the eighteenth century the system of education was used deliberately in an attempt to anglicize the Gaelic-speaking population and to convert them from their 'antiquated' and 'inferior' language and customs. From 1709, the year of its founding, the Society in Scotland for the Propagating of Christian Knowledge (SSPCK), operating under a crown patent, had as one of its major goals the teaching of English to those who did not speak English. Until 1766 the use of Gaelic was forbidden in the Society's schools, their goal being to 'root out the Irish language', as Scots Gaelic was referred to in those days. Only in 1766 was Gaelic allowed into use but even then only so that the process of learning English could be hurried up. In the next century when the Education Act (Scotland) of 1872 extended free primary education to Scotland, it did nothing to encourage the preservation of Gaelic beyond allowing for some use of the language in the teaching of religion.

In matters of education we can see a long and consistent history of a deliberate attempt by Scots who spoke English to convert Scots who did not: they would learn to speak English and they might even be converted from Catholicism. The result has been that over the decades more and more Gaelic-speaking Scots have become bilingual and then their descendants have become English monolinguals. The monolingual Gaelic-speaking population of Scotland has shrunk until it now exists only in the *Gaidhealtachd* (Gaelic-speaking Area) of the Western Isles, the area which has been designated as a kind of preserve for Gaelic.

The 1981 census showed that there are only about 79,000 speakers of Gaelic left in Scotland and all of these also speak English. The census also showed for the first time an increase, small though it was, in the number of those who spoke Gaelic in some Highland and Western Island areas. But native Gaelic-speaking communities today are to be found only on the northwest coastal fringes of the Highlands and in the Hebrides. About half of those who speak Gaelic live in the official Gaidhealtachd and the rest live outside. Within this official area Gaelic is used as the language of the home and of worship, but there is often a noticeable reluctance to transmit the language to children. Some local organizations use it in their work and many meetings are conducted in Gaelic. However, hardly anywhere is it the 'official' or even the most frequently used language, not even in the Western Isles Council. It is also not the language of any town, not even of Stornoway or Lewis. And Gaelic is hardly found at all in any kind of official writing and record keeping. The population of the area is also a skewed one: it is an 'older' population and one that shows the effects of the out-migration of younger workers, particularly of women in the 15–44 age group. In the Gaidhealtachd too younger women seem to be less favorably disposed to the maintenance of Gaelic than any other group but even the general attitude is not positive: it is that Gaelic is somehow inferior to English and hardly worth preserving. Only a few people fight this attitude, most are either apathetic or believe it to be justified, and still others actually work to kill the language hoping that its demise will eliminate the problems that they believe the language creates for those who still use it.

Today, while there are no legal restrictions on the teaching of Gaelic in the schools of Scotland, this does not mean that there is much such teaching or that the teaching itself is pursued with any great enthusiasm. Gaelic is taught in some primary and secondary schools and is actually the medium of instruction in the early years in some schools in the Highlands and Western Isles. But there is a great shortage of both good teaching materials and the kind of administrative support and enthusiasm such teaching usually requires if it is to be effective. There is certainly much less enthusiasm in Scotland for the teaching of Gaelic than there is in Wales for the teaching of Welsh and there is also little doubt the the actual teaching too has proved to be much less effective.

The real problem seems to be that the preservation of Gaelic is very much a peripheral issue in Scotland. Certainly one sees an occasional form or sign written in Gaelic or hears a pronouncement about some way in which Gaelic is acknowledged to exist. And, as we have said, one can even find that it is taught as a school subject in a few places or can be studied at one of the universities. But none of these changes the essential fact about Gaelic in current Scottish life, the fact that the vast majority of Scots regard its existence as a fringe issue. Not even the Scottish National Party regards it otherwise. There is certainly no desire that a Scotland with some kind of independence from England should become a Gaelic-speaking Scotland, even in the symbolic way that Ireland is considered to be Irish-speaking. The English language is much too entrenched historically in Scotland and Scottish identity does not require support from Gaelic. It has always had the support of a separate legal system, a separate educational system including Scottish universities with their own strong identities, and even a separate Church. The survival of Gaelic has always been peripheral to Scottish interests, not just to English interests. The language and the people who spoke it were to be contained and reduced, and this policy has been most successful.

The Gaels themselves can do little to reverse their fortunes and stop their language going the way of Norn. Gaelic is now associated with the Western Isles, with crofting, fishing, and weaving. It is not associated in any way with progress. Consequently, the young see it as an obstacle to their mobility and even many of the older speakers of Gaelic are at least ambivalent about the language. Today, too, everyone who speaks Gaelic also speaks English; the 1961 census showed that there were still about a thousand Gaelic monoglots, but the 1981 census found none. Dorian's work (1981) with speakers of Gaelic in East Sutherland also shows how even those who still speak the language often have but a tenuous hold on it, being what she calls 'semi speakers' rather than fully accomplished speakers of the language. The future prospects for Gaelic are very unpromising indeed; the language is not likely to survive very long into the next century.

IRELAND AND IRISH

Ireland was a Celtic domain outside the Roman Empire and after the Roman legions were withdrawn from England the Celts in Ireland found themselves in a strong enough position either to resist or to assimilate any other non-Celtic people in Ireland. Ireland's 'Golden Age' is the period between the sixth and ninth centuries.. The Irish language flourished during this period and it was the only vernacular language of any western European country that came to rival Latin as a language suitable for education and writing. By the eighth century it had attained sufficient prestige so that it could even replace Latin in monasteries and for religious purposes and by the tenth century the Irish Celts had successfully asserted their hegemony over everyone else in Ireland – other Celts, Picts, Anglo-Saxons, Norse, and Danes alike. All had been successfully gaelicized.

Ireland remained a Celtic domain until well after the Norman Conquest of England. Beginning in 1164, these conquerors turned their attention to Ireland and introduced both English and Norman French there. The two languages came to be known in the towns of the east coast, for example in Dublin, but did not spread into the rural areas. Norman French died out fairly quickly and English had great difficulty maintaining itself in the area that became known as the Pale. It proved impossible to extend the Pale and the influence of the Irish was so strong within it that the English were sometimes gaelicized. It was for this reason that the Statutes of Kilkenny were passed in 1366. These 36 Statutes, written in Norman French, were passed in an attempt to keep settlers from adopting the ways and language of their new country; however, they were not particularly effective in arresting the decline of English.

In the sixteenth century the English once again attempted to settle in Ireland by establishing plantations but this attempt once again met with failure because of Irish resistance. By 1600 the Pale had diminished once more and English was to be found in use only within it and in a few rural enclaves. It was not until the later Protestant settlements of James I and Cromwell that a successful system for the colonization of Ireland began. By the mid-seventeenth century English began to make what was to be its inexorable advance into Ireland.

In the seventeenth and eighteenth centuries people began to abandon Irish as their tongue as, under the new and rapidly developing regime, English became the language of opportunity in Ireland. Irish did hold its own for a while but after about 1800 began the precipitous decline from which it has never been able to recover. As Macnamara (1971, p. 65) has observed: 'The majority of Irish people seem to have dropped Irish in favor of English somewhere between 1750 and 1850 ... .' This process was hastened when the Roman Catholic clergy also decided that it would try to save Irish souls through the medium of English rather than through attempting to maintain Irish in the hope that those who continued to speak Irish would remain loyal to the Church. Even the National Schools, established in 1831 and controlled by the Church, therefore were actively engaged in the promotion of English.

Not even Irish patriots could be counted on to preserve Irish, Daniel O'Connell himself having little use for the language. In addition, the great famine, the mass exodus of people to seek a better life elsewhere – with some five million going to North America and taking English with them not Irish – and the resulting rural depopulation merely sharpened the existing inclination of the Irish people to give up their language. One view is that the English killed Irish; however, an alternative view, which may have more truth to it, is that the language was not killed but committed suicide! One thing appears certain and that is that the particular political arrangements between Engand and Ireland that existed at specific periods of time had little to do with the extent of language loss during those periods. The union with England in 1801 did not change anything: Irish was already in sharp decline before the union and that decline continued unabated after the union was brought about.

By the mid-nineteenth century the number of Irish-speaking monolinguals was very small indeed and the remaining Irish-speaking areas were remote from both Dublin and from one another. Irish had become a west coast phenomenon with Irish-speaking enclaves here and there but with the intervening areas quite clearly anglophone. However, by the end of the nineteenth century it seemed to certain Irish nationalists that the time had come to de-anglicize Ireland and to revive the Irish language while there still existed Irish people who spoke it as a native tongue. This indeed was the theme of Hyde's famous address to the Irish people given before the Irish National Literary Society, a speech that led to the founding of the Gaelic League in 1893 with its objective the maintenance of the Irish language in Ireland. His was also part of a wider European attempt to create a 'Celtic Renaissance' where there had been previously only a 'Celtic Twilight'.

The Gaelic League was dominated by upper-middle-class individuals. While they declared their goal to be no more than the maintenance of the language, they were often seen to want to do more, not just simply maintain what Irish then existed but to extend the language into new areas and among new speakers. The time was also one in which Irish resistance to being governed from Westminster began to meet with success and Home Rule became a real possibility at last. It is interesting to observe that the language of dispute with the English over the future of Ireland was English even though many of the leaders had learned Irish and declared their intention to promote that language once their political objectives had been achieved. Those who favored Home Rule for Ireland spoke and wrote in English and those who supported them in Ireland unified through the medium of English. Such a situation was to recur with considerable frequency in the twentieth century as colonial peoples in general found that their unifying language against the colonial oppressor had necessarily to be that of the colonizer itself: for example, English, French, or Portuguese.

When at last independence did come to Ireland in 1921 the Irish made Irish the first official language of the Irish Free State and later of the Republic. Article 8 of the Constitution states that: 'The Irish language as the national language is the first official language. The English language is recognized as the second official language.' By that time though England and Ireland had become, in Bernard Shaw's words 'two nations divided by a common language', for, in spite of the status given to it in the constitution of the new state, Irish was moribund.

By the time the Irish Free State was established the number of speakers of Irish was very small indeed and Irish had little more than symbolic importance. For example, the 1926 census reported that only 18 per cent of the Irish population could speak Irish and there were very few monoglots left. The 1901 census had found only 21,000 monoglots in the whole of Ireland, about 0.6 per cent of the population. What Irish that was spoken was largely confined to the *Gaeltacht*, a few areas scattered along the western coastline in the counties of Donegal, Mayo, Galway, and Kerry.

The Gaeltacht itself, this last stronghold of Irish, has continued to shrink with every census. Since 1979 the official Gaeltacht has come under the jurisdiction of a special organization, Udaras na Gaeltachta, set up to overseee all aspects of life in the area but specifically to maintain the language and culture. The total population is estimated to be about 70,000 with at most about 50,000 of these being regular speakers of Irish – less than two per cent of Ireland's total population. Today, it is likely that as many as half of the children within the official Gaeltacht are being brought up in English-speaking homes. The people of the area do not appear to be at all enthusiastic about the preservation of Irish, realizing that the price of preservation is a continuation of the isolation that they have experienced, an isolation that has not been at all beneficial to them.

Once the new Irish state was established there was a move afoot to revive Irish and many were the optimistic statements about the chances of success. All that was necessary was to offer children the opportunity to learn Gaelic as part of their schooling and in a generation or two Ireland would once again become an Irish-speaking land! The official goal was the restoration of the Irish language in Ireland., and the actual task of restoring the language was given to the schools. Ardent nationalists such as Timothy Corcoran assumed that the task could be accomplished with few difficulties, being quite sure that the Irish themselves would sacrifice a great deal to speak Irish once again. This has not happened. The Irish school system has lacked the personnel to do such a task as well as the materials and the inclination. But then this explanation for failure presupposes that the task is one that is feasible; there are many who have not thought it to be at all feasible. The language was too moribund to revive when the task was begun. The Irish had won their independence using the English language they had adopted. They had developed a new sense of being Irish without needing the Irish tongue as an expression of that new identity. While they spoke English, they were not English: they were Irish who just happened to speak that language as an accident of history.

The attempt to reintroduce Irish into Ireland through the schools is now acknowledged to have been a dismal failure, even by the Irish Government itself in a 1980 White Paper. The schools cannot possibly accomplish such a task on their own. Irish is still taught at all levels of education in Ireland but no one claims that it is well taught nor that the results of all the teaching are anything but meager. In the 1971 census 28.3 per cent of the population, some 800,000 people, claimed to be able to speak Irish, but most observers regard this as a greatly inflated figure because of the way the question was asked, since a person with only a smattering of Irish would be counted as 'speaking' the language. Those who claim that the 28.3 per cent who claim to speak Irish in 1971 shows some kind of health for the language are surely deceiving themselves! In 1861 24.5 per cent of the population, a smaller percentage, actually did speak the language.

Irish has little more than a symbolic, ceremonial function in Ireland today. Some knowledge of Irish is or has been required at times to practice law, for police work, to be a career soldier, and to be a civil servant. Irish is hardly ever used in business and commerce and even the Church finds little occasion for using it. Most Irish feel no need of any kind for the language and exist quite satisfactorily without it. There is no reason to believe either that they are going to discover that they will need Irish in the future; their own particular variety of English serves them perfectly well.

A very little Irish is still spoken in Northern Ireland, still part of the United Kingdom (or, alternatively, in Ulster, that part of Ireland which continues to be governed from Westminster). This is the part of Ireland that was heavily colonized in the early seventeenth century by English-speaking Presbyterian Scottish Lowlanders, sometimes referred to as the Scots-Irish, in order to break up Celtic power there. These settlers adopted a 'fortress mentality' from the very beginning and this same attitude is apparent among their descendants today. The English and the Irish have always found themselves in confrontation in Ireland and, with the success of Home Rule in the 1920s, Ulster has become the battleground.

The Irish language enjoys no official status of any kind in Northern Ireland: it is never used in any government publications nor on radio or television. Protestants will have little or nothing to do with the language but some Catholics prefer to use it in their worship. It can be taught in the schools but only Catholic schools make such teaching compulsory. To some extent Irish has become identified with the cause of those who seek to unite Ulster to the Republic of Ireland; consequently, it finds most favor among those who protest the policies of the British Government. Anti-British slogans inscribed on buildings are almost invariably written in English, the language of political protest.

PROSPECTS

The Celtic languages and cultures of Britain enjoyed their greatest prosperity between the ninth and sixteenth centuries. However, since the beginning of the seventeenth century they have been more and more pressed to occupy the most isolated western regions of the Isles. Their strong cultural traditions have been assailed and eroded. The main opponent has been the vigorous attempt of the state to assert the power of its central authority. English culture has been deliberately spread to the periphery. Along with such culture also went the spread of the English language. Populations were gradually induced to learn English in addition to the Celtic ancestral language. The next step was to encourage in one way or another the people to abandon the Celtic language, and this step was taken more and more often. English influence was also spread through urbanization, industrialization, and education. When these did not succeed because either the land or the circumstances were unattractive, the native Celtic population tended to get up and leave, as it did in Ireland and in the Highlands of Scotland and to a lesser extent in Wales. In each case the result was the further attrition of the Celtic languages.

Today, we see an attempt being made to stop the decline of the Celtic languages. It is too late for Cornish and Manx where the issue has become their possible revival. The Irish have not been at all successful with even maintaining the Gaeltacht. The future of the language continues to be uncertain and many observers feel that if the Gaeltacht disappears Irish will lose the territorial basis it probably needs. In that event no matter how much the Government of Ireland tries to encourage Irish, it will probably be unsuccessful. Gaelic in Scotland may well be moribund and beyond help too: no one seems to argue otherwise with any conviction. Welsh is also an endangered species, but of all the Celtic languages of the British Isles it is the one that still possesses some viability. However, it is difficult to see Welsh lasting long into the next century if present trends continue. The changes that would have to be made are fundamental and most Welsh people seem unwilling to make them. The present association of Wales with England is by no means perfect but the kind of dissociation and autonomy that would be necessary to maintain the Welsh language at its present level seems to be unpalatabe to most Welsh and any goal of a Welsh-speaking Wales is quite unattainable.

FURTHER READING

Various languages of Britain: Foster 1980, Haugen et al. 1981, McCrum et al. 1986, Price 1984, Stephens 1976, Trudgill 1984; Celtic languages: Durkacz 1983; Cornish: Ellis 1974, Wakelin 1975; Scots Gaelic: Withers 1984; Welsh: Baker 1985, Betts 1976, Lewis 1982, Stephens 1979, Williams 1984.

5

France and Spain

France and Spain are two West European countries with long-established language traditions. Yet each has a variety of problems today that arise from the fact that neither French in France nor Spanish in Spain is everywhere accepted as the everyday language of certain segments of the populations of the two countries. France still has remnants of various other languages on the peripheries of the French state and in recent years the state has found it necessary to meliorate its French-only policy and recognize at last the existence of these languages. The Spanish-only policy of Spain has also given way to a recognition that the country is essentially a multilingual state rather than a unilingual one, and that languages other than Spanish can be recognized without threatening the cohesion of the state.

FRANCE AND THE RISE OF FRENCH

France is still today a country in which various languages are spoken, languages which have a long history in the areas in which they exist. It is also a country that has absorbed large numbers of political refugees, occupants of former imperial possessions, and guestworkers from other countries. All kinds of languages are spoken in France but this fact often goes unrecognized. Most people will tell you that French is spoken everywhere in France, and those who speak French in France will rarely have anything but unkind words to say about any language that is spoken within France that is not French. Such a language will be either quite clearly a foreign language, like English, Arabic, or Vietnamese, or it will be classified as a *dialecte, parler,* or *patois,* and therefore something almost beneath recognition.

The languages with a long history in France are also languages which exist on the territorial periphery of the state. Over the centuries the power of the French state, *la France une et indivisible* (France, one and indivisible), has spread outwards from Paris toward whatever political boundaries existed, and that spread is still apparent. Today, the French state is highly centralized, as it has been for a long time, but peripheral areas are still in the process of being absorbed. That this absorption is still incomplete we can be judge from a variety of factors. Prominent among these are the dissident political movements associated with some of the outlying parts of the state, movements in which language often has a considerable role to play. But French authorities have usually denied such a role to language or to some combination of linguistic and ethnic consciousness: for example, in June 1978, President Giscard d'Estaing declared: 'Contrary to what one often says and writes, there is not a Corsican problem, there are problems in Corsica.'

A glance at a map of France and the languages spoken in the country soon reveals the extent to which linguistic absorption has proceeded within the hexagon of France and the areas in which there is still resistance or work to be done depending on one's point of view concerning the value of attempting to preserve minority languages in the modern state. One part of the state, Corsica, is an island with its own language: it is easy to appreciate how the Corsicans might feel that they are isolated in such circumstances. In the northwest the Bretons speak a language that has no immediate geographical continuity, its nearest kin Celtic language being spoken in Wales across the water in another country. Other peripheral languages in France do have immediate geographical connections to people who speak them. For example, the Dutch-speaking (or Flemish-speaking) people of the northeast and the German-speaking people of the east are immediately adjacent to countries in which Dutch and German are the official languages. This is a very different situation from the one in which the Bretons find themselves: they are not only cut off from Welsh, but Welsh itself, like Breton, is in a precarious position.

The Basques and the Catalans of the southwest have problems that resemble those of their cohorts in Spain; however, the French state has not experienced the same difficulties with its Basque and Catalan populations as the Spanish state. Finally, within France there are those who speak other varieties of the French language itself, varieties which may even be considered to be separate languages. For example, there are speakers of Picardy in the northeast, and in the south there are those who speak the various *parlers d'Oc*. Sometimes these latter varieties are classed together as Occitan with sub-varieties distinguished, e.g., Gascon. Franco-Provençal is another variety.

It is hard to know precisely how many people speak each of the above languages or varieties. The French do not collect certain kinds of information in their periodic censuses. Language ability in any other language than French is regarded as a strictly private matter, just like a person's religious affiliation. Public policy does not allow for the collection of any other language information than information about ability to speak French. One consequence is that sometimes the estimates of the numbers of speakers of these languages and varieties differ widely: 200,000 speakers of Corsican; 50,000–100,000 speakers of Flemish; 1.2–1.4 million speakers of German; 200,000 speakers of Catalan; 80,000–130,000 speakers of Basque; and from two to as many as twelve million speakers of Occitan.

The internal history of the French state is one in which there has been a gradual extension of the power of the Île-de-France outward to the peripheries of the state and in imperial times to the far reaches of the French Empire. This centralizing thrust has been particularly apparent in the nineteenth and twentieth centuries. Although it appears to have picked up much of its momentum during the French Revolution, it was apparent even before that time.

France was Celtic before the Roman invasions and words of Celtic origin have found their way into Modern French, e.g., the names of the rivers Seine, Rhône, and Marne. The French language itself derives from the Vulgar Latin brought by the Roman armies of the first and second centuries BC. This language prospered and later survived the Frankish German-speaking invasions that began in the fifth century AD. The invading Franks were actually romanized, giving up their language and taking over some of the legal, administrative, and religious institutions that they found, and the *Serments de Strasbourg* (Oaths of Strasbourg) of 842 is the first document in which French is distinguished as a separate language. The French kings gradually extended their power within the bounds of what is now modern France: through the crusades into Languedoc in 1270; through marriage into Brittany in 1532; through inheritance into Lorraine in 1766; and through outright conquest. The French language accompanied French power, at least among those who exercised that power if not among those who felt its weight.

So far as language is concerned one of the earliest indicators of the determination of those who ruled France, in this case Francis I, to extend their influence everywhere was the Ordinance of Villers-Cotterêts of 15 August 1539. Its purpose was to replace Latin with French as the language of the law in France so that those who lived in the kingdom might avail themselves of a living language rather than a dead one when they had legal dealings. However, it appears that at the time this change was made only a minority of the population to which the new law applied actually knew any French. It was a time when the regional languages of France still flourished and French was known only to a very few in the peripheral areas of France. What the Ordinance of

Villers-Cotterêts did in effect for such people was to change the language of the law from one inaccessible language to another that was almost as inaccessible. Moreover, it implicitly downgraded all the other living languages of France and conferred on them a status that has changed hardly at all in the subsequent four and a half centuries. The new law applied to affairs of state only. The Roman Catholic Church persisted in its use of Latin and a French translation of the Bible was published over opposition from the Church. What religious works did appear in French were either rare translations of psalms, sermons, etc., popular lives of the saints, or works by Protestants published during the Reformation, e.g., Calvin's writings.

In the late fifteenth and early sixteenth centuries the language of the French court extended itself more and more into the south of France, penetrated the cities, spread along communication routes such as the Rhône, and came into use for all matters of law and administration. A French literature developed and the language began to become attractive to the expanding bourgeoisie.

As French came into greater use people began to pay more and more attention to the characteristics they saw in the language. Du Bellay found it necessary in 1549 to publish his *Défense et illustration de la langue française* and others began to publish on such matters as spelling, grammar, and vocabulary. The first attempts to standardize and glorify the language were under way. In the seventeenth century the work of Malherbe (1555–1628) and de Vaugelas (1585–1650), the founding of the Académie Française in 1635, and the publication of the dictionaries of Pomey (1676), Richelet (1680), and Furetière (1684) were important milestones in the development of the language. The great French writers of the seventeenth and eighteenth centuries also brought enormous prestige to the language: Corneille, Racine, Pascal, Molière, La Fontaine, Descartes, Voltaire, Diderot, and Rousseau.

By the end of the eighteenth century many of those who spoke French were extemely proud of their language. It was no longer felt necessary to 'defend and illustrate' it. In 1784 Rivarol won a prize offered by the Berlin Academy (which called itself L'Académie Berlin) for his *Discours sur l'universalité de la langue française*, in which he glorified the language and its virtues, a language too, which, after the Treaty of Rastadt of 1714, had become the language of international diplomacy. Some of Rivarol's words are worth quoting because they illustrate an attitude toward the French language that one still finds, an attitude which makes it difficult for many who use French to set any high value on other languages:

Il n'y a jamais eu de langue où l'on ait écrit plus purement et plus nettement qu'en la nôtre, qui soit plus ennemie des équivoques et de toute sorte d'obscurité, plus grave et plus douce tout ensemble, plus propre pour toutes sortes de styles, plus chaste en ses locutions, plus judicieuse en ses figures, qui aime plus l'élégance et l'ornement, mais qui craigne plus l'affectation. Elle sait tempérer ces hardiesses, avec la pudeur et la retenue qu'il faut avoir pour ne pas donner dans ses figures monstrueuses où dorment aujourd'hui nos voisins. Il n'y en a point qui observe plus le nombre et la cadence dans ses périodes en quoi consiste la marque véritable de la perfection des langues.

There has never been a language in which you could write more purely and more precisely than in ours, which is more resistant to equivocations and every kind of obscurity, more serious and more gentle at the same time, more suitable for all kinds of styles, purer in its phrases, more judicious in its expressions, which has a greater liking for elegance and ornament, but which is more fearful of affectation. It knows how to moderate its strengths with the modesty and restraint it must have in order to avoid the monstrous expressions in which our neighbours today are fixed. There is none among them which is more attentive to number and rhythm in its declarations, which is the true mark of perfection in languages.

Under the Ancien Régime there was considerable tolerance of local cultures and languages within France. The outlying parts of the country tended to be left much to themselves so long as they caused no trouble and the people paid their taxes. Little attempt was made to force French onto the common people. The élites were won over, though, and French acquired sufficient prestige that it was possible to downgrade every other language or variety of French than that of Paris to patois status. And as the influence of Paris grew that of the provinces fell. On the eve of the French Revolution French had succeeded in becoming the most prestigious language in Europe: however, as we will see, to many millions within the country itself the language was still quite unknown.

When the French Revolution occurred it was necessary at first for the revolutionaries to ignore the fiction that French was spoken everywhere in France. They wanted to be sure of support everywhere. To this end a decree of 14 January 1790 allowed for the translation of official declarations into local languages. However, a few months later on 2 October 1790, another decree required that such official declarations be read in French at the end of Sunday mass. There was therefore some ambivalence during the early years of the revolution about how the different languages of the country were to be treated, but that ambivalence was short-lived.

A survey by the Abbé Grégoire of the linguistic situation in France in 1790 produced some startling results in his report of 1794 , *Rapport sur la nécessité et les moyens d'anéantir les patois et d'universaliser l'usage de la langue française* (Report on the Necessity and the Means for Abolishing the Patois and Universalizing the Use of the French

Language), for those who wanted to see a unified state in which the people shared a common language. Grégoire estimated the population of France to be about 26 million. He identified thirty patois (*trente patois différents*) in what he called the Tower of Babel that France was, including in this number Breton, Basque, Flemish, German, and Italian. For Grégoire anything that was not the French of Paris was a patois! Within France Grégoire found that only 11 million people spoke French as their mother tongue. Well over half the population spoke a language other than French as the mother tongue, and these different languages were spread around the borders of the state. There were certainly speakers of French distributed among such non-French speakers but where such speakers existed there were also clear social divisions. The élites spoke French, the masses did not.

Grégoire estimated that three million of those to whom French was not a mother tongue could still speak French and another six million had some small knowledge of the language. However, six million inhabitants of the French state knew no French at all! Grégoire may actually have overestimated French-speaking ability. What is clear is that at the end of the eighteenth century about half the population of France still had little or no knowledge of French. To the extent that they did not yet know the language they were not yet 'Frenchmen'. The revolutionaries were not prepared to accept this consequence: the population of France were to be turned into Frenchmen and the French language was to be the principal means to effect the necessary change.

The immediate result was the passing of a succession of laws either to promote French or to restrict the use of other languages. In October, 1793 it was decreed that only French could be used as the language of instruction in schools. In December of the same year the use of German was forbidden in Alsace. In January of the following year Barrère, a prominent member of the Committeee of Public Safety, declared that though the overthrown monarchy might have had its reasons for being like a Tower of Babel, the new democracy of free people required the use of one language for all. To this end each commune was ordered to employ a teacher who would be able to teach French. However, it was one thing to so decree and another to be able to find the people who were needed to carry out the decree. Barrère's best-known words, however, are those that directly attacked other languages than French:

Le fédéralisme et la superstition parle bas-breton; l'émigration et la haine de la République parlent allemand; la contre-revolution parle l'italien, et le fanatisme parle le basque. Cassons ces instruments de dommage et d'erreur.... Pour nous, nous devons, à nos concitoyens, nous devons à l'affermissement de la République, de faire parler sur tout son territoire la langue dans laquelle est écrite la Déclaration des droits de l'homme.

This Jacobinian view, which was enacted into law as the *loi du 2 thermidor an II* (the law of 20 July 1794) and which proscribed all other languages than French within the territory of France (*'nul acte public ne pourra, dans quelque partie que se soit du territoire de la République, être écrit qu'en langue française'*), has been very influential in French language policy ever since the revolution, particularly when allied to the view that had developed earlier concerning the unparalleled virtues of the French language itself.

In spite of the measures taken by the Jacobins little actually changed in the countryside to further the advance of French there. France was soon to have other concerns that would attract attention away from the complete francization of the countryside. In 1861, according to Weber (1976, p. 67), official figures showed that no French was spoken in 8,381 of France's 37,510 communes containing about a quarter of the country's population. The Ministry of Public Instruction found that 448,328 of the 4,018,427 schoolchildren between the ages of seven and thirteen spoke no French at all and that another 1,490,269 spoke or understood French but could not write it, suggesting an indifferent grasp of the language. In 24 of the country's 89 departments more than half the people did not speak French. French remained then virtually a foreign language to a substantial proportion of the country's population for much of the nineteenth century.

This situation changed in the last decades of the nineteenth century. Military conscription began in 1875. Under the Third Republic the school laws of Jules Ferry made primary education in French obligatory from 1886 and encouraged the promotion of French language and culture. A rapid development of communication networks occurred, as roads were improved and railways constructed. The result was that the influence of Paris with its strong centralizing tendencies could be felt promptly and consistently everywhere within the hexagon (i.e., metropolitan France). Weber maintains that these were very important years in the formation of French identity and the promotion of the French language. The efforts were to culminate early in the twentieth century with World War I and the patriotism which that war brought forth among the French people.

During the course of the nineteenth century and well into the twentieth it was absolutely forbidden to use any other language than French for purposes of instruction in the schools of France. It did not matter what language the children spoke: Flemish, German, Catalan, Breton, etc. They were living in France and the language of France was French. Every other language in France was inferior to French. It was therefore the responsibility of the schools to teach French and to teach in French, and it was the duty of those who knew no French to repair that deficiency.

It was not until 1951 and the passing of the *loi Deixonne* that this situation changed. This law allowed for the teaching of some of the languages and local dialects of France, specifically Breton, Basque, Catalan, and Occitan. They could be taught for one hour a week on a voluntary basis. They could also be taken as subjects in the French baccalauréat but the results in such subjects were not given the same weighting as other results. Since 1951 the provisions of the law have been extended to Corsican, and provision has also been made for the teaching of Alsatian and Flemish. The results in examinations also now count the same as the results in any other subject. In no case though is it ever obligatory for a student to take one of these languages in school. The only obligatory language in French schools is French. Although the French government has by its *loi Deixonne* and another law of 11 July 1975 authorized the teaching of regional languages and cultures in France as part of the national patrimony, in 1977–8 only some 21,200 out of a total school population of ten million were studying such languages: 12,000 Occitan, 4,900 Breton, 1,800 Corsican, 1,300 Basque, and 1,200 Catalan. There was still a drastic lack of teachers, materials, and possibly too of will.

OCCITAN IN THE SOUTH

The major linguistic division within France is undoubtedly that which is associated with the north–south division between the *langue d'Oil* of the north and the *langue d'Oc* of the south. Standard French is now the prototypical variety of the *langue d'Oil* and it has been spread so successfully into the area once dominated by the *langue d'Oc* that there are no longer any who speak only the latter. There are only those who speak both, the last monoglot speakers of the *langue d'Oc* having died a good half century ago.

The traditional *langue d'Oc* area of the south covers about one-third of the hexagon, i.e., metropolitan France. This area is sometimes called the *Midi* by those who live in the north but it is also called *Occitanie* by many of its actual residents. About a quarter of France's population live in it, that is, about 15 million people. Possibly two-thirds of these still have some knowledge of Occitan and one estimate is that perhaps two million of these use it in their daily lives. It is also acknowledged that since the 1960s there has been a significant decline in the use of the language. Occitan is undoubtedly the largest minority language in

France today, but it is one that has showed, and continues to show, the same decrease in speakers as every other minority language in the country.

The south has been part of France since the thirteenth century when it lost its independence in the Albigensian Crusade. Before then the Occitans had flourished with an independent but never unified civilization of considerable culture. When they lost their independence, they felt themselves swallowed up by an inferior people, the French, a process that has continued to this day. French has long been promoted as the language of the area and Occitan, in spite of its literary tradition, has been downgraded to a patois. As we have just noted, it was not until the end of the nineteenth century that the French met with any great success in francicizing the south but their progress in so doing has been rapid ever since.

The first deliberate attempt to resist this move to eliminate Occitan came in the nineteenth century with the movement known as the *Félibrige* led by the poet Mistral. This movement had as its goals the standardization and unifying of the language of the south of France and some measure of cultural and political autonomy for Occitanie. The movement was not successful in many of its goals: the leaders were often in disagreement about even the most basic issues, e.g., about how language differences in the area should be handled and how to align the cause of Occitanie with the various political factions within the country as a whole. The Félibrige still survives but is often viewed as provincial and reactionary in its goals, particularly by those who espouse quite radical solutions for the problems they believe the south of France has with the north.

World War II did little to help the political cause of the south: it was after all the seat of the Vichy government under Pétain. Nor has the economy of the country been kind to the south. Not only does political power lie in the north where the mass of the French population resides but so does the economic power of the state. The south of France is a neglected area. People have moved away in large numbers and when they have been replaced it has been by tourists and people who buy second homes for vacations. The result has been a serious decline in the language. Bec (1986, p. 120) describes the current situation as follows:

Ce qui tue la langue, ce sont les moyens modernes de diffusion de la pensée, presse industrialisée, radio, cinéma, télévision qui vont au plus profond des campagnes comme véhicule d'un français imposé aux consciences; ce sont les pénétrations d'une population permanente de fonctionnaires déracinés, d'ouvriers étrangers et maintenant d'entreprises agricoles qui s'installent dans les réserves les plus reculées; ce sont les arrivées periodiques de touristes.

One of the main objectives of those who seek to preserve Occitan language and culture is that Occitan should be taught in the schools and not just at the secondary level as an optional subject for the *baccalauréat*. As a result of the *loi Deixonne* more and more students do take this option each year but, if the language is ever to flourish again, it must be available in the elementary schools and it must be used as a language of instruction and be more than just another subject. Furthermore, adequate time must be provided in the school curriculum for more teaching about the history and culture of Occitanie. Since the founding of the Institut d'Estudis Occitans (Institute of Occitan Studies) in Toulouse in 1945 there has been a considerable standardization of the language but not, unfortunately, an end to the disputes over which variety of Occitan is to be promoted, the standardized variety or more traditional varieties. Some of the dialectal and orthographic problems that have stood in the way of teaching Occitan as a written language may have been resolved, but it is not at all clear which spoken variety will prevail, if any. The creation in 1981 of L'Association Internationale d'Etudes Occitanes (International Association of Occitan Studies) may also be expected to provide some impetus for the language and culture.

Occitanie now has an intellectual and middle-class leadership devoted to the goal of improving the lot of the south. This leadership also finds much support among the working people of the area. Consequently, Occitanie is one place in the world where the working and middle classes seem to share a set of common objectives, even though to outsiders these often appear to be diffuse and sometimes quite unrealistic. Critics have wondered what possibly can come from a movement which unites, temporarily at least, language groups, folk singers and folklorists, disillusioned winegrowers and miners, teachers, and trade unionists. There are also groups with more radical persuasions than those who just want to see a greater recognition given to the language and culture of the area. For example, the Lutte Occitane (Lucha Occitana) is a small Marxist revolutionary group which claims that the French state is trying to liquidate a national minority. This group seeks autonomy for the region and places its cause within the context of the Marxist class struggle. The group also claims that in Occitanie we find a classic example of the exploitation of one of the outlying regional areas of France by the centre of the state.

So far the various groups that have claimed leadership in this region have not been able to unite successfully in a common cause. The region is an area in decline. It is also an area without any strong sense of 'national' identity and it has so far been impossible to create such an identity. Political discontent in the south of France seems to be occasioned more by social and class issues than by those that we usually associate with language and ethnicity. Possibly for this reason the future of Occitanie does not appear as a large issue in contemporary French political life.

BRETON IN BRITTANY

The French view the problems posed by the Bretons much more seriously than those that discontent in the south creates, even though the Bretons are a much smaller group. Brittany with a population of about two and a half million is mainly an agricultural area although it also has an important fishing industry. Its administrative centre is Rennes but it also contains the major ports of Brest and Nantes. Only in Lower Brittany (Basse Bretagne) is Breton still spoken; it has long disappeared from Upper Brittany (Haute Bretagne). The language is now in a considerable state of decline and that decline has been particularly rapid in recent years.

The present inhabitants of Brittany are descended from the Celts who began to settle in this northwest corner of what is now France in the fifth century. These Celts were in flight from Wales and particularly Cornwall, where their lands were being encroached upon by the invading Anglo-Saxons and to a lesser extent by Irish Celts. They fled across the sea to found a Britannia Minor as opposed to the Britannia Major which they had left. In the new land they soon found themselves in competition with the Frankish invaders, but by 845 they had managed to found an independent kingdom, all the while continuing to maintain contact with Cornwall. The Bretons later managed to extend this original kingdom but not to extend their language to it, mainly because of the Viking incursions which produced considerable chaos. For example, Rennes, the capital city of the area, and Nantes were not part of the original kingdom and have never been Breton-speaking even though some people today regard these cities as part of the 'historical Brittany' that merits special treatment.

For about six centuries Brittany experienced a somewhat uneasy independence. The successful Normans influenced many of the upper-class Bretons and there was considerable intermarriage which harmed Breton. The language of the nobility became French; the language of the peasantry remained Breton. Brittany itself was in an uncomfortable position between England and France and, as the English and French fought each other, first one of these countries and then the other held sway over Brittany. By the fifteenth century it was apparent that Brittany could no longer maintain its full independence from France but it was not until 1532 that an Act of Union was effected. By the terms of this union the Kings of France became Dukes of Brittany, the French agreed to respect the political and administrative rights that the Bretons had, and the Bretons were allowed a considerable amount of autonomy.

The 1539 Ordinance of Villers-Cotterêts was of little immediate consequence to Brittany. It required French to be used for all official purposes in the kingdom but since Breton had no official recognition in Brittany (with first Latin and later French the languages of law and French the language of administration) the new law changed nothing. Brittany's grievances were other than linguistic: the people were strongly opposed to a variety of measures imposed by the French and in the seventeenth and eighteenth centuries there were bloody rebellions against moves to centralize power in Paris. The Bretons welcomed the French Revolution when it came, believing that it would gain them a new measure of freedom, but their joy was not to last long. At the time of the revolution only the eastern half of Brittany, Upper Brittany, was at all integrated into France, being francophone. The western half, Lower Brittany, was monolingually celtophone with few exceptions: the few aristocrats, the petite bourgeoisie, and some linguistically mixed towns.

In the initial revolutionary period it did appear that the Bretons would regain some of their autonomy and some recognition of their language. But the revolutionaries quickly identified the French language with their cause and set out to make France entirely francophone. The Breton Parliament was dissolved, Brittany was subdivided into five departments, and the Breton language was virtually proscribed outside the home following Barrère's attack. Not even open rebellion would deter the central government from its intentions. The Breton language was to be destroyed and teachers were instructed 'to kill the Breton language'.

No matter who held power in the nineteenth century this policy of francization prevailed. In 1858, for example, the government banned a Breton association, *Kevredigez Vreiz*. The notorious *symbole* was used to enforce compliance with the requirement that only the French language could be used in the schools and examples of its use are attested until as late as the mid-twentieth century. Popular resistance to the influence of French and its culture did continue into the nineteenth century and, because of Brittany's location on the geographical perimeter of the state, Bretons were able to maintain their language and culture until the end of the century.

World War I had a drastic effect so far as isolation was concerned. Before 1914 the French state had been actively involved in turning all those who resided in France into Frenchmen and Frenchwomen. The war of 1914–18 provided a unique opportunity to further that goal. In this protracted engagement, much of it conducted on French soil, it became necessary to marshal all the forces of France if victory were to be achieved: the people of every part of France had to be brought into the fray. The policy was so successful in Brittany that this part of France was actually over-represented in the casualty lists. By the end of the war most Bretons had experienced France in a way that was to have serious consequences for the future. Some felt that Brittany's contribution should be recognized in the peace that resulted but the French Government thwarted attempts to have Brittany's claims put directly to the peace-makers at Versailles. However, Bretons did succeed in presenting to President Wilson and other participants at the peace conference a petition signed by 800 of its most prominent citizens.

The twentieth century has seen the concurrent sharp decline of the language and growth of various groups determined to change Brittany's status. The inter-war years were particularly lively ones in this respect. However, World War II was a disaster for Brittany. The occupying Germans were able to use some of the anti-French Breton sentiment for their own purposes: they promoted the Breton language and culture and co-opted and recruited some Bretons to work for them to such an extent that the Vichy Government was stirred to object that German support for Brittany should fall far short of encouraging separatist ambitions. When the war ended the French took their revenge through executions, imprisonment, and the confiscation of property, and Breton nationalism was thoroughly discredited. Undoubtedly the French government overre-acted against Brittany at the end of the war. The French were still intent on ridding themselves of this little pocket of linguistic and cultural resistance and the events of wartime provided a convenient excuse for the suppressive measures that were taken. The few gains made during the German occupation were lost and it was not until the 1960s and 1970s that the lost ground was recovered.

The post-war decline of French agriculture hit Brittany particularly hard. Farmer-led strikes and demonstrations became a feature of life in Brittany in the 1960s. These led eventually to a demand for more local control of Brittany's economy and for a degree of political autonomy. In the late 1960s and 1970s the movemant took some violent turns, e.g., the destruction of the main French television tower in Brittany. Today, although there is still a flourishing Breton culture, it remains poorly served by the media which fall under the control of the state and it often must express itself through the French language.

The decline of the language itself is mainly a twentieth-century phenomenon. It has been estimated that at the beginning of the century about 90 per cent of the inhabitants of Lower Brittany spoke Breton with about 1.3 million speakers altogether. By 1952 that number seems to have fallen to about 700,000 people who 'used French only in the case of necessity', and another 300,000 who could speak it 'if the need arose'. Twenty years later apparently only about 25 per cent of the population of Lower Brittany spoke Breton during the course of their daily lives and very few of these were young people. Breton had become the language of the older rural population, a population moreover that can speak the language but cannot read or write it. Learning to write Breton is also not made any easier by the existence of two competing orthographies.

Currently, little use is made of Breton in Brittany. The language is not being passed on to the children. French immigrants to the area and foreign workers there, mainly from Portugal and Algeria, have no use for the language. Men do use Breton in the male-oriented cafés and in the fields, this latter use adding, of course, to the association the language has with backwardness and drudgery, but in the bars, which cater to both men and women, the language is usually French. Women prefer to use French when they can, and French, the symbol of modernity and mobility, is overwhelmingly the choice of the young. The French language is even the language that is most frequently used in Brittany's cultural festivals.

The group most concerned with perpetuating Breton is a middle-class group of néo-bretonnants (new-Bretonists). However, their efforts to promote the language appear to bypass most Bretons, particularly those who actually use the language, who find the goals of the néo-bretonnants largely irrelevant to their needs. Most inhabitants of Brittany seem only too ready to give up the language and accept French in its place. Some are even suspicious of any movement to support the language that is encouraged by Paris, regarding such support as no more than a cynical ploy to win friends against the encroachments of English. The effort to preserve Breton seems to be a case of too little done too late. Bretons are therefore much more likely to be concerned with trying to maintain certain cultural differences that are still left – using French to do so – than with maintaining or reviving Breton.

If the language itself seems doomed, there is still a considerable Breton consciousness which exists independently of language. Brittany has found itself at the periphery of the French state, and regional consciousness has solidified along ethnic, political, and economic lines rather than linguistic ones. One consequence of the state's success in imposing its will on Brittany is that the various processes involved, such as urbanization and modernization, have drawn attention to disparities between life in Brittany and life in the more prosperous regions. Many Bretons feel that only if they unite around their common ethnicity and act as a unified group will they be able to effect the changes they regard as necessary. While it may be too late to save their language, their separate identity as a people is not yet lost if they are prepared to act.

GERMAN IN ALSACE

Alsace, like Brittany, is a part of modern France that is still undergoing the process of absorption. In this case the process is complicated by the fact that Alsace lies between France and Germany; consequently, it has proved to be a constant source of dispute between the two powers. Today, Alsace seems to be firmly part of France and Alsatians make little secret of the fact that they are loyal to the French state. They might speak one of the German dialects at home but they are French at heart.

Before 1648 Alsace was unquestionably part of Germany. In that year it was annexed to France by the Treaty of Westphalia and France began a somewhat uneasy occupation. That occupation was possible in large measure because the French decided to respect the region's frontiers and its language and traditions. The French also avoided inflicting alien practices on the local citizens, who were not only allowed to keep their schools but were also excused from military conscription. In 1789, when the French Revolution occurred, Alsace was relatively untouched by French influence. The French revolutionaries were determined to integrate Alsace fully into France and so they were particularly severe on the German-speaking Alsatians. It was not until the time of Napoleon that this harshness was eased. Napoleon himself is said to have remarked of the linguistic issue as follows: '*Laissez-les parler allemand, pourvu qu'ils sabrent en français.*' ('Let them speak German as long as they use their swords in French.')

During the first two-thirds of the nineteenth century the French spread their influence and their language into Alsace. French became the medium of instruction in the secondary schools and universities of the province and then, in 1853, of the primary schools. French also became the language of the bourgeoisie and of the growing world of industry. More and more young people elected to use it, but German remained the language of the home, of the churches, and of daily living.

Bismarck annexed Alsace after the Franco-Prussian War of 1870 and the German state set out to make the province a part of Germany. A deliberate policy of germanization was pursued. The success of this policy can be judged from the divided loyalties of the people of Alsace during World War I. The Germans conscripted 250,000 Alsatians to serve in their armies but at least 20,000 others went to France to volunteer for the French side. Following the war, the Treaty of Versailles restored Alsace to France.

The French government decided that the two generations of German rule had to be undone and that severe measures were necessary. German was therefore banned from the schools and it was also proposed that the laws on the separation of Church and State would be extended to Alsace so that religious instruction would no longer be allowed in the schools. The majority of Alsatians were glad to be part of France again but did not believe that they should have to give up their language. They opposed the government's proposals and it backed down: German was allowed in the classrooms and Alsace was excluded from the laws governing the separation of Church and State. There was some pro-German sentiment in Alsace between the two wars and some of this sentiment allied itself to a movement for the autonomy of Alsace, a movement which the majority of the French regarded as treasonous.

The Germans reoccupied Alsace during World War II and proceeded to treat it as part of Germany. The French language was banned and the population was conscripted to the war effort. Little mercy was shown to either conscripts or those who resisted conscription: the first were sent to fight against the allies of France and the second were sent to concentration camps. The brutality of the German occupation produced a pro-French sentiment within Alsace but, when the war ended, there were numerous reprisals against those who had collaborated with the occupying German forces. Unfortunately, the majority of the French people seems to have suspected the loyalty of Alsatians during the war and Alsatians became, like Bretons, scapegoats for the French conscience.

At the war's end the teaching of German was once again banned in the schools of Alsace and French was deliberately promoted. It was estimated in 1964 that although 80 per cent of Alsatians could speak one of the Alsatian dialects, few could either read or write Standard German. This situation appears to have changed little since that time in spite of the provisions of the *loi Deixonne*. The local dialects remain secure in Alsace. Nearly all eight-year-old Alsatians know the local dialect and achieve mastery of French as a result of schooling. In contrast, in Occitanie all children are completely fluent in French by the time they are eight and less than half know any of the local dialect by the time they are fourteen.

Bilingualism is a fact of life in Alsace but it is a bilingualism on the wane. Young Alsatians are turning more and more to French and use it in more and more circumstances. Alsatian still has a considerable hold in the family, leisure-time activities, and the workplace but young people are being attracted to use French increasingly in their lives. Many now even report that French has become the language in which they dream. The current linguistic situation in Alsace is probably best described as one that is essentially diglossic, with one language, French, used for the prestige functions and the other language, German, confined to a restricted set of lower-status functions. Knowledge of Standard German is also declining in Alsace. The Alsatians are constantly reminded that to be French one must speak French. The unitary French state does not easily tolerate languages other than French within its borders and there is little reason to suppose that in the long run the Alsatians will be better able to resist francization than the Occitans or the Bretons.

FLEMISH IN THE NORTH

The long campaign of the French to assimilate the Flemish (i.e., Dutch)-speaking population along the border with Belgium has been very successful indeed. Today fewer than 100,000 speakers of the language remain and these are concentrated in the rural areas that border on Belgium. The Flemish-speaking area, Westhoek was much greater as recently as the end of the nineteenth century but French gained all along the coastline and in all the large towns.

The decline of Flemish actually began in the seventeenth century when it was banned for official purposes for the first time. Little changed during the centuries that followed. One could be dismissed or even imprisoned for either teaching or preaching in Flemish. The nineteenth and early twentieth centuries did see the rise of several movements that sought recognition for the language but these usually provoked an official reaction that such moves were reactionary, even treasonous. In World War II there was indeed some collaboration with the German occupying forces which did nothing to further the cause of the Flemish in France. After 1951 one of the greatest concerns was to have Flemish recognized as one of the languages that would benefit from the *loi Deixonne*. Even though the government has now acceded to the request that Flemish be taught in the schools of the areas, it appears that it is much too late to arrest the decline of the language. Extinction seems imminent.

CORSICAN IN CORSICA

Unlike Westhoek, the Flemish-speaking part of France, the island of Corsica is separated from the mainland by a considerable body of water. It actually lies much closer to Italy than it does to France. But unlike the residents of Westhoek the residents of the island do not speak a language that is the standard language of the nearest country. Corsica is the third largest island of the Mediterranean; only Sicily and Sardinia are larger. But it is a poor, sparsely populated island with a population of a little over 200,000, the vast majority of whom speak Corsican. Corsican itself is a dialect of Italian and is actually spoken in two varieties on the island. As a result of the growing Corsican-consciousness of the nineteenth and twentieth centuries, there is now a Corsican literature in a somewhat standardized form.

Most Corsicans do not live on the island, as a result of the long history of economic decline. Like Napoleon, the island's most famous native son, many have gone to live on the mainland of France but without achieving Napoleon's distinction. Indeed the opposite is the case: rightly or wrongly the majority of Frenchmen evince a fairly strong dislike for Corsicans partly because of the kinds of jobs they prefer to fill. Recent protests by Corsicans about what they perceive to be their 'internal colonial' status within France have done nothing to change that feeling.

Corsica has been part of France since the French purchased the island from Genoa in 1768. Previous to that purchase Genoa had tried to assert its control over the island for a number of centuries but had not been particularly successful and the French were no more successful for many years. Corsica is either the last part of France's territory to be completely occupied or one of the first of its colonies, one still not yet 'freed'. For two decades after 1768 the French pursued a policy of 'pacification', with all the brutality and horrors that usually attend such a policy. By the outbreak of the French Revolution, Corsican opposition had been suppressed and the revolutionaries pursued there the same integrating policies as elsewhere. The later rise of Napoleon to power may have established a connection between Corsica and France that had not previously existed, for Corsicans took a great pride in the Emperor's accomplishments even though he showed no particular generosity to either the island or its people.

The nineteenth century brought a great decline to the island. Its economy and agriculture collapsed and many people left. There was a feeling of nostalgia about both the remote past, when the island was largely independent, and about the recent past, when Napoleon, its native son, had so dominated the world. Autonomy for the island became a goal for a new cultural leadership, and one of the focal issues was the separate language the people had and their desire to use it in every walk of life. The central government resisted such goals, regarding them as anti-French. In the twentieth century the events of World War II once again appeared to confirm to many Frenchmen that citizens of France who did not speak French were untrustworthy. Those who had sought autonomy for Corsica were accused of collaboration with the enemy during that war. Once again the French government found reason to suppress both a movement for some kind of regional autonomy and a language that was not that of the majority.

Today, there is a strong movement for autonomy for Corsica. Many Corsicans feel that they have been neglected and that they are losing their land to people from the outside or for purposes that do not meet with their approval. There have been violent political demonstrations and boycotts of elections when the issues have seemed either irrelevant or deliberately evasive. Many Corsicans believe that the French have used and manipulated the traditional clan system of the island, in which certain families effectively wield power, so as to deprive ordinary Corsicans of their full political rights. There was a long and bitter struggle to have the *loi Deixonne* applied to Corsica, a struggle not won until 1974. Corsicans want their language to be taught in the schools. There are grammars now available and a growing literature. The majority of Corsicans can still unite around their language. They still experience linguistic discrimination in such incidents as one in 1986 when the use of Corsican first names in electoral documents resulted in a government official rejecting lists of candidates submitted by two autonomist parties on the grounds that French law did not allow for the use of such names. Corsicans can still use Corsican to express among themselves their hostility to the central government and its two centuries of suppression, neglect, and indifference. In this respect they are different from any other group in France, and it may be for this reason that the French often perceive Corsica to be one of their most troublesome regions.

CATALAN AND BASQUE IN THE SOUTHWEST

France shares two minority peoples with Spain, the Catalans and the Basques. Most Catalans live in Spain but there about 260,000 who live in France, in Rousillon and Cerdagne, an area that has been part of France since 1659. Even before that time this territory had gone back and forth between France and Spain for two centuries until the Treaty of the Pyrenees finally acknowledged that it would belong to France. The French initiated a policy of francization to ensure the loyalty of the people and as early as 1700 proclaimed that French would be the only language recognized for legal purposes.

This policy has been pursued ever since. The French state has actively promoted French, and the *loi Deixonne* has had almost no effect. The official view seems to be that Catalan is the language of a peasantry. It is not the language of opportunity. Since the area in which Catalan is spoken is not at all prosperous, it is also easy to make such an association.

The French Catalans are also cut off from the Spanish Catalans. Originally they were cut off because of the political choice they made when they preferred French rule to Castilian rule. Then, after their absorption into the French state, they were cut off by the political boundary. When the French built roads and railways, the Catalans of France were drawn toward the north in the direction of Paris rather than toward the south in the direction of Barcelona. In the twentieth century French Catalans also found the Franco regime in Spain with its latent hostility to minorities and republicans to be a further factor in directing attention away from Spain no matter how sympathetic many of them were to the plight of Spain's Catalan population.

The Catalans are a very small group in France; in Spain they are a large group. On the whole, French Catalans have been successful in retaining their language. They have tended to identify in their cultural and linguistic struggles with the Occitans. The problems of the Spanish Catalans under Franco seemed somewhat remote and there was really very little contact with them. The economic problems of this part of France are also considerable: French Catalans have not prospered economically like Spanish Catalans. Their region does attract migrants but these weaken their language and culture. Unlike the Spanish Catalans they do not convert some of these immigrants to their ways and sometimes even to their language. However, language retention is very high in the region and the French have not had their way entirely. The *loi Deixonne* is now available to the people if they can persuade the authorities to implement its provisions. The French Catalans can look now to the new post-Franco Spanish Catalonia and see it as an example of how a region can rapidly be transformed under a new political system. There is, therefore, a small but growing feeling in the region that it may have a future under some other arrangement either within or without the French state.

The Basques are another people divided by a state boundary. This division again dates from 1659 when the Spanish–French boundary was finally fixed. At that time the seven Basque provinces were divided with the four southern ones going to Spain and the three northern ones to France. Immediately the French began the process of assimilating this new population. The French Revolution hastened this process. To the revolutionaries the Basque provinces were symbols of reaction and catholicism. As we have seen, Barrère, for example, went so far as to declare that 'fanaticism speaks Basque'. Ever since, the French government has tried to promote French in the area much as it did in Brittany, employing many of the same means.

The Basque area of France is also a poor area economically, and the people have always had a struggle to survive and have lacked the resources needed to combat state policies which they have found to be inimical. Young people leave to seek employment in other parts of France. If they are replaced, it is by francophones. Basque culture has also been quite attenuated and is disappearing along with the language. Now it is only the very old who speak Basque, but some Basque consciousness remains. Today, only about a quarter of French Basques regard themselves as Basques; one in five actually declares for a French identity; and the remaining 55 per cent choose a 'hyphenated' identity, either Basque-French or French-Basque.

There has been some response to the example of the Basques who live in Spain and to their long struggle against Spanish oppression. French Basques, and even, to some extent, the French government, were sympathetic to the aspirations of the Spanish Basques. However, this sympathy was not translated by the state into support for the Basque language and culture within France. The state quite clearly failed to provide such support in its pursuit of policies aimed at spreading French into all domains of life. But, even if Basque and much of the culture associated with it are on the verge of disappearing, the feeling that the majority of people have that they are Basques, or at least hyphenated Basques rather than French, has not. Many still pursue the vision of some kind of association with the Basques of Spain, and some kind of control of their destiny within a different political arrangement with France.

FRENCH ATTITUDES

Some common factors emerge from a consideration of the minority languages that continue to exist in France. While these were able to remain largely intact before the French Revolution, the events of that era brought about changes which threatened them all. One such change was the abolition of the old provinces, each with its own special association with the Crown. In place of the old provinces a system of departments was developed and each of the departments was controlled from Paris in a highly centralized uniform state. The state had exhibited centralizing tendencies well before the French Revolution but these became much stronger after.

Through much of the nineteenth century the old provinces were often viewed as the bastions of royalism and clericalism opposed to a republic in which anti-clericalism was a strong force. Only the Basques and the Catalans escaped criticism on these grounds. The two catastrophic wars of the twentieth century did nothing to help regional aspirations. They confirmed to many Frenchmen the suspicion that those who were French but did not speak the language were somehow untrustworthy even though many non-francophone Frenchmen died in those wars and many others accepted a French identity for the first time.

The particular attitude that the French have toward their language also encourages them to want others to learn it. A language praised for its *clarté, beauté, perfection, stabilité, utilité,* and *simplicité,* just to name a few of the 'virtues' which have been ascribed to it, obviously deserves widespread dissemination, especially in France itself. There is also the pervasive myth that the French are all one people, sharing both a common language and a common culture. All national political parties seem to subscribe to that myth. When, for example, the *Soviet Encyclopedia* pointed out in 1978 that ten per cent of France's population belonged to minority nationalities, even *L'Humanité* objected, declaring for *'l'unité nationale du peuple français'* and denying any reality to a multinational French state. As President Pompidou remarked in 1972 : *'Il n'y a pas de place pour les langues minoritaires dans une France destinée à marquer l'Europe de son sceau.'* ('There is no place for minority languages in a France destined to make its mark in Europe.')

The *loi Deixonne* has really done very little to help preserve the minority languages of France. It has proved to be little more than an empty gesture. The election of a Socialist administration under President Mitterand seemed for a while to promise change. The Giordan Report of 1982, *Démocratie culturelle et droit à la différence,* commissioned by the French government, did recognize the existence in France of authentic regional and minority cultures and argued that these should be subsidized through a National Commission for Minorities. However, other problems became more urgent in the mid-1980s and no significant changes in language policy toward minorities have resulted. The minority groups have banded together to form an umbrella organization to promote their interests, the Conseil de Défense et Promotion des Langues de France.

Finally, we should add that whereas in the period up to the end of World War II ethnic movements in France were associated with reactionary politics, when a resurgence of such movements occurred about a decade after that war's end, they had taken on a left-wing association. This is mainly because national liberation movements throughout the world are associated with the political aspirations of the left. That is where the examples and the rhetoric come from. However, it is not always clear that those who lead such movements are genuinely of the left; there are those who feel that a number of rightists are quite content to cling to the coat-tails of left-wing politics so long as it is both safe and convenient to do so. In other words, many French people still perceive regional movements aimed at providing a better deal for the surviving languages or for some kind of local autonomy to be motivated by old hatreds rather by a genuine desire to build a new political consensus. Without such a consensus the future is likely to be very much like the past so far as minority languages and cultures are concerned. A continuation of old policies must inevitably lead to a France which will be entirely French in both language and culture. The Jacobinian ideal will have been achieved at long last.

SPAIN AND ITS LANGUAGES

It is useful to contrast the linguistic situation in France with that which exists in neighbouring Spain. Each country is a large, long-established Western European state. Each is assumed by many of its citizens to be monolingual, and those who do not subscribe to this belief are regarded as being somewhat disloyal. But each state has important linguistic and ethnic minorities. In addition, two of these minorities, the Basques and the Catalans, are minorities in both states and form majorities nowhere. According to Linz (1975, p. 367): 'Spain is ... in population after the Soviet Union the largest economically developed multi-lingual country, followed by Canada and Yugoslavia. Outside of the USSR, it is the largest multi-lingual country in Europe and the oldest multi-lingual state in Europe.'

Spain has a population of 37 million nearly all of whom speak Castilian, known everywhere in the world as Spanish and acknowledged to be one of the world's great languages because of its history, literary and cultural associations, and diffusion across the world, particularly to South America. It is difficult for many Castilians to think that any other language can compare with their own, but millions of Spaniards who speak either Catalan, Basque, or Galician do not share this opinion. There are no exact figures as to how many people speak each of these languages because the Spanish census avoids inquiring into the matter. The official view has long been that the language of Spain is Spanish and that there is no need to probe the issue further. Most people in Spain do speak Spanish but many are bilingual, speaking both Spanish and one of those other languages. But even those who most ardently pursue the goal of promoting one of the other languages do not tend to push too hard for official counts of speakers. Such information might weaken some of the claims they make. As Linz says (p. 369): 'The Spanish-Castilian nationalists want to ignore the fact of multi-lingualism and the regional linguistic nationalists probably would not be happy in discovering the weakness of some of the local languages.' There is some agreement, though, that there are about six million speakers of Catalan, a half million speakers of Basque, and about three million speakers of Galician in Spain.

It was the Castilians who unified Spain. The small kingdom of Castile led the struggle against the Arab invaders, developed a literature, and encouraged the use of the language for a wide variety of purposes. Politically, the country developed through the union of the crowns of Castile and Aragon (which then included Catalonia) in 1476; the conquest of Granada in 1492; and the annexation of Navarre in 1512. As the country developed, the use of Castilian was also extended to these possessions, for example to Catalonia from 1707 on, as the sole official language and as the language of education. Until very recently little or no recognition was given to the fact that millions of Spaniards preferred to use some other language than Spanish for the affairs of daily life and had succeeded in keeping these other languages alive in spite of restrictive measures and even persecution. Franco's proscription of all other languages than Spanish was harsh but it was not new. From the eighteenth century on a succession of Spanish governments had severely restricted the use of the other languages of Spain, forbidding their use in education, administration, and public life, and severely curtailing what was written in them and their use in religious worship.

The post-Franco years have brought important changes to Spain. The new 1978 Constitution recognizes the other languages of Spain. Article 3 declares that: 'Castilian is the official Spanish language of the state. All Spaniards are obliged to know it and have the right to use it. The other Spanish languages will also be official in their respective Autonomous Communities, in accordance with the Statutes.' These communities, the result of an attempt to bring a measure of decentralization to a heavily centralized Spanish state, are now in operation in the Basque country, Catalonia, Galicia, and Andalusia. Local control of internal language affairs is an important issue within each of the first three communities and bilingualism is now an acknowledged fact of life in all the non-Castilian regions of Spain. It also seems to be politically irreversible. The real issue is how bilingualism can be maintained when there are so many competing pressures and interests. As we will see, even Catalonia is not at all secure in its bilingualism, the Basques seem to emphasize cultural differences rather than linguistic ones and a minority are the most violent separatists in Western Europe, and the Galicians do almost nothing to resist the dominant state language. Even though Spain is multilingual at present, there is no guarantee that it will continue to be so. The freedom that the present rather fragile democracy has brought could turn out to be even more harmful to the minority languages of Spain than oppressive dictatorship!

CATALAN IN SPAIN

Catalan is the minority language of Spain that has the widest distribution on Spanish territory and the greatest number of speakers. Catalonia has been part of Spain since 1476 when Isabel of Castile married Ferdinand of the Catalonia–Aragonese federation. It is difficult to give the present Catalan-speaking area precise bounds: historical, cultural, and linguistic boundaries no longer coincide in Spain and no region can claim not to have a strong 'Spanish' component within it. The area in which Catalan is spoken today comprises approximately an eighth of Spain's territory and includes about a quarter of the total population. It is on the whole a prosperous area, and its capital Barcelona, a city of over two million people, is the most important industrial city of the Iberian peninsula. The language is also spoken on the Balearic Islands of Majorca, Minorca, Ibiza, and Formentera. Catalan is acknowledged to be a different language from Castilian, in fact probably more different than Portuguese. Catalans can also look back at least a thousand years over a history that shows periods of independence from Castile, periods of marked opposition, and periods of subjection. There is therefore a strong Catalan consciousness of a separate history and of resistance to Castilian domination. The Catalans also take considerable pride in being an outward-looking, intellectually-oriented people who have suffered from the constraints imposed on them by the much more insular Castilians.

Until the nineteenth century the efforts of the Spanish government to suppress Catalan and promote Spanish were quite successful and even the loss of the right to use Catalan in the schools stirred little protest. However, the same period showed the beginnings of a cultural and linguistic revival in Catalonia. Catalan nationalism grew rapidly in the nineteenth century in response to the loss of the South American colonies. That loss deprived the Catalans of valuable markets and led to a decline in prosperity within Catalonia. The final blow was the loss of Cuba in 1898. Discontent turned into outright rebellion and by the end of the century many Catalans were determined to change a political system which favoured the Castilians at their expense. From that time date the various movements to achieve some form of independence for Catalonia.

The Spanish state dissolved into civil war in the 1930s and for a time the people of Catalonia were able to achieve the autonomy they had sought. Franco's victory ended this brief experience of freedom. To Franco, Catalan was the 'language of dogs' and he banned it from the schools and insisted on a unitary Spanish-speaking state. Catalan could no longer be used on the airwaves or in any kind of administrative activity. Castilian ways were reimposed on the Catalans: no longer could they have trade unions and no longer were Church and State to be separate or would land reform and divorce be possible. It was not until 1961 that the government felt secure enough to once again allow the publication of books in Catalan or the existence of Catalan cultural organizations. At the end of Franco's regime about 90 per cent of Catalans could understand Catalan, about 75 per cent could speak it, about two-thirds could read it, and about a half could write it. While there is reason to believe that these figures over-represent the vitality of Catalan, nevertheless the language had managed to endure a long period of suppression.

Today, Catalan has an official status within Catalonia. Under the 1979 Statute of Autonomy of Catalonia Catalan is acknowledged to be the official language of Catalonia and Castilian the official language of the entire Spanish state, but both languages are to be promoted within Catalonia. The main beneficiary of this policy is, of course, Catalan, which can now be taught on a systematic basis. The *Generalitat* of Catalonia has proposed that all children in Catalonia should receive primary instruction in their mother tongue, either Catalan or Castilian, so that all will be bilingual when they reach adolescence. This policy is being implemented slowly. Since 1978 Catalan has been an obligatory subject of instruction in schools of the area and since 1982 it must be used as a language of instruction for at least one subject. It is also obligatory to teach Castilian but it is quite possible for Castilian to be the only subject that is taught in Castilian in some schools if parents so choose. At the moment there are various kinds of schools in Catalonia with some teaching in Catalan, others in Castilian, and the remainder bilingual with different proportions of the two languages. The new system is not fully implemented and opinions vary from place to place concerning the kind of school that is most desirable. There is also in many places a shortage of instructors who are really comfortable in using Catalan as a language of instruction.

Since Franco's death and the return of democracy to Spain, Catalan has made much progress. It is now recognized as a language of culture, one with a long and proud history. There is a flourishing Catalan book industry and the language is used, though not as much as many Catalans would wish, in the daily press, radio, and television. It is possibly a majority language in its own territory, there are no social class distinctions since its use extends across all classes, and Catalans strongly identify with the language. Their language is what makes them special within Spain. They have no cause for shame either: Catalonia is one of the richest parts of Spain so one can in no way attach the stigmata of poverty and failure to speaking Catalan.

But how secure is Catalan within Catalonia? Here opinions differ. Some estimates are that little more than half of the adult population of Catalonia actually speak Catalan. The percentage is even lower in the cities falling to as low as 40 per cent, even in Barcelona itself, and in immigrant-dominated areas to as low as a quarter of the total population. These immigrants, who comprise at least a third of the population, are mainly Castilians who are attracted to the area because of its economic prosperity. In one view many of these willingly set about the task of learning Catalan – or at least their children learn the language – because it is socially and economically advantageous to do so. Another view is that little such learning occurs, Castilian being so well entrenched in Catalonia and the supporting facilities so adequate that there is no need for immigrants to learn Catalan. Non-Catalans are also more fertile than Catalans so that Catalans appear to be becoming more and more of a minority in their own area. They are already a minority in the school population as only 37 per cent of primary school children in the province of Barcelona are native speakers of Catalan.

There is therefore disagreement about whether Catalan is holding its own, losing, or gaining in Catalonia. The lack of accurate census information does little to help resolve matters either. The current post-Franco years are transitional ones but it is not at all clear what the transition will be to. Catalan may prove to be attractive to newcomers to the area and there may be a successful amalgamation of linguistic and regional consciousnesses. However, Castilian immigrants to Catalonia have begun to express their concerns about what they perceive to be language policies and practices that discriminate against them. They tend to see themselves as being already socially and economically disadvantaged and to these disadvantages the regional government in Catalonia is adding a linguistic one. Catalans themselves can no longer unite against the Spanish state. Now they must turn their attention to Castilian–Catalan linguistic competition within their own region, but it is not at all clear, nor may it be for quite a while, which language will be the winner and which the loser in that struggle.

BASQUE IN SPAIN

The Basques of Spain have become known as one of the most militant minorities in the world. *Euzkadi*, the homeland of the Basques, covers territory in both France and Spain, but the four provinces of Euzkadi that lie in Spain (Vizcaya, Guipuzcoa, Alava, and Navarra) contain many more Basques than the three provinces that lie in France (Basse Navarre, Soule, and Labourd), well over ten times as many in fact, i.e., well over 2 million people as compared with 200,000 people. The Basques appear to be the original inhabitants of the area in which they now reside. At one time this area was much larger but it was considerably reduced as the French and Spanish states absorbed Basque territory and attempted to absorb the people too. The Basque language, which the Basques call *Euskera*, is unrelated to any other language in the world, and the Basque people have the highest incidence of the Rh negative blood factor of any people. The Basques are 'unique' therefore in these two respects but different views exist concerning what value should be placed on that 'uniqueness'.

The Basques have never been comfortable within either state and have resisted various moves by the central governments. Spain contains the larger number of Basques, and its recent history has been a more troubled one than that of France so far as the treatment of minorities has been concerned. In large measure this difficulty stems from the events of the bloody civil war of the 1930s. During that war the Basques were able to establish an autonomous republic for a short while. The victorious Franco had to fight hard and even vindictively, as in the bombing of Guernica, to overcome Basque opposition, and at the end of the war he did everything in his power to suppress the Basque people. He persecuted the language even to the extent of having books burned, banning the language entirely from public life, forbidding the use of Basque names in public documents, and removing Basque inscriptions from public buildings and even tombstones. Basque cultural organizations were also banned, and it was not until the 1950s that Franco felt sufficiently confident to relax some of the oppressive measures and allow, either officially or unofficially, certain Basque cultural activities as the founding of *ikastolak*, i.e., privately-sponsored schools outside the educational system in which Basque could be taught.

The consequence of Franco's policies was a further reduction of the ability of Basques to speak their language. The estimates vary on how many Basques continue to use the language but no estimate ever claims that more than 20 per cent of the people retain use of their language. Basque is also spoken in several different dialects and the lack of a universally agreed to standard form of the language has also proved to be something of an obstacle in promoting literacy. Basque is no longer the language of the cities of Euzkadi; it is the language only of some of the rural areas and of some smaller towns. Other Spaniards who move to the Basque area – and there is considerable migration to this the wealthiest part of Spain with its shipyards, steel mills, and manufacturing centres – do not learn Basque. Indeed they further weaken the claims of the language since they are usually not at all sympathetic to Basque claims. The Basques are also not a minority who can use discriminatory economic treatment by the central state as a rallying cry. The Basques actually see themselves exploited in the opposite way, claiming that they give more to the state than they receive in benefits. For the radical minority of the region not even the granting of a form of regional autonomy to the provinces of Vizcaya, Alava, and Guipuzcoa in 1980 with rights to a regional government, to control of the police force, and to the levying of taxes, meets their minimum demands.

Some Basques seek considerably more autonomy than was granted in 1980: their goal is the unification of the Basque provinces of France and Spain in order to establish a Basque state. The most radical group is Euzkadi ta Askatasuna, the ETA, (Basque Homeland and Freedom), with its unification slogans of '3+4=7' and *zazpiak bat* (the seven are one), both referring to the number of Basque provinces in France and Spain. ETA is not widely supported in the polls with perhaps only as few as 15 per cent of the population sympathetic to its goals; however, its activities have cost the lives of nearly 600 people in the last two decades. Basque separatism is now associated in many people's minds with some of the most violent terrorism in Europe. This violence began under Franco as an expression of protest against his policies. The convenience of a border with France with fellow Basques residing across that border also allowed a measure of external support for such activities at a time when such support was critical. Today, these activities are not directed against specific state policies but rather against the Spanish state itself because separatism is the avowed goal of this radical minority.

There are other groups in the region with aspirations for the Basques as a people. What characterizes all the groups is a strong commitment to a Basque identity, a commitment which to some observers appears almost to be xenophobic in the expression it often takes, and a belief in territorial integrity. Language is less important: one is Basque by descent; if one can speak Basque that is a good thing but if one does not speak it there are still plenty of reasons to be Basque rather than something else. Some Basques now find it particularly galling to be a minority in their own territory, and the Castilian intruders are made to bear the brunt of their displeasure. Others are willing to acknowledge that the region has prospered under the Spanish state and that, although it might contribute to that state more than its fair share of taxes and get less than its fair share of benefits, its economic viability would be seriously impaired if it were independent.

Current Spanish policy encourages the use of languages other than Spanish in those regions in which such languages are spoken. The Basques are now free to teach their language to their children, but they do not appear to be as keen to do so as the Catalans are to teach Catalan to their children. Among the Basques today less than half understand or speak the language, about a quarter can read Basque, and as few as 10 per cent are able to write in it.

The Basques have always regarded ethnicity and their claim to a territory as their key identifying characteristics. They regard themselves as a separate group of people with a long historical association to a particular piece of territory. To many Basques language is a secondary issue. Franco successfully suppressed the people and their language for many years but in no way did he suppress the feeling they had that they were different from all other residents of the Iberian peninsula. Basques are also not particularly anxious that Spanish immigrants to Euzkadi learn Basque. Such immigrants do not learn the language for this reason among others – it is generally acknowledged to be a difficult language for an adult to learn – whereas immigrants to Catalonia are sometimes won over to Catalan or deliberately courted. The Basques believe that you do not become a Basque by learning Basque: you are either a Basque by birth or you are never a Basque. While there is some evidence that this attitude is changing, the Basque language may already have declined to such a point that ethnicity rather than language must provide the rallying point for any aspirations that the Basques might continue to pursue as a people.

GALICIAN IN SPAIN

The third linguistic minority in Spain is the Galician minority. There are about three million people in that part of Spain in the northwest which has Portugal directly to the south. Many of these people speak Galician, a language that evolved from a common Galician-Portuguese language. However, Castilian conquest cut Galician off from Portuguese in the fifteenth century. Portuguese continued to evolve into a standard language, but Galician did not evolve in the same way. It was dominated by Castilian, devoid of a literature, and without access to the written medium. It was a spoken language only and eventually came to exist in a diglossic relationship with Spanish within its own area of Spain. Today, the written form of Galician is hardly distinguishable from Portuguese; the spoken form tends to strike speakers of Portuguese as a somewhat archaic form of their language. A popular myth among many Galicians is that there is a considerable Celtic content to Galician; however, there is no convincing evidence to support such a belief.

Galicia is a poor and isolated part of Spain. It is still an undeveloped, marginal region of subsistence agriculture and the out-migration of the surplus peasant population, a region that lacks either a local intelligentsia or leadership and one still dominated by the central state, its institutions, and bureaucracy. Galician has never had any status in administration, education, or law. Only in recent years have the Galicians begun to take any pride in the language they use for everyday conversation but which they do not use in other circumstances. There is now some desire to end the diglossic situation that Galician has in relation to Spanish in favour of one in which there is genuine bilingualism. However, that will require the development of literacy in Galician and at the moment it is only a very small minority who can claim to be able to write the language. Interest in the language itself also appears to be low. There is as yet little overt Galician opposition to the central government and the Galicians are one of the most dormant linguistic minorities in Europe today. The limited autonomy of the post-Franco years may prove to be largely irrelevant to the future of the language, which is not at all a promising one, unless some drastic change of attitude occurs in the region in which it is spoken.

FURTHER READING

French in modern times: Weber 1976, Gordon 1978; minority languages of France: Berthet 1982, Calvet 1974, Esman 1977a, Foster 1980, Stephens 1976; Occitan: Bec 1986; Breton: Lebesque 1970.

6

Promoting English and French

English is now by far the most widespread of the world's languages. Hundreds of millions use English as a native tongue but it also serves perhaps an even greater number as a second language even though the forms it takes as such an additional language may differ widely from place to place. There is also no indication that English is in any way ceasing to spread; indeed it seems to be on the ascendant in the world with no serious competitor. In contrast, French, while not a threatened language, is struggling to maintain its former glories as a world language and even to preserve its integrity within France itself. However, the efforts the French are currently making may be quite unsuccessful. The international linguistic tide has turned in favour of English, and French is in danger of being left high and dry on the shore along with all other possible contenders as a world language. That tide may someday change and come to favour some other language than English but only in a very different world from the one that currently exists and one that those who presently speak the language would likely view as catastrophically different.

THE ASCENDANCY OF ENGLISH

The language that the Anglo-Saxons brought with them to England and which later withstood the invasion of the Normans is now not only the language of the British Isles but also the language of many other countries in the world. In some it is the official language or one of the official languages. In others it is accepted as the official language although not recognized in law as such. In a still greater number it is the language in which much work is done by those who necessarily deal with matters that transcend state boundaries, whether these are political, cultural, or economic. People throughout the world, particularly young people, also want to learn English, a language they often associate with ideas of 'progress' and 'modernity'.

English has been spread throughout the world until it is now undoubtedly the most important language in the world if importance is measured by the kinds of activities for which the language is used and not just by the sheer numbers of speakers involved. By that last criterion the most important language would be the Mandarin variety of Chinese, for there are more native speakers of this variety of Chinese than of any other language. However, it would be difficult to make any kind of case that at the present time those who speak Mandarin exert more than a fraction of the power and influence in the world of those who speak English.

In the late twentieth century the influence of English radiates from a variety of sources. The influence of the British variety continues to be felt through many of Britain's former colonial and imperial possessions. But at least one of these, the United States, is now several times larger and wealthier than the original homeland. The 'centre' of English has shifted across the Atlantic and some states are torn because of that shift, one group in those states preferring the 'older' British variety of the language and another group the 'modern' American variety. Whereas the British variety is still associated in many people's minds with ideas about 'culture', the North American variety benefits from its associations with science, technology, the media, and raw political, economic, and military power.

As English has spread, not only has there been this pull between the two major varieties but there have also been moves to assert the legitimacy of other varieties. In some cases in which there is a clear 'ethnic' continuity (i.e., English was brought to a particular place in the world by native speakers of the language who settled there permanently rather than was adopted by non-speakers of the language) that recognition has occurred without much opposition. Few would dispute that, if it is legitimate to talk about the British and American varieties of English, it is no less legitimate to talk about the Australian, Canadian, and South African varieties. But can one talk in the same way about Indian, Nigerian, and Singaporean varieties? Do the varieties of English spoken in such countries in which there is no such 'ethnic' continuity and in which the English language is a second language qualify as legitimate examples of English? As English spreads, the diversity of the language increases, and questions are raised from time to time about this diversity and even about who 'owns' English today.

The Constitution of the United States makes no mention of the English language. In fact, there seems to have been a deliberate move in the early years of the new republic to be exceedingly tolerant of linguistic diversity. Consequently, in the early nineteenth century many different languages were spoken in the United States and little concern was expressed about even the fairly widespread systems of education in tongues other than English. The English language seemed to be self-evidently the right language for people to adopt at this time and there is little reason to suppose that this benign view was incorrect. People who spoke a language other than English may indeed have sent their children to what schools existed at the time with the aim of retaining that language but the strong social pressure to learn English tended to prevail. It was not believed to be necessary to compel children to learn English – unless they were aboriginal peoples – since they would acquire the language naturally, it being in their best interests to do so as quickly as possible.

This situation changed somewhat in the second half of the nineteenth century. As Heath and Mandabach (1983) indicate, various moves were made in that period to promote English. Some of those arose from the sudden influx of non-anglophone immigrants and others from the extension of the state overseas into Puerto Rico, Hawaii, and the Philippines. Many felt that the language of the law and of education should be mandated and that the *laisser faire* situation that existed was not in the country's best interests. Consequently, various laws were passed forbidding the teaching of languages other than English and by 1923 English was the only permissible language of instruction in 34 states. Such laws, however, were not the principal means for either encouraging English or curtailing other languages. It was above all the desire of the élites who controlled the various social institutions that English would be the language of the United States and its possessions and the willingness of the masses to accept this point of view, which was so influential in giving English the status that it eventually achieved, that of being if not the official language of the nation at least its quasi-official one. That language is also the American variety of English, not the British one, a development foreshadowed in Noah Webster's words of 1789 in his *Dissertations on the English Language*: 'As an independent nation, our honor requires us to have a system of our own, in language as well as government. Great Britain whose children we are, and whose language we speak, should no longer be our standard; for the taste of her writers is already corrupted and her language on the decline'. Webster's stated reasons for rejecting the British variety of the language were undoubtedly incorrect – Mencken (1919) was to echo them quite forcefully in the twentieth century – but there can be no doubt that independence did bring forth a new and potent variety of the English language.

As we will see in the final chapter, in the last quarter century a number of questions have been raised concerning language in the United States. On the one hand, there are those who seek to make English the official language of the United States and have gone so far as to propose that the constitution be amended so as to do this. Proponents of this course of action believe that the English language is a key instrument in the americanization of both immigrants and those indigenous residents who have managed to keep their languages. In this view it is somehow 'un-American' not to be able to speak English if one is a citizen of the United States. Moreover, the unity of the whole state would be threatened if various parts of it were to have the right to pick and choose what languages should be official in particular jurisdictions. On the other hand, there are those who claim that the present quasi-official status of English is harmful to minorities. It seriously disadvantages those who do not speak English when, for example, they seek schooling or jobs. Since the constitution declares against such discrimination, it is the duty of the state to recognize other languages when such recognition is necessary so as to ensure the equality of all citizens. What has resulted from these concerns is a long and somewhat inconclusive debate about bilingual education in the United States, with the various issues as yet still far from being resolved.

It was during the nineteenth century that English spread throughout the United States and consolidated its position there. It was also during the same century that English spread over the whole world as the British Empire came into existence. There have been numerous other imperial languages, and others too have outlasted their empires. English is therefore not unique in having survived the decline of the British Empire for even today other post-imperial languages continue to exist in former domains – Arabic, French, and Spanish to cite but a few examples. What is remarkable about English and what makes it unique is the extent to which it has spread throughout the world. No other language has ever been spread so far and wide. No other language has ever had the influence in world affairs that English has today.

English competes with other languages in various parts of the world but that competition is often one-sided. It is the major language of science and technology, particularly of the new computer technology, of international business, banking, trade, and tourism, and often the preferred language of education at the higher levels. Until recently French was its most serious competitor, but few today would dispute the claim that English has clearly triumphed in the struggle between the two languages. As Fishman has observed (1983, p. 20) of the two languages: 'English is less loved but more used; French is more loved but less used.'

In some parts of the world English is now viewed as an intruding language that threatens one or more local languages. That threat may take the form of widespread borrowing from English, and actions are sometimes taken in an attempt to control or restrict the importation of words from English. Countries as diverse as France, India, Japan, and Tanzania have all had to recognize this problem and have found it necessary to establish agencies with a double function: to control the effects of English on the language of the state – even to 'purify' it – and to encourage the use and development of that state language.

A second kind of threat is the threat to the state's educational system when the vernaculars and English find themselves in competition as possible languages of instruction. English has advantages to offer that many vernacular languages lack. But national policy (whether motivated by a desire to achieve some form of national consensus or to make a clean break with the colonial past) and simple economics may dictate that the educational medium be one or more of the vernaculars. Some states have found that attempts to vernacularize their educational systems may meet with resistance when English is the prestige language in the state, and vernacularization of education results in a decrease in the amount of English that is taught. People may resist such attempts to discourage the use of English and to encourage use of the vernaculars.

Sometimes the issue is clearly one of values. Those who seek to acquire English often subscribe to values they feel are associated with the language, that is, the values they associate with the United States and Great Britain. Others seek to resist the spread of English because they seek to resist those same values. In some cases there are mixed feelings: the government of Singapore has very actively encouraged the use of English in the Republic, stating that it is the language all Singaporeans must learn in order to guarantee a future for the island in a world that English dominates, but at the same time expressing serious concern at some of the values that it feels should be resisted.

There are those who believe that along with the English language, which is disseminated widely by radio, subsidized books, international news services, and potent satellite communication systems, goes a particular point of view of the world seen fron a Western 'developed' perspective. This perspective is possibly more subtle than the one the French have developed, with its very conscious promotion of French language and culture, but it is probably much more pervasive. The resources that support it are much greater and it encroaches on many more areas of existence. According to those who hold such a view, when the perspective on the world masquerades as the 'truth' about the world, it can be, and often is, a source of conflict among peoples.

There is an alternative 'value-free' view of English in the world. A number of observers and commentators on the spread of English have argued that one of the principal reasons for the rapid spread of English is its actual 'neutrality' so far as values are concerned. In this view

English now belongs to no one. It is a world language with no single proprietor. It is associated with all kinds and colours of people, and with very different political, social, cultural, and religious systems. Nor is it tied to a particular view of the world or a particular culture. They cite the case of French as a language which does not enjoy this same neutrality. The French insist on identifying that language with their culture and maintain that France and its ways are somehow centrally involved in the French language, the language and the culture being inseparable.

The French continue to insist that they 'own' French and that the standards for French are to be set in France. It is a rare Frenchman who is willing to make a strong case in support of a patois. It is also rare for a citizen of a country once colonized by France who, having been exposed to French language and culture, is unwilling to defend French or who has anything positive to say about a local or creole variety of the language, e.g., the English spoken in Quebec. English has proved much more accepting of local varieties and standards. Most users of English accept the existence of standards themselves even though the pronouncements of particular individuals as to what these standards are or should be do not go without comment. However, users of English look to no one established authority for a standard: they have nothing equivalent to the Académie Française. Instead they recognize that local standards can and do exist. There is not only a British standard but an American one, and the inhabitants of Australia and Canada will refer to Australian standards and Canadian ones too.

There is even a growing acknowledgement that the term *standard* may be appropriate to the Englishes of such countries as India, Nigeria, and Singapore. Platt et al. (1984, pp. 2–3) refer to what they call 'New Englishes,' localized' or 'nationized' varieties of English characterized by being developed through educational systems in which English is either a subject of instruction or the medium of instruction in areas in which English is not a native language. These varieties may have a limited or full range of uses and are usually perpetuated with little or no input from native speakers of the 'Old Englishes', i.e., the British or American varieties. The Englishes of India, Ghana, and Nigeria are good examples of such New Englishes. In India, for example, English is spoken in all kinds of varieties to the extent that some are not intelligible outside India or even outside the particular region in which they are spoken. But these varieties are grammatical, there are local standards and norms, and often these are preferred to those of the Old Englishes. Local élites will often reject what they now regard as the 'foreign' standards and norms of either British or American English. We can contrast this tolerance for local standards with the attitude that the

French almost invariably adopt to the French spoken in Quebec, that it is something to be regretted rather than something to be proud of as a distinctive and legitimate variety of French.

All of this is not to suggest that those to whom English is a native language are extremely tolerant of the different ways in which English is spoken and used in the world or even within the particular states in which they happen to live. They are actually not much more tolerant than the French in this regard. However, the widespread distribution of English in the world and the fact that it is not strongly identified with a particular culture quite often exposes speakers of English to those who speak the language somewhat differently. They may not easily be able to associate these differences with the criteria they customarily use to stereotype speakers of more familiar varieties; therefore, the wisest course may require them to be neutral about such differences as do exist rather than to attempt to use them to judge and classify.

THE USES AND USERS OF ENGLISH

English has the most widespread distribution of any language in the world. However, there is considerable disagreement about exactly how many people speak English altogether. There are at least two major difficulties in arriving at a figure. One has to do with counting who speaks what language in any country, a problem that almost every census-taker interested in language issues must confront almost everywhere. The second has to do with specifying what it means to say that someone speaks English. English is spoken as a first language and as an only language by millions of people. It is also a second language for many millions of others and many additional millions know some English as a foreign language. In the second and third cases that knowledge may enable a speaker to do everything that a native can do with the language, but, on the other hand, it may be very restricted, confined to enough vocabulary to do a little bit of business or for minimal use as a lingua franca. Nor can one be sure that being a citizen of a particular country means that one can speak the official language of that country: few Haitians speak French, and it is fairly easy to find naturalized citizens of Australia, Canada, and the United States who cannot follow a simple conversation in English.

One estimate is that there are well over 300 million speakers of English who speak the language as a first language with a large majority of these residing in the United States. The rest are in Great Britain and such Commonwealth countries as Australia, Canada, and New Zealand. Then there is at least an equal number of people for whom English is a second language. These are spread throughout the world but with the largest group in Asia. Finally, there are at least another 100 million for whom English is a foreign language and these may be found throughout the world. The total figure, well in excess of 700 million, seems to be the smallest figure that one can arrive at. It is a conservative estimate. Less conservative estimates can double this figure, for example by assuming that everyone who lives in a country in which English is recognized as an official language be counted as having some knowledge of English. Such a procedure immediately adds 700 million to the overall figure, the entire population of India, where English still has an 'associate official' status. However, any visitor to India who expects to be able to use English with everyone he or she is likely to meet will be sorely disappointed even though the odd word or two may communicate something. Whatever figure one arrives at for the world there seems to be little doubt that about one-fifth of the world's population of better than five billion people has reason to use some English almost every day.

We should observe that while English has spread dramatically as a lingua franca in the modern world, it has shrunk proportionally to certain other languages so far as the number of native speakers is concerned. Population growth in Asia, India, Africa, and South America has led to English today being spoken as a first language by a diminishing proportion of the world's population. The Mandarin variety of Chinese has at least twice as many speakers and the numbers who speak languages such as Spanish (in South America), Hindi, Arabic, and Portuguese (in Brazil) are increasing so fast that each may come to surpass English in terms of numbers of native speakers. The future of English is therefore tied to its ability to capture those who are willing to learn a second language, i.e., to the usefulness of English as a lingua franca.

English is the most widely-spread official language in the world, either de facto or de jure. It is the sole official language of 25 countries with the runner-up languages being Spanish (21), French (19), and Arabic (18). Portuguese, German, and Malay lag far behind these with totals of seven, three, and three respectively. English is the co-official language of a further seventeen countries. French again is its nearest competitor but French is the co-official language in only nine countries. No other language is co-official in more than two countries.

In world trade English is used far more than any other language. Whether one counts imports or exports or adds the two together, countries using English far surpass those using any competing language. The German, Japanese, and French languages are the nearest competitors but use of these in trade lags far behind the use of English. The English-speaking countries of the world are also responsible for one-third of the world's gross national product; in this case the nearest competitor is Russian. French lags far behind, French-speaking countries accounting for a mere one-fifteenth of all goods and services in the world.

English has also spread for special uses. In 1980 for example 72.6 per cent of the articles indexed in the *Index Medicus* were published in English. The nearest competing languages were Russian, German, and French with 6.3 per cent, 4.9 per cent, and 4.1 per cent respectively. In the same year 64.7 per cent of the articles indexed in *Chemical Abstracts* were published in English. Again the nearest competitors were Russian, Japanese, and German with 17.8 per cent, 5.2 per cent, and 4.0 per cent respectively. While English does not completely monopolize the scientific literature, it is difficult to understand how a scientist who cannot read English or who does not have immediate access to good translations from English can hope to keep up with current scientific activity. The French have found this situation to be particularly irritating. French researchers find they must publish their work in English if it is to gain international attention and French libraries are full of English books in the sciences. In Quebec the Conseil de la Langue Française reported that between 1980 and 1983 75 per cent of the articles from the province's francophone universities and research institutes were published in English. In physical sciences the percentage was as high as 90 per cent and in the biological and medical sciences it was 76 per cent. Only in the humanities and social sciences were the majority of articles published in French but even in those areas a quarter found their way into print in English. The Third World too finds English attractive as the language of publication of scholarly work: in 1971 74 per cent of India's scientific journals and 83 per cent of its non-scientific journals were published in English.

English also predominates in the production of new book titles: each year about one-fifth of all new titles are books published in English: French accounts for one-twelfth. English also provides by far the major source language for books translated into other languages – for 39 per cent of these, according to a UNESCO survey of books published in 1976. The nearest runner-up languages in this case were French (12.7 per cent), Russian (10.8 per cent), and German (9.0 per cent). Millions of English books are disseminated throughout the world by such programmes as the United Kingdom's English Language Book Scheme and the United States Information Agency's various programmes. One consequence is that books in English are to be found everywhere in the world. Countries such as India may themselves devote much of their annual book production to publishing books in English, in India's case as much as 45 per cent in 1973, an increase from the 33 per cent of 1969.

Much of higher education in the world is carried out in English or requires some knowledge of English, and the educational systems of many countries acknowledge that students should be given some instruction in English if they are to be adequately prepared to meet the needs of the late twentieth century. For example, China is seeking to enlarge the English-language capability of its best science students. English is also the language of international banking and trade. It is the major language used in international relations, conferences, travel, and tourism. In many parts of the world it is also highly influential as the language of local élites, much popular culture, music, movies, etc.

English has become the lingua franca of the modern world. As Conrad and Fishman (1977, p. 6) observe: 'It is the language of diplomacy, the predominant language in which mail is written, the principal language of aviation and of radio broadcasting, the first language of nearly 300 million people, and an additional language of perhaps that many more'. After surveying how English is used throughout the world and the various attractions it has to those who might seek to learn it, they arrive at certain conclusions. One is that the use of English as an official language in a country is almost exclusively related to that country's control or former control by an English-speaking power. English-medium instruction is not widely found in countries that were not controlled in this way. In such circumstances while there is often a demand for such instruction, that demand may not be met because of urgent needs to promote some other official language. Over 40 per cent of non-English-speaking foreign students study in English mother-tongue countries, and such countries are most attractive of all to students from the less developed parts of the world. There is an extensive English-language press in the non-English-speaking parts of the world, and the newspaper and book production of this press far outstrips that in any other language that may lay claim to have an international status, most specifically French. In fact there are plenty of signs that English is superseding French for various purposes and in numerous places. Conrad and Fishman conclude (p. 56): 'All in all, the data we have accumulated ... indicate that English is clearly the major link-language in the world today and that it alone shows signs of continuing as such, at least in the short run, while the use of local languages for official literacy/education related purposes is also likely to increase'. Such a conclusion seems warranted by the facts and there seems to be little reason to suppose that any drastic change will occur in the near future. In still another study, Fishman, Cooper, and Rosenbaum (1977) used secondary source material from 102 non-English-mother-tongue countries in an attempt to discover what factors were important in the spread of English there. They found that in addition to the four factors that Brosnahan (1963) had mentioned in accounting for the spread of Arabic, Greek, and Latin, four others were important in accounting for the spread of English, factors they described as urbanization, economic development, educational development, and religious composition. They noted that the first three are closely related to one another. They observed (p. 137), however: 'Poorer nations ... were more likely to rely on English as a medium of instruction and to stress English as a subject of instruction than were richer nations, but poorer nations were less likely to provide equal opportunity to learn English through formal schooling'.

One important consequence of this world-wide desire to learn English is the spread of the language into the foreign-language component of the curricula of schools just about everywhere. At any one time at least a 100 million students of various ages are enrolled in classes in which English is being taught as a foreign language. In the majority of cases that teaching is being done by teachers who are not native speakers of the language. English has even replaced French as the preferred foreign language nearly everywhere that French had the ascendancy, e.g., in South America, parts of the Near East, and Romania. The French have tried to maintain their share of the linguisic market in each of these areas, particularly in South America, but the usefulness of English in science, technology, and higher education generally proves to be more potent than the attractiveness of French culture.

In a number of places there is of course resistance to English. That resistance can be the kind that the French have tried to organize through *la Francophonie*, an informal association of francophone states with very deliberate leadership provided from Paris. It is also seen in attempts to keep languages free of English influences. One indicator of how much English has spread in the world is the attention given by language-planning authorities in non-English-speaking countries to the influence of English – always regarded as harmful – on the languages of those countries. Among languages requiring such 'protection' are German, French (in both France and Quebec), Spanish, Hindi, Indonesian, Hebrew, and Swahili. Further incursions of English may also be resisted by providing an indigenous language with the means to compete, e.g., dictionaries, glossaries, etc. Of course, the development of adequate primary and secondary school systems has its place too, and, if it is possible to provide tertiary education in the language of the country, so much the better. But there is also informal resistance, especially that which a local competing lingua franca provides. We can find instances of such competition throughout the world whether these are Swahili in

East Africa, Hindi in India, or pidginized varieties of English in West Africa.

The governments of countries in which English is the native language of the majority of the population often take an active role in promoting English. They not only see that people from other parts of the world are allowed to visit and study but they also quite often support speakers of English as teachers in other parts of the world or make available opportunities to use the English language. In the mid-1960s, for example, the United States was promoting English abroad through at least five different government agencies: the United States Information Agency (USIA), the Agency for International Development (AID), the State Department, the Peace Corps, and the Department of Defense.

One of the most influential organizations for the promotion of English abroad is the British Council which is supported by the Government of the United Kingdom. Another is the British Broadcasting Corporation (BBC). The aim of the British Council founded in 1934, is to promote a wider knowledge of Britain and of the English language by developing closer cultural relations with other countries. Three quarters of the Council's annual budget of about £200 million comes from the Overseas Development Administration and the Foreign and Commonwealth Office in Westminster. Among other activities such as educational exchanges, a book programme, and arranging exhibitions and tours, this budget supports 43 English teaching centres in 32 countries with an average enrolment at any one time of over 50,000 students who are taught by about one thousand teachers, the majority of whom are native speakers of English. In some countries this teaching of English is very closely linked with British culture but in other countries it reflects only the importance that English has in international communications and development. However, both the 4,000 employees of the Council and governments of all political persuasions who have supported its work see that work as an important and essential component of Britain's effort to win and maintain friends overseas now and in the future. There is consequently a strong political motivation to the work of the British Council.

The BBC is another organization subsidized by the British Government which is actively involved in the spread of English. It does this through both its World Service and its *English by Radio and Television* series. The broadcasts emanate from both London and locally from stations in over a 100 countries. The BBC promotes English not only through the medium of English but also through the use of some 30 different foreign languages, ranging alphabetically from Arabic to Vietnamese. Many millions of people around the world listen to or view these programmes to the extent that this may be the largest language-teaching enterprise in existence. For example, BBC *English by Radio* lessons presented solely in English are followed regularly by 700,000 listeners in France and by 800,000 listeners in Germany. Even in francophone Africa it seems that more people listen to bilingual *English by Radio* lessons than listen to news bulletins in French. A television programme for beginners entitled *Follow Me* has been broadcast in over forty countries and was particularly well received in China. At one time the BBC strongly favoured the exclusive use of Received Pronunciation in such lessons and even today that is the pronunciation which is preferred in teaching. However, students are asked to listen to a variety of accents for the purposes of comprehension of spoken English. The BBC's programmes are supplemented by readily available books, materials, and cassettes which can be bought locally, and many millions of such items are bought each year. Those in charge of these BBC programmes readily acknowledge that English has long ceased to be the exclusive possession of one country and now belongs to all those who care to use it: their goal is the promotion of English as an instrument of international understanding.

The English-Speaking Union is still another agency that helps to promote English. It is a world-wide organization with a membership estimated to number about 50,000. While the Union's principal goal is the promotion of understanding and friendship, it sponsors various programmes designed to encourage the use of English. It has also tried to adopt a flexible attitude toward the many varieties of English found in its various branches. As its Director-General A. L. Williams observed in an interview reported in the journal *English Today* in 1985: 'Our criteria are acceptability and suitability for any linguistic situation. We are interested in but not sympathetic with the aims of the Académie Française to "purify the language". The ESU would not support prescriptive pronouncements by official bodies.' Time and time again we find this same tolerant attitude to varieties of English expressed by those who seek to promote the language. When we look at how the French have gone about promoting their language, we will find a somewhat different attitude, one that shows little tolerance for anything but the French of Paris. Just how different the consequences have been for the spread of the two languages is a matter for conjecture.

FRENCH IN THE WORLD

French has been spread far beyond the territory of France. It has been spread through conquest or dominance, through colonization, and through cultural influences. It is conquest or dominance that accounts for the use of French in such countries as Belgium, Luxembourg, and Switzerland, in each of which French has an official status. Conquest also accounts for the French that is still spoken in the Val d'Aoste in Italy. The spread through colonization has occurred in two waves. In the first of these French spread to such places as Canada, Louisiana, the Antilles, and India. The second wave of colonization accounts for the presence of French in North and West Africa, in the Near East, and in Indochina. French has also spread as a language of culture almost everywhere in the world. In some cases it was even adopted as the language of a certain segment of society for a while, as, for example, in pre-unification Germany, Poland, and Russia among the upper classes at various times in the seventeenth to nineteenth centuries. Finally, French became the language of European diplomacy and international relations until it was eclipsed by English at the end of World War I.

As the French spread their influence in the world in one way or another they deliberately spread their language too, but not to everyone. Much of the spread was selective, a selectivity that arose from the attitudes that many speakers of French have adopted toward their language. As we saw in the previous chapter, the French easily write such self-serving proclamations about the French language as the one that follows (Reboullet, 1976, p.3):

[La] double expansion . . . serait légitimée par les caractères privilégiés de cette langue. Rappelons-les: la clarté, la beauté, la perfection; d'où sur des plans différents, la stabilité (une langue parfaite ne saurait évoluer sans déchoir); l'utilité (comme langue internationale, par rapport à d'autres langues moins bien dotées); la simplicité (une langue claire, plus qu'une autre, facilite l'apprentissage).

The double expansion ... would be legitimized by the privileged characteristics of this language. Recall them: clarity, beauty, perfection; whence at different levels, stability (a perfect language may evolve without harm); utility (as an international language, in comparison with other less well endowed languages); simplicity (a transparent language, more than another, facilitates learning).

There is no doubt that the French are imbued almost from birth with ideas about the superiority of French as a language. As Harzic (1976, p. 157) says: '*les Français ont une conviction innée dans la supériorité de leur langue*' (the French have an innate conviction in the superiority of their language). One consequence of this attitude is that the language has to be guarded while it is being spread so as to prevent any harm being done to it. In the French view it is better therefore to see that it is acquired perfectly by a few who will learn to prize what they have acquired than imperfectly by the many who might abuse it.

The French do point to the fact that the French that is spoken in the world is much more homogeneous than the English that is spoken. There is also much less tolerance of local varieties, and the metropolitan variety is almost everywhere promoted as the only 'correct' variety. The French of France are therefore seen as setting the standards for the language. In this way the language is kept uniform wherever it is spoken, but some critics also view the result as another aspect of French neo-colonialism, this insistence that they still 'own' the language. They advocate the development of local varieties of French, e.g., of Joual in Quebec, but not with any great success.

It is sometimes rather surprising to see how highly valued the Standard French of France is today in those countries which have large francophone populations. The Belgians still seem to look to Paris for their standard. Luxembourg also shares this orientation. The Swiss are a little more independent and there are Swiss characteristics of speaking French which are at least as highly valued in Switzerland as the corresponding characteristics of Parisian French. The French of Canada are much more ambivalent. Many are proud to speak Canadian French, even those varieties which are full of anglicisms. Education at the higher levels, however, encourages the use of the metropolitan variety. The official view, as one would expect, is that the kind of French that should be spoken in Quebec is indeed this last variety. That this variety is not spoken by the majority becomes quite obvious to many Québécois who venture to vacation in France and find the variety of French they speak treated, in large towns and cities in particular, as just another unfortunate patois.

One important consequence of this attitude is that the French have often been somewhat reluctant to spread their language along with their power. They have reserved French for dominated élites. They have shown considerable intolerance of local varieties of the language and frowned on any derivative pidgins or creoles. They are likely to be scornful of the kind of new French that is found in West Africa, as this is described by the Zaire writer Valenti Mudimbe (Coste 1984, p. 223):

prononciation approximative, syntaxe réprimée, vocabulaire boursouflé ou supplicié, intonation, rhythme et accent englués à l'écoulement de la langue originelle du locuteur africain; en tout cas, des 'africanismes' phonétiques, morphologiques, syntaxiques et lexicaux.

approximate pronunciation, repressed syntax, inflated or tortured vocabulary, intonation, rhythm and accent caught up in the flow of the original African language; everywhere phonetic, morphological, syntactic and lexical 'Africanisms'.

In their Jacobinian fervour, they are likely to heap the same scorn on such French as they have been wont to do on the minority languages that have managed to survive in France itself. The French strive to maintain the purity of their language. To this end they have opposed borrowing from other languages, e.g., of German chemical terminology in the early twentieth century, and of anglicisms today. They are very prescriptive of correct linguistic behaviour: *Ne dites pas ..., mais dites ...* (Don't say ..., but say ...). They have also established a variety of organizations to police the language: in addition to the Académie Française there is L'Office de la Langue Française, founded in 1937 and refounded in 1945, L'Office du Vocabulaire Français, founded in 1957, and Le Comité d'Étude des Termes Techniques Français, founded in 1954, none of which has been particularly successful in its efforts.

We can contrast these attitudes with those that speakers of English have customarily adopted toward their language. English has been spread in the world rather differently. There has never been the same concern for purity and correctness. There has never been an academy looking over the shoulders of those who have taken English to the far reaches of the world. There has also never been any feeling that English is a particularly fine language that somehow must be protected at all costs. English is to be used. If it gets changed in use, then that is generally accepted as the price one must pay. Admittedly there are those who bewail what has happened to the language and who decry the 'falling standards' they claim to be apparent everywhere in the use of English. Fortunately perhaps, little heed is paid to these views and the language continues to retain its vitality. French appears to lack that same vitality and many French people today are concerned about what can be done to revitalize their language. While they continue to acknowledge that French is a fine cultural instrument, they are very conscious that in the competition with English in the world French does very poorly indeed.

As a result of French colonization sub-Saharan Africa today contains 24 francophone states, that is two dozen states in which the French language has an important official role. Before independence nearly all were part of the French African Empire. Like most African states that emerged from post-imperial Africa, these francophone states are usually linguistically, culturally, and ethnically heterogeneous. Quite often the only common experience the people of an African state have shared has been rule by a particular European power for less than a century with the language of such rule being that of the European power. The francophone states of Africa fit this pattern perfectly.

These states have emerged from a period of French rule in which indigenous languages were treated as primitive dialects or patois and Standard French was used in government, business, and education. The vernacular languages were not allowed in education; children had to learn French if they wanted any education at all and, in that learning, they had to acquire the same attitudes to French language and culture as children in France itself if they were to be regarded as successful. Many members of the local élites accepted such a philosophy. They learned to prize their knowledge of French; it marked them off from their less fortunate compatriots. They also were able to use French against the French, for it was the French language which served as a lingua franca among those who eventually came to oppose the French presence in their lands. French was the language of revolt. But once independence had been gained this same knowledge of French meant that for a while very little changed in the new states so far as the use of the various languages was concerned. French continued in its privileged position and little has changed in this respect in the last quarter of a century in most of the former French possessions in Africa. Some of the leaders of the new Black Africa were actually ardent francophiles, particularly President Léopold Senghor of Senegal.

French is still the sole official language in most of these former French possessions. It is likely to be the only language that members of all the. élites know everywhere in a plurilingual country. It remains the language of all official publications, of most government communications among the various departments, of banking, and of education. However, in some countries one or more local languages may have extensive use: e.g., Bambara in Mali, Wolof in Senegal, and Sango in the Central African Republic. In is only rarely that a local language has a full and equal status with French: e.g., Arabic in Mauritania, Malagasy in Madagascar, and Kinyarwanda in Rwanda.

French is actually not widely known in many of these countries. The French did not develop extensive systems of education. They preferred to educate small local élites and indoctrinate these with their own linguistic and cultural attitudes. Since independence France has continued to support these former élites. They still have access to the French system of higher education, and France still continues to support them in their post-independence positions in the political, social, economic, and military hierarchies, and still continues its *mission civilisatrice*. As much as 90 per cent of France's foreign aid budget goes to former colonies, a little more than the United Kingdom's 80 per cent. There is, therefore, still a very considerable French influence in these states though it does not spread too far down from the top in most cases.

French influence may be lessening somewhat today. The new countries of Africa have become less dependent on France for economic and military assistance. There is more cooperation among the African countries themselves and English has become important as these cooperative endeavours increase in scope. African languages are increasingly being recognized as having an important part to play in primary education. French is more and more regarded as a 'foreign' language, an important one to be sure but no longer as the language through which the future of genuine African nations can be expressed. In 1967 Tougas could claim that French language and culture would be more appealing to black Africans than the pragmatic English language, declaring (1967, p. 167):

La culture française, parce qu'elle implique d'équilibre entre les facultés créatrices et l'enracinement au cosmos, répond aux aspirations profondes de l'âme noire. Quel homme sent plus intensément l'appel des forces telluriques que l'Africain?

French culture, because it implies equilibrium between the creative faculties and rootedness in the cosmos, responds to the deep aspirations of the black soul. Who feels more intensely the call of telluric forces than the African?

Deniau (1983, p. 98) can also nearly echo those words with his approval of another's declaration '*L'anglais c'est le téléphone, le français c'est un système culturel de référence*' (English is the telephone, French is a cultural reference system). But somehow each seems to be just another instance of special pleading.

The real issue for the countries of francophone Africa is much the same as the one that confronts the anglophone countries of that continent: how to promote the various competing local languages or to choose among these in such a way that ethnic conflict is not encouraged while maintaining contact with the outside world through the continued use of a European language. French is therefore more and more becoming a subject of instruction in the schools of francophone Africa; less and less is it the medium of instruction and taught as though it were actually the native language of the children. Only among very privileged élites is French today a language that some African children acquire natively. For the vast majority of children a little knowledge of French is something they might acquire if they are able to spend a number of years in school.

As local languages are encouraged in Africa there is a growing concern about the amount and kind of French that is now spoken there. The French government has tried to stop the erosion of French in Africa by promoting la Francophonie, described in more detail below. Of course, many of the nations characterized as 'French-speaking' have only a minority of francophones. However, the French see such nations allying with them to oppose the spread of English in the world. In particular, they deplore the spread of English into areas they once controlled themselves. English has spread into francophone Africa and that is one of the reasons why the French language is declining there. English is also attractive to the new élites, particularly those that have emerged a generation or so after independence.

In North Africa French now competes directly with a single language, Arabic, in those countries that have emerged from French rule. Algeria, Morocco, and Tunisia do not have the linguistic diversity of most of the countries that emerged from the collapse of French West Africa. In each of these countries French found itself in opposition to Arabic, a language with a long presence in North Africa, an associated religion, Islam, and a strong cultural tradition. The French tried to replace Arabic with their language while they were in control of this part of the world. In the struggle for independence from France it was Arabic that served as a unifying language among those who felt oppressed. Consequently, at independence a major goal of each of the new states was to undo what the French had done linguistically: in this case to replace French with Arabic. As we will see in chapter 8, this has not been an easy task.

When the French eventually left North Africa, the French language had become strongly identified with modernization, education, and international communication. Arabic had been neglected. Moreover, while the written form of Arabic existed in a classical version associated with religious practice, the spoken language had diverged into a number of very different regional varieties. There was also very little correspondence between that written variety and the different local vernaculars, a classic diglossic situation. Consequently, after independence had been achieved there was no standardized form of Arabic that could easily replace French.

Each of the three countries has followed a process of arabization since independence. French still has a strong presence in each country. Gordon (1978) says that in 1975 the presence was felt in Tunisia by choice, in Morocco partly through inertia, and in Algeria only provisionally. Many North Africans in these former French possessions see themselves as both Arabs for whom Arabic is important for their personal identity and citizens of a world of culture in which the language is French. French, therefore, continues to exert a tremendous appeal in these countries, particularly among the élites. Again, the variety of French spoken in each of the countries is different from that spoken across the Mediterranean. These varieties do not find ready acceptance in France, being associated in the minds of many French people with what they consider to be the problems created by an unwelcome North African presence in France itself.

Elsewhere in the Middle East French is in marked decline. Such decline is particularly noticeable in Lebanon where until very recently it was a major language and successfully competed with both Arabic and English.

In particular, French was the language of much of the banking of the Middle East, which centred in Beirut. There were francophone lycées and a francophone university and knowledge of the French language was regarded as a sign of culture in the Christian community. In the recent civil war the French language has declined along with the country. The Arabic language has reasserted itself: it is the language of the large Muslim factions. The social disruption and destruction of a decade of civil strife has considerably weakened the system that has supported French to the extent that it is unlikely to continue to serve even as a language of a prestigious minority in Lebanon. In this respect Lebanon is likely to follow the example of countries such as Egypt, Syria, Iran, and Turkey, in each of which a rapid decline of French followed immediately on independence. The élites gave up French in favour of the local language for internal use and sometimes adopted English for external use.

The French language also once had a considerable presence in Southeast Asia. Vietnam, Laos, and Cambodia were all part of French Indochina. The French established their language as the language of education and administration and the élites of each country easily adopted the language as theirs. Those selected for higher education were indoctrinated into a system which stressed the importance of French language and culture and many came to accept what they were taught. A few did not and it was this French-educated minority which tended to assume the leadership of dissidents in each country. However, the masses in each country remained quite unaffected by what was happening in the larger towns and cities. They had no access to French, the pattern of their lives continued much as it had over the years before French rule, and most experienced that rule as merely that of still another foreign oppressor, the last in a long line of such oppressors.

The Vietnamese were able to throw off the French in a bloody war, but they were not allowed to reunite. It took another long and bitter war for that to happen. The result of the first war was to eliminate French from Vietnam and the result of the second war was to eliminate English, the language that had replaced French. Today, the language of the reunified Vietnam is Vietnamese. Many Vietnamese who now live abroad left the country with some knowledge of one or both languages, but there is little reason to assume that today either language has any large number of adherents in Vietnam itself. The new Vietnamese nationalism requires Vietnamese for its expression and a firm rejection of French and English, the languages of the country's most recent oppressors. The French-speaking élites who controlled both Laos and Cambodia after independence finally lost their power in the early 1970s. The new rulers reestablished the ancestral languages as the languages of government and of what education they were able to provide.

French has virtually disappeared from Southeast Asia. The various national struggles have meant that French is regarded as a language of oppression rather than of culture. National pride requires the use of ancestral languages. Since in each of the three countries these language can be asssociated with rich and esteemed cultures there is no lack of associated symbols. The new countries are also far removed from France both geographically and ideologically. Each has a new élite in no way tied to a colonial past. If any French remains it does so either as a decaying relic of the past or as no more than one of a number of foreign languages that one might learn which may be useful for a limited set of external activities. Certainly French in Southeast Asia is no longer admired for the cultural claims so often made for it, and once those claims are denied its position is drastically weakened anywhere in the world, not only in Southeast Asia.

The French people are acutely conscious of the fact that their language is in a very precarious position in the world. Some claim that as many as 200 million people speak the language but that figure seems to be considerably inflated. French is certainly shrinking as a European language. Whereas 28 per cent of the population of Western Europe is estimated to have spoken French in 1750, that proportion dropped to 19 per cent by 1900 and may be no larger than 15 per cent today. France itself contains only about one per cent of the world's population so it is vital to the French to preserve their language outside the hexagon itself. That task has not been an easy one and it is made more difficult by the fact that French does not appear to be winning new converts. Many French also apparently feel that the language itself is quite often not spoken as well as it should be by those who do speak it. Above all, though, the French see English as the language which is taking away speakers and weakening French itself through the kinds of borrowings from English that creep into the language.

French is still used as one of the languages of a number of international organizations. However, it is the exclusive language only of the International Postal Union and of the Vatican in its diplomatic dealings. French was almost not recognized at all as one of the languages of the United Nations, gaining official status there by only a single vote. It was not until the break-up of the French Empire that a strong francophone presence arose in the United Nations with the admission to that organization of many of the former French colonies as newly independent states whose élites had been used to working in French. French still dominates in the European Economic Community (EEC) although English is a potent rival. The influence of French there is partly the result of the headquarters of that organization being in Brussels so that much of the permanent secretariat is francophone. However, we can also observe that until recently at least the presence of the UNESCO headquarters in Paris itself did not prevent much of the internal work of that organization from being done in English. As anglophone support for UNESCO has diminished for ideological reasons, it is quite possible that French will gain in UNESCO at the expense of English. French is also used as a working language in such organizations as the World Health Organization, the International Labour Organization, the Council of Europe, the Red Cross, the International Court of Justice, and so on, such uses attesting to the continued staying power of a language once it becomes a lingua franca of international diplomacy.

LA FRANCOPHONIE

The French have developed la Francophonie, a loose alliance of francophone nations, in order to try to safeguard French influence in the world and to arrest any further decline of their language and culture. Through la Francophonie they seek to maintain the purity of the language, to promote its continued use as a world language, and to provide an effective opposition to English. The power of France as a country has declined in the twentieth century just as has the power of England. However, the loss of England's power has been more than offset by the rise to world ascendancy of the United States, another anglophone state. France has no similar francophone state to offset the losses she has sustained in the same period. While the English language continues to spread in the world, the French struggle to arrest the decline of their language and to prevent that decline from becoming a rout.

La Francophonie has different meanings to those who use it as a device for drawing francophones together. It can be used to cover all those who speak French anywhere in the world and becomes synonymous with the ability to speak French. Hence there is an interest in promoting French so as to maintain the language. But many of those who speak French also have an interest in French life and culture. Consequently, la Francophonie can be viewed as as attempt to promote that life and culture so that it keeps its place in the world. In this view French language and culture have a role to play in the world, and la Francophonie becomes a kind of spiritual union in which France has an important role to play. Deniau (1983, p. 5), the President of the Comité de la Francophonie, states such a view:

La langue, la culture et la civilisation française appartiennent à toutes les familles spirituelles et politiques de notre pays et des autres pays qui se réfèrent à notre langue. La langue française est médiatrice et non pas impératrice.

French language, culture and civilization belong to all the spiritual and political families of our country and of other countries that share our language. The French language is a mediator not an imperialist.

La Francophonie can also be defined to include those states in which French still has some official role to play, where for example it is still the official language or one of the official languages or, if it is not an official language any more, it still continues to have a strong presence, as it does in the Maghreb. Most of these latter countries once formed part of the French Empire and in many ways la Francophonie is a French counterpart to the British Commonwealth, the successor to the defunct British Empire. Alternatively, la Francophonie is the collectivity of institutions that exist to unite French-speaking people everywhere and to promote French in the world. But whatever else it is, la Francophonie is first of all a language movement designed to counteract the influence of English in the world.

The idea of a formal francophonic union of some kind dates back to the early 1960s. Much of the early initiative came from outside France from people such as Presidents Senghor of Senegal and Bourguiba of Tunisia. Senghor, for example, saw no contradiction between supporting French language and culture and supporting national cultures in Africa, *négritude*, and arabism. The people of Quebec were also interested in the idea, seeing the French of other countries as possible allies in their struggle with the English within Canada. However, France under President de Gaulle remained aloof, and Belgium and Switzerland in Europe and Algeria, Guinea, and Mauritania in North Africa were not at all sympathetic.

A series of meetings in the late 1960s led to the setting up of the Agence de Coopération Culturelle et Technique in 1970 which included France, Canada, and Belgium among its 21 member states. The aims of the organization were to act as a clearing house for the member countries in the areas of technology and culture, to eliminate duplication of efforts in education, to provide technical assistance when needed, and to provide for cultural exchanges. The French language was to provide the common basis for association and the headquarters of the organization were to be located in Paris. Major funding was to come from France (45 per cent), Canada (33 per cent), and Belgium (12 per cent), and general meetings were to be held every two years on a rotating basis. Thus did la Francophonie come into existence.

As we will see, la Francophonie has expanded considerably since its beginnings. Many different countries and other political units are now involved one way or another in its activities. These range from the three countries mentioned above to a province like Quebec in Canada, a state like Louisiana in the USA, overseas departments and territories of France such as Guadaloupe and New Caledonia, creolophone countries such as Haiti, francophone African countries, and even Poland and Romania. The appeal is not to the masses in such places but rather to the élites, who find they are able to enhance their stature through participation in this international movement. As we will see, the range of supporting organizations is equally large. The French government is now also an enthusiastic supporter of la Francophonie. Whereas the Jeanneney Report to that government in 1963 saw only altruistic motives for such an organization, it is quite clear today that French motives have a political and economic dimension: la Francophonie enhances France's power and prestige in the world and provides outlets for her industry. But France is not the only participant in the movement with political and economic goals for la Francophonie: various African participants and Quebec have their own goals too. What is not clear is how to make the various goals compatible. Whether to allow France to dominate or to insist on a decision-making structure that is 'multilateral' in nature is also a controversial issue. For example, the *Tribune de Genève* expressed a fear (19 April 1968) that a francophonic union would become '*la recherche d'un super-État réunissant tous ceux qui parlent français, mais sous la domination de Paris*'('the quest for a super-state reuniting all those who speak French but under the domination of Paris'). That such suspicions are warranted is confirmed by statements such as the one Giscard d'Estaing made during his presidential election campaign of 1974 when he declared that the francophonic movement should form an essential part of France's political policy.

Numerous organizations now exist to support la Francophonie. There are various intergovernmental agencies: the Agence de Coopération Culturelle et Technique (ACCT), founded in 1970, with its permanent secretariat and meetings held every two years; the Conférences des Ministres de l'Éducation des Pays d'Expression Française (CONFEMEN) and other like conferences bringing together those who share interests in such matters as justice, public health, youth, sports, etc.; a francophone caucus at the United Nations; and the Haut Comité de la Francophonie, founded in 1984. There are semi-official organizations: the Association Internationale des Parlementaires de Langue Française (AIPELF), founded in 1967, with its regular meetings to seek out cooperative measures to promote, for example, an anti-drought campaign in Africa; the Association des Universités Partiellement ou Entièrement de Langue Française (AUPELF), founded in 1961, which provides liaison and cooperation among its 120 members and French departments in another 350 institutions; the Conseil International de la Langue Française (CILF), founded in 1967, aimed at '*la sauvegarde et l'unité de la langue française dans le monde*'; and so on.

Private organizations abound too: L'Association Nationale des Scientifiques pour l'Usage de la Langue Française (ANSULF); the Association des Écrivains de Langue Française (ADELF); L'Alliance Française, founded in 1883; the Mission Laïque Française, founded in 1902; and so on. Institutions supported directly or indirectly by the French government are also numerous; some such as the Centre de Recherche et d'Étude pour la Diffusion du Français (CREDIF), founded in 1959, and the Bureau pour l'Enseignement de la Langue et de la Civilisation Françaises à l'Étranger (BELC), founded in 1966, are mainly oriented to promoting the French language through improving how it is taught; other recent creations such as the Haut Conseil de la Francophonie, the Commissariat Général de la Langue Française, and the Comité Consultatif pour la Francophonie have a much broader scope.

France also attempts to spread French influence throughout the world in other ways. By 1978 France had signed at least 350 treaties, accords, conventions, or protocols dealing with cultural, scientific, and technical matters with 117 countries; these involved nearly 200 different commissions and committees. In 1983 France also supported about 80,000 'cultural ambassadors' in various places in the world, the large majority in teaching French. The French Ministry of Foreign Affairs is estimated to spend about 40 per cent of its budget through its Direction Générale des Relations Culturelles, Scientifiques et Techniques (DGRCST). According to its 1980 report, the DGRCST supported 274 schools outside of France, 5,000 teachers, 1,000 cultural missions, 164 cultural centres, and 7,600 scholarships.

France is particularly concerned with maintaining a presence in sub-Saharan Africa. In the years that immediately followed the end of direct French rule in sub-Saharan Africa France continued to exert considerable pressure on the new states. A series of bilateral treaties allowed France to maintain important military bases and even to intervene militarily in the internal affairs of various states. (France has intervened in the affairs of a number of African states since their independence, the most recent example being the prolonged intervention in Chad.) French economic, administrative, educational, and technical assistance was also sought and given, and it took well over a decade for these initial arrangements to be changed in any important respect.

Today, French influence in Africa extends beyond its former colonies to include three former Belgian colonies: Zaire, Rwanda, and Burundi. Thirteen of these are bound together in the Franc Zone, the currencies of which are tied to the French franc. All the West African francophone states, except Guinea, have military assistance or defence agreements with France and there are French military bases in Djibouti, Gabon, Ivory Coast, Senegal, and the Central African Republic. A typical French accord with an African state is the one signed with Ivory Coast in April 1961 covering such matters as defence, economy, finance, justice, higher education, culture, post and telecommunications, civil avaiation, merchant marine, and technical cooperation. The accord was renegotiated in 1973 but the substance was left largely unchanged; Ivory Coast did however gain some recognition of her right to enter into additional trade agreements with the United Kingdom and Japan. The French also direct much of their external radio broadcasting to an African audience.

La Francophonie lacks the official organization and periodical meetings associated with the British Commonwealth. Consequently, the French set about remedying that deficiency when it held a meeting attended by 42 delegations in Paris between 17 and 19 February 1986, La Francophonie's first 'summit'. Sixteen heads of state and a dozen heads of government were present. Representatives came from all over the world: Canada and Quebec, Haiti and St Lucia, North and West Africa (but not Algeria), Egypt and Lebanon, Laos and Vietnam, Vanuatu and New Caledonia, and so on. While a common interest in the French language brought these governments together, there were so many differences that little was accomplished at that meeting other than to set a tentative date and place for a second meeting – in 1988 in Quebec. The cultural, political, economic, and geographic differences among the representatives were only too readily apparent. However, those present at the francophone summit did unite to call for greater economic assistance to be given to Third World nations and resolved to see how French could be used increasingly in the new telecommunications and computer industries which English now dominates.

The French are very seriously concerned about the position of their language in the world. In 1980 the National Assembly created a Commission d'Enquête sur la Langue Française to inquire into the state of the French language both within and without France and to make recommendations concerning measures to promote the language – what its terms referred to as *'un ensemble cohérent de mesures constituant une véritable politique de la langue française, tant en France qu'à l'étranger'*, ('a coherent set of measures constituting a true policy for the French language both within France and outside'). In its report of 1981 the Commission recommended that French should be made the language of work in France, particularly in scientific matters, that French scientific work should be published in French, that there should be a greater emphasis on the teaching of French in French schools and good foreign students should be encouraged to study in France, that greater emphasis should also be placed on teaching French outside France and on exporting French books, sending teachers abroad, developing contacts, and promoting French culture, and that France should spend more effort on developing francophonic institutions and the personnel they required for their proper functioning. La Francophonie should be regarded as a kind of 'mission' to the world, an obligation that France could not turn its back on.

Very obviously the French find themselves engaged in a struggle to preserve their language and culture against the dominating influence of English. They see themselves at a considerable disadvantage in that competition. Much of their recent effort has gone into the organization of an infrastructure for the francophone community. There is good reason, however, to believe that there is more hope than substance in some of the efforts and that French leadership itself is still suspect in many parts of the francophone world. The English language has also become increasingly attractive to people in countries in which French has historic roots of one kind or another. It remains to be seen how effective la Francophonie will be as a kind of holding action on behalf of a beleaguered language.

FURTHER READING

The spread of English: Ferguson and Heath 1981, Fishman et al. 1977, Greenbaum 1985, Kachru 1983, McCrum et al. 1986, Smith, L.E. 1981; varieties of English: Bailey and Görlach 1982, Platt et al. 1984, Price 1982; journals dealing with English in the world: *English Today, English World-Wide, World Englishes*; the spread of French: Gordon 1978; varieties of French: Valdman 1979; la Francophonie: Bengtsson 1968, Blancpain and Reboullet 1976, Bourhis 1982, Bostock 1983, Coste 1984, Deniau 1983, Tougas 1967, Viatte 1969.

7

English and French in Sub-Saharan Africa

Africa offers anyone who is concerned with relationships among languages one of the most interesting situations in the world. It is a continent of over half a billion people, i.e., about 10 per cent of the world's population. The African population is also estimated to be growing by 2.7 per cent annually, the highest rate of increase of any area in the world. Africa contains a rich diversity of languages. Most African states have only recently emerged from colonial status, and there is little in most of them that resembles the kinds of 'national consciousness' found in Europe. European languages, particularly English and French, came to dominate much of Africa during the colonial period and they still continue to possess an enormous attraction in the 'neo-colonialism' that now prevails in the continent. However, these languages must compete with a large number of vernaculars, trade languages, and at least two other very important languages, Arabic and Swahili. The new states have adopted a variety of approaches in dealing with pressing language issues. Just how great has been that variety and how effective some of the solutions have been we will see in the pages that follow when we look particularly at a variety of language issues in sub-Saharan Africa, particularly in West Africa.

THE PRE-INDEPENDENCE PERIOD

The linguistic situation in sub-Saharan Africa is an extremely complex one. It is estimated that at least a thousand different languages are spoken in Africa, almost certainly a higher proportion of languages in relation to population than in any other part of the world. Africa is also a continent in which there have been large movements of populations over the centuries so that it is not easy to determine how the various languages are related to one another or to arrive at a definitive linguistic history of the continent. Nor can we associate particular languages with particular types of Africans or cultural traits. As Alexandre (1972, p. 75) has said:

The only general affirmation which can confidently be put forward about the situation in precolonial Africa is that there was almost never an exact coincidence of physical type, language, and civilization. The most notable exception ... is that of the Bushmen of the Kalahari, among whom a specific physical type, a unique civilization, and a special language coexist.

It is into this complicated linguistic situation that the colonizing European powers brought their languages in the late nineteenth century.

A pervasive myth about sub-Saharan Africa is that it was like a Tower of Babel before European colonization, that intertribal warfare was endemic, and that it had no history of large-scale political and economic organization. In fact, Europeans did not come to a 'dark continent': that is a convenient self-serving justification for much that was done later in the name of 'civilizing the African'. Many Africans are indeed multilingual but language itself seems never to have been a divisive issue. Warfare too was unknown on the scale that it had been experienced in Europe and Africans had had experience of large-scale organizations. There had been various African empires, e.g., those of Ghana in the eleventh century, of Mali in the fourteenth century, and of Songhay in the fifteenth and sixteenth centuries, each with its armies, wealth, trade, cities, and extensive administrative machinery. In the nineteenth century the Ashanti, Oyo, Baganda, Masai, Katanga, and Zulu were all sufficiently well organized that they were regarded as either formidable opponents of the invading Europeans or necessary allies. Extensive trade routes had also existed over the centuries reaching from the coasts far into the interior to allow Africans to deal in various goods and particularly in ivory and slaves. And, finally, one of the world's great religions, Islam, had spread extensively across the north, down the east coast, and even into some west and central areas.

Before colonization the major contact Africans had with Europeans was along the coasts. Portuguese, English, Dutch, and French traders had long plied the coasts, particularly in the lucrative slave trade. But they had not penetrated far into the interior. Arabs engaged in the slave trade penetrated into Africa far deeper than Europeans, who relied on exploiting the coasts. Europeans bought slaves with cheap European goods, took those slaves to the Americas, exchanged them for sugar, cotton, and tobacco there, and sold these in Europe in the infamous 'trade triangle' that existed. The main linguistic consequence of this activity had been the development of a number of pidgins along the west coast to facilitate trade. There was some missionary activity but not a great deal since the involvement of the European powers in the slave trade severely hindered missionary work.

The European powers finally decided to carve up Africa among themselves in the late nineteenth century in what has been called 'the rape of geography by history'. Most of the new colonies were arbitrary creations. Ethnic groups were divided among the resulting colonies: consequently, today there are Ewe in Ghana and Togo, Hausa in Niger and Nigeria, Yoruba in Nigeria and Benin, Wolof in Senegal, Gambia, and Mauritania, Fulani in a wide area of West and Central Africa, and Fang in Cameroon, Gabon, and Equatorial Guinea. Sometimes certain groups did manage to survive largely intact: Burundi is now homogeneous linguistically (Kirundi-speaking) because it was administered as a single unit; both the Baganda of Uganda and the Kikuyu of Kenya were able to profit not only because they were left intact but also because of the privileged positions they came to hold in their respective colonies, the British choosing to co-opt the Kabaka (king) of the Baganda in the first case and administer the colony from Kikuyu territory in the second.

The new colonies were almost entirely European creations. In a typical case various ethnic groups speaking numerous languages found themselves under a single administration. That administration necessarily had to develop an infrastructure if it was to be successful. At independence the new state that came into existence often had only a a very few of the characteristics typical of the older European states. Among the most important of these would be a rudimentary infrastucture with a European language one of its essential components. It would be a new state not a new nation, instant membership in the United Nations notwithstanding.

What we observe in Africa today are states with a variety of linguistic characteristics. According to Alexandre (1972, pp. 88–91), there are four linguistically homogeneous states but each of these is very small: Rwanda, Burundi, Botswana, and Lesotho. There are linguistically heterogeneous states with one or several dominant African languages. Some of these are very important states possessing non-European languages which could serve them well for education, administration, etc., even if only sometimes on a regional basis. The best example is Nigeria with languages like Yoruba, Ibo, and Hausa. There are also Tanzania and to a lesser extent Kenya and Uganda with Swahili, Malawi with Nyanja, Zimbabwe with Shona, Zambia with Bemba, and Swaziland with Swazi.

According to Alexandre, certain other states have no immediately useful language or languages. In this number he includes Senegal and Gambia while noting that in each Wolof predominates. He also includes Mali, Upper Volta (now Burkina Faso), and Gabon in this category.

There are states with moderate linguistic homogeneity. Some of these have immediately usable languages: Ghana with languages like Ewe, Twa, and Fanti; and Togo, also with Ewe. Niger, Dahomey, and Guinea have various less usable languages. Finally, there are those states with great linguistic heterogeneity. These include Sierra Leone, Liberia, Ivory Coast, Cameroon, Chad, and the Central African Republic. It is not surprising that many of these states still use English or French as an official language even after independence. A European language was often the only thing that the members of the native élite of an African colony shared; it sometimes even allowed them to unite against the European power.

COLONIAL LANGUAGE POLICIES

Much of the influence that English and French have in sub-Saharan Africa today derives from the ways in which the languages were promoted during the colonial era and from the roles they play in the world today. The colonial powers had different attitudes toward indigenous languages . The British, German, and Belgian colonizers were quite willing to learn one or more of the native languages and conduct much of their business through the vernaculars. Colonial administrators often stayed in particular colonies for long periods, learned one or more local languages, and took considerable pride in trying to understand the local languages and cultures. They also allowed native children to be educated in the local language in what few schools were available to them. The French attitude was quite different. French was the language of a high culture and an advanced civilization. An élite had to be educated in French and civilized through that education. Local languages were almost beneath contempt. In fact, the French adopted the same language policies in their colonies as they had adopted at home. Just as Breton and Basque were despised in the hexagon itself, all the indigenous languages of the colonies were treated with the same contempt.

The European colonists had to develop language policies alongside other policies. Just as they had to make administrative and economic decisions so thay also had to make linguistic and social ones. Almost invariably these decisions led to there being little access to education for Africans either through European languages or through the vernaculars. There would be just enough education in either or both to satisfy the needs the colonies had for low-level functionaries and in some cases to satisfy European consciences about the 'mission' to Africa.

In the British colonies the English language was spread through the limited number of schools that existed usually as a subject of instruction with the language of instruction being one of the local languages. This system led to a certain amount of literacy in the local languages but it did not encourage a very high standard of English proficiency. In fact, those who went only to primary school usually acquired very little knowledge of English. Those who graduated from secondary schools in which English was the language of instruction were much better prepared, and it was from the ranks of these graduates that local élites were formed. Like colonial educational systems elsewhere in Africa, the British system had as its goal the inculcation of the values of the colonial society and the training of individuals to serve the colonial state. The British attitude to the educated colonial was also decidedly ambivalent. On the one hand, education and English were to be available; on the other hand, those who took full advantage came to be regarded as 'uppity' and 'people who did not know their place'.

Like the British, the Belgians also favored a limited use of the vernaculars in education. But their goal was quite clearly to keep Africans subservient and deny all but a very few access to French. They did not want an educated African élite, so they encouraged the use of Lingala, Kikongo, Ciluba, and Swahili in the schools of the Belgian Congo and they also encouraged Belgians working there to learn the local vernaculars.

The Africans who lived in the British colonies generally wanted to have their children educated in English – if they received any schooling at all. The schools in these colonies were initially the creation of missionary groups, with colonial administrations generally not being very interested in promoting education until the twentieth century. The missions tended to favour vernacular education but did teach English, often as an inducement to parents to send their children to school. As the colonial educational systems developed, English became more and more important. The Phelps-Stokes Commission reported in 1927 that one of the major incentives for Africans to send their children to school was the opportunity to learn English. The commission itself favoured a greater expansion of vernacular education believing that such education would prove to be more valuable to Africans than education in a European language.

There was always conflict in the British colonies as to the right balance between the teaching of the vernaculars and the teaching of English. The vernaculars could be used to promote religious values and much of colonial education was in the hands of missionaries. For a while translations into various vernaculars of such works as Bunyan's *Pilgrim's Progress*, *Aesop's Fables*, and Lamb's *Tales from Shakespeare* came into wide use in Africa. The vernaculars could also be taught by native teachers; using English as the language of instruction would require the development and funding of massive teacher-training programmes. Moreover, it was not necessary that everyone in the colonies should learn to speak English. A colony's needs could be well served by training a rather small cadre of natives in English and allowing these to mediate between the colonial power and the local population.

There were certain other consequences of the language policies adopted in the colonies. Africans living in towns had better access both to schooling and to education in English than did rural-dwelling Africans, such education being largely unavailable in the countryside. Vernacular education was seen everywhere as a preparation for 'real' education, the education that one gained through knowing English. Finally, English education in Africa led to the creation of new élites, dividing those who could speak English from those who could not, and introducing into the former group attitudes about government service, 'white collar' jobs, and academic certification that are still widespread.

There was not even a uniform British policy concerning education in the colonies. Each colony could do almost as it pleased in matters of education. Local pragmatic solutions were worked out and varied according to the nature of the particular crisis that had arisen or the need to appease a specific ethnic group. It was not until well into the twentieth century that any but piecemeal solutions were developed. That this was so is really not surprising: British education has always been heavily decentralized, in comparison to the French system, and even today individual schools are allowed a latitude that administrators elsewhere might consider to verge on anarchy! Changes in policy did result in more and more English being taught in African schools after the end of World War II, but by 1950 91 different African languages were also in use in the primary schools of British Africa.

One result of this activity was that at independence the former British colonies in Africa found themselves with different systems of education and very little commonality in the language problems they faced. They were also left with at least two important attitudes toward English and other languages. One was that English was a pragmatic language, a language that should be learned because it was useful rather than because it symbolized all that was best in civilization. The other was that vernacular languages themselves were of some worth: pupils could be educated in them, and they could be used to unite people in a region or state. But another reality was that only a very few could be educated in English and that in most cases the majority of school-age childen had not even been exposed to education in a vernacular.

French colonial policy was quite different from English colonial policy. Education was to be the same outside France as it was within. The Ordinance of Villers-Cotterêts of 1539 which forbade the use of languages other than French in all official functions within the territories of France applied outside France as well. As Alexandre (1972, p. 77) says:

Only one language is taught in the schools, recognized in law courts, and used in administration: French, as defined by the opinions of the Academy and the decrees of the minister of public education. All other languages belong to the realm of folklore, dancing around the maypole, and riding hobbyhorses and are signs of disintegration of the French Republic.

In the French colonies, therefore, French was to be the language of instruction in whatever education was made available to the indigenous populations. Only the catechism could be taught in the vernaculars.

In 1928 the Governor-General of French West Africa declared that:

le but de l'enseignement ... est de former des collaborateurs indigènes dont nous avons besoin dans l'œuvre administrative et dans l'œuvre de colonisation, dont la direction seule incombé aux Européens.

the goal of teaching ... is to provide the native collaborators whom we need in administrative work and in the work of colonization, the sole control of which falls on Europeans.

A decree of January 31, 1938 applying to schools in French West Africa declared that:

L'enseignement doit être donné exclusivement en langue française. L'emploi des idiomes indigènes est interdit. L'usage des langues maternelles n'est autorisé que dans les écoles coraniques et les écoles de catéchisme, les écoles religieuses n'étant pas considérées comme des établissements d'enseignement.

Instruction must be given exclusively in the French language. The use of indigenous vernaculars is forbidden. The use of mother tongues is authorized only in Koranic schools and schools for the catechism, religious schools not being considered as educational institutions.

The teaching of French was initially a rarity, but an ability to speak the language soon became so prestigious that parents began to demand more and more opportunities for their children to learn the language.

Between the wars the French continued to provide only a very limited amount of education in West Africa through the medium of French in spite of local demands. Less than 0.5 per cent of the children in the area received any education at all, and this mostly confined to primary education, in the haphazard system that came into existence. Such education as did exist was also directed toward local élites with the aim of co-opting these. It emphasized spoken French and demanded little in the way of real literacy and thorough learning. In content it stressed the good relationships that should exist between blacks and whites and kept clear of criticizing local ways.

Promoting French even in this extremely limited way did arouse some opposition though. In some places the French found educational systems already in place and their attempt to supplant these with francophone systems met with local opposition. The Muslims of several of the colonies had well developed Koranic schools which used Arabic as the language of instruction; they resisted as much as they could the attempts the French made to establish French-only education. In such circumstances the French tended to leave these opposing systems alone and turned their attention to educating non-Muslims who better fitted into their plans.

The French system did encourage a small number of people in each colony to become speakers of French at a very high level of skill. Since the French, unlike the English, tended to rotate their colonial administrators with great frequency, and these administrators almost never acquired even a smattering of the local language, such educated natives gained considerable power and prestige with their own people. By the end of World War II they formed the élites from which the post-independence leadership came. They were also to be élites who subscribed to many of the same values that the French themselves had subscribed to, particularly beliefs about the values to be placed on French language and culture. For a while a number among them were more concerned about working out what it meant to be black – *négritude* – within the French cultural context than with independence. De Gaulle's first offer of independence in 1958 was actually rejected by all the colonies except Guinea. When the French finally did withdraw from Africa, they left their language developed for only a narrow range of activities among local élites, a body of myth about French and other languages, and little knowledge of, or interest in, the local vernaculars. Alexandre (1972, p. 124) observes, for example, that in '1964 there were more teachers of African linguistics at the University of London alone than qualified students and researchers in France and francophone Africa combined'.

In their colonizing activities the French regarded themselves as the successors to the Romans. They were a superior people blessed with a superior language and culture and it was their mission, the *mission civilisatrice*, to extend the benefits of their civilization to the backward peoples of their empire. Individuals in that empire would be awarded full French citizenship when they gave proper evidence that they were indeed civilized. In practice, however, the French did little to see that the masses of colonized peoples had any real opportunity to achieve such a state as *évolués*; it was only a very few selected individuals who managed. French colonial policy may have been less 'racist' than that of other European powers but certain aspects of it were to create difficulties. French colonies were regarded as part of France itself; while France was able to free herself from the colonies in West Africa without much difficulty, in at least two cases, Vietnam and Algeria, struggles for independence roused strong passions within France because of a reluctance to give up 'French' territory.

The legacy of the British and French Empires in Africa was some teaching in most of sub-Saharan Africa of one or other of these languages. There was also teaching of French in the Belgian possessions in Africa, French being the language that Belgian colonizers took with them rather than Dutch, which at that time was heavily disfavoured in Belgium. Only those parts of Africa colonized by the Portuguese did not have some contact with one or other of the languages. What little German presence there had been was ended after World War 1 when Germany was dispossessed of its African colonies. The Germans had also administered their part of East Africa largely through Swahili. By the time the colonies finally achieved independence Africa had effectively been divided in two so far English and French are concerned. There was an anglophone Africa and a francophone Africa with the English and French languages lying like a veneer over the new states of Africa. One immediate problem that each new state had to confront was what it would make of that veneer. Was it desirable? Should it be removed? What would take its place? How would any changes be made? What would they cost? It is questions like these which still pose many problems for various African states.

THE RESIDUE OF ENGLISH AND FRENCH

There are several reasons why the former colonies often maintain either French or English as an official language or give it some other recognition. The colonial powers left behind their languages along with institutions that functioned through the use of those languages. Consequently, in each former colony the areas of law, administration, and education are very likely to be the preserves of a former colonial language. Sometimes the choice of a language such as English or French is seen to be expedient in that it guarantees a certain amount of continuity and efficiency in conducting the affairs of the state. It may even serve to unify a state in which a variety of languages exist and in which choosing to promote one language over the others might bring about ethnic conflict. English and French are also associated with notions of progress and modernization and the United Kingdom and France have continued to provide various forms of assistance; therefore, the languages remain attractive to those who seek certain kinds of developments in the new states.

In each former colony the European language dominated the infrastructure, at least at the higher levels. At independence it was the local élites functioning in the European language who took over the affairs of state, but in most cases maintained a connection with the former controlling power. Civil servants, teachers, lawyers, judges, administrators, army personnel, and so on immediately assumed important positions. Their future depended on the skills they brought with them and one of the most important of those skills was a command of a European language. It is not surprising therefore that English and French maintained their privileged positions in the new states of Africa; their privileges also guaranteed the privileges of those who used them. Only now, a full generation later, as the old élites give way, often reluctantly, is it becoming apparent that local languages must also be recognized to accommodate local demands.

The argument for expediency and efficiency rests on a belief that European languages are developed in ways that the indigenous languages are not. They have vocabularies and literatures which allow for the easy accomplishment of any and every task. In comparison, the local vernaculars reveal gross deficiencies. Some advocates of the continued use of European languages in Africa also believe that it would ultimately be more productive to educate children from the very beginning of their schooling in a European language so as not to waste valuable years of education using languages which have serious limitations.

Many African states use a European language as the official language of the state in order to avoid factionalism. Most African states are both ethnically and linguistically heterogeneous. Moreover, many do not contain a majority group of any kind. Some Africans argue that a European language may be a good 'neutral' choice as the official language in such circumstances in that it favours no indigenous language over any other. The alternative would be to make all the languages of the state – or at least the most important ones – official. This solution is often seen as one that promotes factionalism in that it tends to encourage individuals to identify with sub-groups within the state rather than with the state as a whole. However, this is exactly how individuals often do tend to identify themselves, and the state's failure to recognize local vernaculars in any way may just as likely encourage such identification as discourage it.

One consequence of colonialism is that many Africans have come to acknowledge how languages like English and French are related to certain ways of life they seek to emulate. They are languages of cultures that have spread throughout the world. They are also languages that are associated with science and technology and all the benefits that accrue from these. Within each state too those who speak the European language generally have more advantages than those who do not. Even after independence English and French continue to be associated with the élites of African states. It is therefore easy to believe that one must acquire one of these languages in order to join an élite. One interesting shift that is occurring in Africa is that in the francophone states English is winning converts from French because of the greater value it appears to have as a language of progress and prestige. There is no comparable loss to French in the anglophone part of Africa.

There are several consequences of such residual feelings for English and French in sub-Saharan Africa. One is that the two languages are still widely recognized as official languages. Another is that different states have adopted different policies so far as the use of the various indigenous languages of the states is concerned. In some states there is a considerable vernacularization of education; in others there is much less. But in just about all states either English or French still has some role to play in the educational process. English or French will be important no matter how great or small that role because customs of language use developed through the colonial period still exert considerable influence everywhere.

English and French therefore continue to be taught. They are essentially languages that Africans learn at school; in contrast, Africans often learn languages like Arabic, Swahili, Wolof, and Sango outside the school. Learning English or French well is the mark of either an expensive education or a privileged position. Some critics claim that many African states spend an entirely disproportionate part of their educational budgets on teaching English or French to the detriment of local languages and deplore the way in which the United Kingdom and France support what they regard as a completely misdirected activity. Most students seem to learn only a little English or French and much of that is quickly forgotten since it is not very useful, certainly not in most cases as useful as an informally acquired regional lingua franca such as Swahili rather than English in East Africa, or Wolof rather than French in Senegal.

Some critics are really quite vocal in their opposition to the continued teaching of English and French. Makouta-Mboukou (1973, p. 50) characterizes their views concerning the use of French as follows. He says that they regard French as:

l'instrument d'aliénation par excellence: alienation mentale et culturelle. La langue française ne libère plus, mais opprime; elle n'élargit plus l'horizon, mais le restreint; elle n'est plus une langue d'ouverture au monde, mais un voile qui, comme une gangue, enveloppe les consciences; elle n'est plus un facteur de rapprochement, mais de division, de désunion, ou simplement d'éloignement.

the most notable instrument of alienation: mental and cultural alienation. The French language no longer liberates, but oppresses; it no longer widens the horizon, but narrows it; it is no longer a language of openness to the world, but a veil which, like waste, smothers minds; it is no longer an instrument of accommodation, but of division, disunity, or simply distancing.

Still others, e. g., Manessy and Wald (1984, pp. 108–9), find much of the teaching of a language like French in West Africa to be inadequate because the teaching bears no relationship to pupils' lives:

Ceci explique alors la fréquente ritualisation de son enseignement apparament détaché des réalités contingentes, comme si la langue était non seulement étrangère, mais inopérante dans la vie quotidienne, comme si l'élève devait se préparer à la visite de l'Europe plutôt qu'a l'usage du français dans la société africaine.

This explains then the frequent ritualization of teaching apparently detached from contingent realities, as if the language was not only foreign but inapplicable to daily living, as if the student should prepare himself for a visit to Europe rather than to use French in African society.

Not all Africans welcome the opportunity to learn English or French; some see such learning as an obstacle to achieving a genuine African identity for themselves, as still another example of neo-colonialism.

The emphasis placed on making sure that a few people learn English or French well may be either very wasteful if many must fall by the wayside in the learning process or very selective and élitist. Nor can it do anything to raise the esteem of the vernaculars. Alternatively, if the teaching of English and French is carried out half-heartedly, that can result only in very little learning and a very poor knowledge of the languages. When this has indeed happened, the French have been particularly critical because of their feelings of 'purism' about their language. The English are much more accepting of the consequences of such poor learning and of local developments in English.

After achieving independence, the government of each sub-Saharan country had to make an immediate decision as to the language it would use in internal communication with its people. That language was almost always English or French (or Portuguese in those states which had been colonies of Portugal). Tanzania was the only exception, the government choosing Swahili as the official language. Even Burundi, Lesotho, and Rwanda chose a European language as an official language although each has an indigenous language known to almost everyone, respectively Kirundi, Sesotho, and Nyarwanda. In each case the African language achieved a status that was really no better than the non-indigenous language although it was to be the national language. The European language was declared to be an *official* language rather than a *national* language, governments realizing that whereas an official language may be necessary for pragmatic reasons, a national language has an additional symbolic value. No government wanted to have a European language holding such a symbolic position in a state so recently freed from European dominance. In many cases too this designation also set aside the issue of deciding which language or languages should be given the *national* label, an issue that would probably be divisive.

The movement to designate more African languages as national languages proceeded slowly. Botswana designated Setswana, the Central African Republic added Sango, a widely spoken lingua franca, Ethiopia and Kenya substituted Amharic and Swahili respectively for English, and Nigeria, having avoided any choice at all at independence, adopted English and Hausa, the latter only in the northern region. This slow progress in adding an official language or designating a national language has become the established pattern in Africa. It has seemed best to make haste slowly. Most states have very serious internal problems when judged by the standards of Western democracies. Anything that exacerbates these problems is to be avoided. Since favouring one language over another is likely to create rather than reduce ethnic friction, decisions are best avoided. Far better to opt for a pragmatic solution to the linguistic problems of a particular state than to promote an ideologically-oriented one that might further tear at its delicate fabric.

One pragmatic solution is to require that people who work for the government control not only the official language and the national language, if there is a designated national language, but also one or more local languages. Being able to use the language of the particular part of the state in which a civil servant works would appear to be a totally reasonable requirement in an efficient system. However, it is still a fairly rare requirement in sub-Saharan states. Governments, even local governments, continue to work in one of the European languages in almost all instances. The only real exceptions are those states with national languages, where these are also used, and one or two states, such as Guinea and Burkina Faso, where some small use is made of local languages. Little headway therefore has been made in reducing the dependence on languages like English and French in internal administration: most former French colonies continue to be administered in French and most former British colonies continue to be administered in English.

THE USE OF VERNACULAR LANGUAGES

Any movement to promote the use of vernacular languages in Africa must confront the fact that many African states contain dozens, even hundreds, of such languages. There is also, as we have indicated, the potential for interethnic conflict when one language is preferred over another. And there are the costs that are involved. Fortunately, in Africa there are several languages with widespread distribution, and that makes the task of selection and promotion just a little easier. Swahili is spoken extensively in Rwanda, Burundi, Zaire, Tanzania, Kenya, and Uganda; Lingala is spoken in Zaire and Congo; Kikongo is spoken in Zaire, Congo, and Angola; Hausa is spoken in Niger and Nigeria; Peul is spoken in Mali, Senegal, Burkina Faso, Niger, Benin, and Cameroon; and members of the group of languages known as Mandingo are spoken in Mali, Burkina Faso, Guinea, Senegal, Ivory Coast, and Guinea-Bissau.

Ever since 1953 and the release of a UNESCO report entitled *The Use of Vernacular Languages in Education*, there has been considerable pressure to promote the teaching of the vernaculars in Africa. The report said that since 'the mother tongue is a person's natural means of self-expression, and one of his first needs is to develop his power of self-expression to the full', then 'every pupil should begin his formal education in his mother tongue'. Critics have pointed out that the report's recommendations were based on opinions rather than on research and that several decades of research have proved to be inconclusive. Be that as it may, there is no doubt that a belief in the virtues and rightness of vernacular education is now an article of faith in many parts of the world and is a belief that one is unwise to ignore.

Promoting vernaculars is a long and sometimes perilous undertaking. Many are first used by missionaries in their work and in this way gain alphabets and a basic literature. Then they become used increasingly in the media, particularly on the radio and for information-giving purposes. Informal uses for them tend to develop in education, religion, and politics. As demand increases, the languages find their way into the schools on a more regular basis, and they are used in a wider variety of publications and functions. At this stage they require more deliberate promotion: agencies must be established to encourage use; curriculum materials must be developed and teachers trained; researchers must be encouraged to study them; 'official' blessing of some kind must be given; and money must be spent. But only when the language achieves a full range of functions and no stigma is attached to its use has it 'arrived'.

Some African vernaculars are somewhere on the journey just described; none is yet near the end.

In the 1960s almost no use was made of local vernaculars in the educational systems of the emerging African states. French was used entirely from the beginning in states such as Senegal, Mali, Niger, Upper Volta (as it was then known), Ivory Coast, Togo, and Benin. In Sierra Leone, Liberia, Gambia, and northern Nigeria the language was English. In the rest of Nigeria, Ghana, Uganda, and Kenya there was a bridging use of local languages. A significant change occurred in the 1970s when demands for 'authenticity' led to more and more use of vernaculars in education. Now there is a wide variety of experiments: for example, with Bambara, Peul, Songhay, and Tamasheq in Mali; with Moore, Dagari, and Peul in Burkina Faso; with Wolof, Peul, Serere, Diola, Mandingo, and Soninke in Senegal; and with Kabre and Ewe in Togo. Local languages are now being promoted for purposes of education in most of francophone Africa but no clear pattern of use emerges, with the choice an entirely local matter. As a 1986 report (Conférence des Ministres de l'Éducation des États d'Expression Française 1986, p. 22) says: '*la décision politique apparaît véritablement comme la clé de l'avenir social des langues nationales*' ('political decision making truly appears to be the key to the social future of national languages'). There is everywhere a noticeable growth in literacy programmes in local languages, and in their use in such media as radio, television, and newspapers, and as languages of instruction and administration.

A very brief look at what has happened in a number of African states quickly reveals some of the issues and difficulties involved in switching from a European language to one or more local languages. Nigeria is a country of some 80 million people who speak over 300 different languages. However, the dominant vernaculars are Hausa in the north, Ibo in the southeast, and Yoruba in the southwest. The Hausa north is also largely Muslim. It was British policy under Lord Lugard in the early twentieth century not to allow Christian missionaries into the Islamic north of Nigeria and not to spread English there. Administrative help was provided by Ibos who were brought to the north to help the British run the colony. Following independence, Nigeria suffered a bloody civil war when the Ibos seemed to adopt a policy which gave preference to those who spoke Ibo. Other Nigerians resisted what they saw as an Ibo attempt to dominate the state. The Ibos then decided to separate and found their own state, to be called Biafra. They were unsuccessful. Nigeria has tried various internal political systems since the civil war but one thing has been common to them all: the continued use of English after the early levels of education and a recognition of the need to use Hausa, Ibo, and Yoruba in at least the first three years of schooling.

Nigeria is still struggling in its educational system to find a balance among English, its three major regional languages, and the hundreds of minor local languages. A 1979 government policy statement entitled *Federal Republic of Nigeria National Policy on Education* did try to recognize all these languages and assign each a place in the overall system, but the practical diificulties of finding a balance acceptable to all Nigerians and the resources to maintain it if it could be found seem almost insurmountable. English is still the language of all higher levels of education in Nigeria, of the government itself and its agencies, of commerce, and even of most of the media. Moreover, it has become a distinctive indigenized variety so that one can now just as easily speak of Nigerian English as of Australian English or Indian English.

Another anglophone country of West Africa, Ghana, has probably become even more dependent on English since independence than before. Ghanaians have placed more emphasis on English as the medium of instruction in their schools than the British did in the colonial era. There has even been a marked decline in the teaching of local languages such as Twi, Ga, Ewe, and Fanti since independence. English is regarded as an indispensable language; local languages can be rejected because of their extremely limited usefulness.

In francophone Africa Senegal is a good example of a state that still exhibits a strong attachment to French even though it has a very good alternative language. Over one-third of the people speak Wolof as a native language and about four out of five can use it. Wolof is the language of the towns, of African trade, of the schoolyard in contrast to the schoolroom, and of interethnic marriages. But French, known by about 10 per cent of the population, still retains its privileged status as the language of government and of record. Senghor, the first President of Senegal, was an ardent francophile, even owning a vacation home in Normandy, and he merely continued the language policies of the French during his long rule. Since 1971 six languages have been recognized as national languages – Wolof, Peul, Serere, Diola, Mandingo, and Soninke – but French is the state's official language. The national languages get little exposure in the media, little use is made of them in the schools, and no real attempt is being made to exploit Wolof, by far the most useful. Those who control Senegal apparently still find French sufficiently alluring to prevent any substantive changes being made.

In Ivory Coast there is perhaps an even stronger insistence on the continued use of French as the language of administration, education, and social advancement than in Senegal. French is regarded as the national unifying language. Unlike Senegal, Ivory Coast has no language which is a native language to more than about 20 per cent of its population although as many as a half of the people have some familiarity with Diola. Dozens of languages are also spoken in the country, French has a neutral status, and most citizens support its continued use in the schools. Only a very few experiments have been conducted using local languages and these languages do not even find favour in adult literacy programmes. This reliance on French does have its opponents, e.g., some intellectuals at the University of Abidjan, but they find almost no support for their views. Young Ivory Coast speakers of French will sometimes today even openly support the local variety of French that they have acquired, 'un français populaire', against 'purists' of the older generation.

Mali, Niger, and the Central African Republic are also states in which there has been considerable reluctance to opt for the use of vernacular languages. The first two states have confined their efforts largely to experiments with literacy programmes. In the case of the Central African Republic there is available a widespread lingua franca, Sango, known to perhaps as many as 98 per cent of the population, but the government continues to insist on French as the official language. French is also the language of instruction except in a few experimental primary programmes and a few literacy programmes. Guinea, the first French colony to claim independence and therefore one that the French made to suffer for this 'mistake', has tried to promote local languages in education while keeping French as the official language of the state. In 1984, however, Guinea decided to reinstitute instruction in French for a period of six years because the results of using the local languages had proved to be unsatisfactory in the absence of adequate preparation.

In Malagasy French is rapidly disappearing from the schools except as a foreign language. After independence the people were able to use their own language, spread everywhere on the island but spoken in numerous dialects, as their national language. All that was necessary was to develop it to meet modern needs, but that has not been an easy task to accomplish. There have been problems in resolving issues concerned both with differences among the variety of 'low' dialects that exist and between those dialects and a 'high' literary variety of the language. Consequently, even though bilingualism in French and Malagasy was officially ended in 1972, French still continues to be used in a variety of circumstances on the island.

The official language of Zaire is French but widespread use is made of Swahili, Ciluba, Lingala, and Kikongo. The Belgians used all these languages in education. At independence French replaced them for a time at all levels of education, but in the mid-1970s they were reinstituted for use in primary education and in adult literacy programmes. This reinstitution did not meet with the approval of all, nor has it been conducted with much planning and any great enthusiasm. Although Burundi, another former Belgian colony, possessed a national language, Kirundi, at independence in 1962, the new state opted for a continuation of French as one of its two official languages. Kirundi was also made official but little use has been made of the language in the state because of problems with an orthography which does not adequately represent vowel tones and quality, a shortage of materials in the language, a lack of resources, and the limited usefulness of the language outside of what is really a very small country.

Finally, we should mention Cameroon, formed out of the union of a French colony with a British colony. French Cameroon was typically French in its governance. The French took over this territory from the Germans at the end of World War I and ended the pluralistic language policy of the Germans, a policy that had allowed German, Pidgin English, and the vernaculars to be used in different schools according to the local situation. Under the French the French language alone became the language of primary education, and the vernaculars and Pidgin English were banned from the schools, as obviously was German. Only French textbooks could be used. In contrast, the British at first used the vernaculars in primary education in the one-fifth of Cameroon that was theirs. But over the years, pressured by the Cameroonians, they began to place more and more emphasis on education in English so that by 1958 vernacular education was extinct.

Since 1972 English and French have had equal status in the unitary bilingual Cameroon that came into existence then. However, in practice the five francophone provinces contain 80 per cent of the population and the two anglophone provinces the rest. In the French provinces English is taught as a second language and English is the language of instruction in the English part of the country. The more than 200 indigenous languages have no official status but they are used – orally at least – in both administration and justice and also occasionally in radio programmes. Only a very few experiments have been conducted in using them in schooling and literacy. General promotion of the vernaculars is regarded as quite impracticable. There is also widespread official resistance to any recognition of Cameroonian Pidgin English, which is a widespread lingua franca even in the French provinces. The state's emphasis is on developing bilingualism in French and English, but Cameroonians do make extensive use of the pidgin. With the majority of children still not in school, it is not surprising that the pidgin, which can be very easily acquired informally, has perhaps become

Cameroon's real national language. However, there appears to be no way in which it will ever be given official recognition.

THE UNCERTAIN FUTURE

Landman (1978, p. 80) comments as follows on the pattern of language use that has developed in sub-Saharan African states:

> As is evident, public policy decisions have tended to favor minority, exogenous languages and have given little support to the large variety of indigenous tongues. I suggest that the relationships between this stress on the minority language competence and majority language repertoires are explicable on three major grounds: traditional patterns of language acquisition, a widespread instrumental attitude toward language, and the maximization strategies of the small groups who assumed power with the transition to independence.

Many Africans are multilingual and have no hesitation in learning a new language if it is in any way useful to them. English and French are often viewed as just other useful languages to be added to sometimes already extensive linguistic repertoires. They are particularly useful languages to have in dealing with the various parts of the states' infrastructures. In the years after independence those infrastructures depended on the colonial languages. Guinea was the only state that attempted to break away almost entirely from its colonial language, in this case French. It tried to use several of the major languages spoken by its citizens for administration and education but was forced to keep French as well.

It was just not possible for the new African states to do without the European languages in their early years and other problems proved more pressing than trying to find new languages in which to conduct the internal affairs of the states. Moreover, the new leaderships felt entirely comfortable speaking either English or French: these languages were very useful to them in their dealings with one another and in their dealings with governments that might give them the various kinds of assistance they soon sought. English and French were the languages of power, of power within the African states themselves and very obviously of power outside those states. However, it soon became obvious that of the two languages English was the one with the greater external power.

Today, there is considerable variation from state to state in the influence that either English or French has. There is also competition to these languages from various other languages. Several states make use of a lingua franca that is not English or French and are discovering how useful such a language can be. In particular, Swahili in East Africa is competing with English and this spread of Swahili merits separate consideration. It can be likened to the resurgence of Arabic in North Africa. Consequently, we will consider both languages together in the chapter that follows.

In francophone West Africa more and more use is being made of the local vernaculars in elementary education. French still retains its prestige and the French government still tries to provide certain resources to maintain a French presence in the area. However, it seems likely that the growing African nationalism will continue to require that still greater emphasis be placed on local languages and that their use will spread even further. It is also unlikely that France will have the resources to match this growth in interest. Therefore, the French language must almost inevitably decline in influence in West Africa. We must remember too that it was never very deep: it was really very few who ever learned much French. Admittedly, some of those learned what French they learned very well indeed and became recognized by the French themselves as fully assimilated. The opportunities today to join that group are fewer and the rewards are also fewer: it makes greater political sense today in Africa to be 'African' than to be thoroughly civilized in French language and culture.

English in Africa has to meet some of the same challenges. There is the same growth in the use of local and regional languages in education and the same competition from other widespread languages, particularly in East Africa from Swahili. One of the major countries of West Africa, Nigeria, is also a multilingual country in which as many as 300 different languages are spoken. It is also a country in which strong local passions have been aroused, to the extent that it underwent a bloody civil war. English is still widely used in Nigeria, as it is in most of the other former British colonial possessions. However, in Africa more and more people are being educated through languages other than English. English does still retain its hold in the higher levels of education, in the law, and in governmental administration almost everywhere it controlled in colonial times. It also cannot be matched by any of the local languages, not even by Swahili, in the appeal it exerts on those who aspire to join the social and political élites, and it is the language of science and technology. Furthermore, it exists in any number of varieties so that one does not have to speak one particular variety to be accepted. English, therefore, continues to be a very attractive language in those parts of Africa into which it was introduced in colonial times. There seems to be no sign at all that it is losing converts. Indeed, the opposite appears to be the case.

English is even winning converts from French in Africa. The so-called francophone countries in West Africa are becoming more and more reliant on trade with anglophone countries. They are finding it increasingly necessary to link themselves to the English-speaking world through their commercial and banking requirements. Even Senegal, long regarded as the most pro-French of these states, is developing more ties with the English-speaking world. Such ties require that some citizens of these francophone countries develop competence in English. Consequently, more and more programmes are being established in these countries to give a number of people the linguistic skills in English that will be needed if the countries are to participate fully in international life, a life that the English language dominates. There is no comparable movement in anglophone Africa to learn French: one just does not need French to make one's way in the world.

Language issues may be difficult to resolve in sub-Saharan Africa but they do tend to pale before certain other issues. It may well be, as Gérard (1981, p. xv) says, that: 'Whether Europe's languages are in Africa to stay, or whether they will go the way of Latin, to become dead languages there and making room for triumphant vernaculars, is a matter that is not likely to be known until a few centuries to come'. In the meantime this part of Africa has many other problems to solve. There have been frequent outbreaks of ethnic strife, including attempts at secession in Nigeria and Zaire, open interethnic conflict in Rwanda, Burundi, Uganda, Sudan, Chad, Ethiopia, Somalia, etc., and the expulsion of minority groups or threats of such expulsion, as in Uganda, Ghana, and Ivory Coast. The area is one of widespread poverty, economic decline, and illiteracy. For example, according to a 1980 World Bank report entitled *Education Sector Policy Paper*, in many countries at least half the children of elementary school-age are still not in school. It is also an area of authoritarian rule and changes of government through coups rather than elections. The phrase 'downward spiral' is sometimes used to describe the overall situation that exists in this part of the world. Language is just one factor in that spiral; it also seems less important than many others. It may well be that most African countries have not reached the stage in which they can indulge in battles over language. Such battles require that there be spoils that can be fought for using language issues as the battleground, that is, that language issues can be used to mobilize interest groups. Language has not yet been tied to the spoils system in this part of the world. Other issues seem much more important to Africans. At some point language issues may become important, but at the moment what we observe is the dissolution of the system the colonial powers left in Africa and the failure to replace it with a system that meets the needs of those it should serve.

FURTHER READING

General issues: Altbach and Kelly 1984, Richmond 1983, Treffgarne 1981; the French language: Bamgbose 1976, Corbett 1972, Kelly 1984, Kwofie 1979, Makouta-Mboukou 1973, Manessy and Wald 1984, Turcotte 1981, 1983, Weinstein 1980; Cameroon: Todd 1982, 1983; Nigeria: Afoloyan 1984.

8

Competition from Arabic and Swahili

The two major competitors to French and English in Africa are Arabic and Swahili respectively. Arabic has long played an important role in Africa, having been spread through much of North Africa along with the Islamic faith. For a while French replaced it as the language of administration, law, and what little education there was in much of the area that Arabic had dominated for centuries. Now that the French have been forced to leave North Africa Arabic is reclaiming its historic territory, although not without difficulty, since French retains much of its former importance. As the countries of the Maghreb arabize, they still cling to French because it offers many advantages to them that Arabic does not, Swahili – also known as Kiswahili – has been a very important African lingua franca for many centuries, particularly in East Africa. It is a major competitor to English in various countries there, and serious attempts are being made in several to replace English with Swahili as the official language and to make it more than just a symbolic national language. However, English is still enormously attractive to those who aspire to recognition of various kinds and is therefore likely to continue to play an important role even in those countries in which Swahili is spreading.

ARABIC AND ISLAM

Arabic is a Semitic language and therefore related to languages such as Hebrew and Aramaic. It owes its great influence in the world to its use, in one of its written forms now known as Classical Arabic, by the prophet Muhammad in the writing of the Koran. Arabs themselves are one people to the extent that they are united by a common language (although this is spoken in a variety of dialects), a common religion, a common cultural tradition, and a common history. They are a nomadic people who trace their history back to the Bedouins of the Arabian peninsula. When they embraced Muhammad (d. 632), they carried the Islamic faith far and wide, for Islam was a militant faith, one which also did not separate the temporal and the spiritual.

The Arabs spread their culture and their language along with their faith. Conquered peoples became Arabs as they were assimilated into the new faith and adopted the new language, and most other faiths and languages died out in the lands that the Arabs came to occupy permanently. Islam was, however, sometimes able to tolerate two faiths with which it had certain similarities, Judaism and Christianity, and sometimes Jews and Christians were able to continue their ways of life in the self-ruling millets of the Arabic and Ottoman worlds.

Today, there are Arabs who are not Muslims, e.g., the Maronites of Lebanon and the Copts of Egypt, and there are Muslims who are not Arabs, e.g., Kurds, Berbers, Malays, Pakistanis, Indonesians, etc. Islam itself possesses none of the unity of some parts of the Christian faith, e.g., Roman Catholicism. In particular, there is a great internal schism between Shiites and Sunnis and there are different views as to Islam's relationship to various political movements and to secularism itself. Above all, it is the five pillars of the faith that unite Muslims: a confession of the faith ('There is no god but Allah and Muhammad is his Prophet'), the five daily prayers, the month-long fast at Ramadan, the pilgrimage to Mecca, and the giving of alms.

The Arabs were able to create for themselves a considerable empire. Arab armies penetrated through Persia to the Indus and the borders of China in the east, to the borders of Armenia in the north in the area of the Black and Caspian Seas, to the Persian Gulf in the south, right across the north of Africa with a swing northward into Spain, and into the Mediterranean to Cyprus, Crete, Sardinia, and Sicily. By the middle of the eighth century a unified Islamic Empire existed. In North Africa the islamization of the Maghreb preceded arabization and the latter was never completed. The consequence is that while there are no Berbers in Tunisia, there are to its west in both Algeria and Morocco. The empire proved to be shortlived since political intrigue and religious schisms – particularly between Shiites and Sunnis – soon resulted in its break-up into independent Muslim states. But Islam itself continued to spread in Africa for another millenium, down the eastern seabord and also into the central and western areas, with Timbuctoo, for example, an important trade and cultural centre in the fifteenth and sixteenth centuries. A further important consequence of the initial expansion was the development of an extensive network of caravan routes across the north of Africa, routes which connected to those leading to Arabia, to the eastern coasts of Africa, into the Mediterranean, and still further afield to the Orient.

Almost as quickly as the empire achieved its glory, it lost it. Even in the eighth century various provinces began to assert their autonomy. Spain became virtually independent as early as 756 and Morocco (788), Tunisia (800), and Egypt (868) followed. By the eleventh century the glory was gone and the remnants of the empire were assaulted on all sides and even from within – by Christians, Berbers, Turks and dissident Arabs. Later, in the thirteenth century, we can add the Mongols to this list. But some of the force of the imperial connection still prevailed long after the decline was apparent; it was not until 1492, for example, that the Spanish finally recaptured Granada from Islam. Eventually, the Turks and Persians of the Ottoman Empire replaced the Arabs, who found themselves dominated, disunited, and localized with little left but their language and faith and a remembrance of past glories. Even the Arabic language faded as a language of prestige before both Turkish and Persian. It ceased to be a language of learning, dialect differences became increasingly apparent, and the great diglossic split developed between the classical written variety and the various spoken varieties.

Even though the Arab Empire broke up, the language continued to fare quite well as a spoken medium. Along the edges of the empire the various vernaculars reasserted themselves, e.g., in India, Persia, and Spain, but in the central parts it was Arabic that maintained its dominance over all competitors. It submerged most of the other Semitic languages, displaced Greek, which had been the regional lingua franca for many centuries, became the language of Egypt, where it pushed aside Coptic, and encroached considerably into the Berber-speaking area of North Africa. By the sixteenth century Arabic was 'the general language of all the peoples from Aleppo to Aden and from Oman to Morocco' (Brosnahan, 1963, p. 13). Brosnahan adds:

It is still today the main, and in most places the only, language of this whole area. In addition, as the language of the Koran and of a rich literary inheritance, as the language of learning and of the law, it is the classical language of the religious and the educated through the whole Islamic world which stretches far beyond these boundaries. It is without question one of the great languages of the world.

In Africa, for example, the Islamic religion has spread southward everywhere through the desert area almost to the Equator and in the east down the coast far to the south of the Equator. Spoken Arabic has not always accompanied that spread; the influence that Arabic has in the area comes from the place that Classical Arabic holds in religious practice. Likewise Arabic has not accompanied the spread of Islam into

Persia, Turkey, East Africa, where Swahili is the language associated with Islam, and countries as distant as Pakistan, Malaysia, and Indonesia. Arabic has, however, left its mark on each of the languages used in these countries.

At the beginning of the nineteenth century Arab culture had fallen to its lowest ebb since the rise of Islam. The rulers of the Ottoman Empire dominated most of the Arab lands and Turkish had become the primary language of administration. Arabic was still the language of religion but had little influence outside the religious domain. Spoken Arabic had diversified into a series of dialects that were not easily intelligible to one another and classical scholarship was moribund. There seemed little hope that Arabic would reassert itself in the world, particularly as the Ottoman Empire appeared so strong and, even if it faltered, the various European powers seemed all too ready to fill any void that might result. There was also no sense of a common Arab identity, and it was not until near the end of the century that a revival of Arab consciousness occurred. Arab nationalism did grow as the Ottoman Empire declined. However, it was not until the final demise of that empire in World War I that Arabs were seriously able to consider alternative systems of organizing their affairs, either through greater political autonomy, some kind of pan-Arabism, or a revival of Islam. But by that time the European powers had indeed stepped in to fill the void.

The Ottoman Empire broke up with growing Arab nationalism an important contributory cause. One by one the provinces of the Ottoman Empire sought more and more local control and gained some success. But they would have a long wait to achieve full autonomy. Various European powers decided to send their armies into the Arab world, there to claim possessions and to fight one another. North Africa was to be colonized just like the rest of the continent.

Initially, it was economic motives that led to European interest in the Ottoman Empire. From the sixteenth century on various European countries were able to negotiate trade concessions. The first military intervention did not occur until Napoleon's shortlived invasion of Egypt in 1798. This event led to further interventions in the following century when European countries used their military power to gain control of areas that would enhance their trade and communications. Britain penetrated into the Persian Gulf and Red Sea, and into the Sudan, Egypt, and Palestine. The opening of the Suez Canal in 1869 was a milestone event in the development of the British Empire. France moved into Algeria (1830), Tunisia (1881), and Morocco (1912), and gained control over Lebanon and Syria; Spain also moved into part of Morocco, and Italy moved into Tripolitania. This European penetration eventually did help bring about a resurgence of Arab feeling, but it was not until the 1950s and 1960s that many of the Arab states were able to achieve independence, e.g., Tunisia and Morocco in 1956 and Algeria in 1962.

In this part of the world most of the twentieth century has been devoted to freeing the area of European influence and reestablishing an Arab identity. However, in each of the newly emergent states there is also a need to establish a local identity. Therefore, pan-Arab feelings must often be circumscribed in order to realize local goals. In addition, the Arab world must continue to rely on its contacts with Europe if it is to participate fully in the process of modernization. For that reason English and French still exert a strong hold in the area.

Today, the Arab world stretches 5,000 miles from Oman in the Persian Gulf to Mauritania on Africa's west coast. Beyond it is the further Islamic world of which it is a part, a world of possibly as many as a billion people on various continents, some one-fifth of the global population. The major Arab areas are: first, the Arabian peninsula itself, containing Saudi Arabia; second, the Fertile Crescent to its north, containing countries such as Syria and Jordan with their considerable Arab consciousnesses and with Israel in their midst; third, Egypt, the largest Arab state but one with its own brand of Arab nationalism; fourth, the militant Libya; and, finally, the countries of the Maghreb, long subject to French domination and possibly least affected by strong Arab sentiment. The Arab world tends to unite through language, the Islamic faith, and anti-West, anti-Israeli, and pan-Arab feelings. But it also divides through religious factionalism, in the forms of government the various states have adopted, in the variety of its social, economic, and educational developments, and in conflicting views over Islam's proper role in the state. At the boundaries of the Arab world in Africa lie such countries as Chad, Mauritania, and Sudan. Each of these states is split to the point of conflict on whether it is an Arab state or an African state. Finally, Arabic itself is not Islam's only language in Africa. In its way each of Swahili, Hausa, and Wolof is also an Islamic language.

FRENCH AND ARABIC IN THE MAGHREB

Of particular interest to us is the competition between Arabic and French in the Maghreb, i.e., Algeria, Tunisia, and Morocco. In many ways these were the most settled of the European colonies and they avoided much of the recurrent warfare of colonial possessions elsewhere in the Arab world, particularly in Egypt and the Levant. There was even a deliberate policy of European settlement so that one of these countries,

Algeria, came to be regarded as an integral part of France. Tunisia and Morocco were protectorates but Algeria was considered to be a territorial extension of France itself. It was this view of Algeria that was largely responsible for the horrors of the Algerian War. Many French tended to regard the violence in Algeria as an insurrection, a civil war, rather than as the struggle of a colonial people for independence.

From the very beginning of French rule in the Maghreb the French insisted that their language would be used as the language of administration. Since Algeria was regarded as part of France Arabic was suppressed there just as every other language had been suppressed on French territory. French would be the sole official language. Not even interpreters were available in government offices for those who had to deal with French-speaking officials but did not know the language. The two local languages, Arabic and Berber, were not recognized at all officially, although some use was made of Berber in an attempt to win Berber support against the Arabs in Algeria. Between 15 per cent and 20 per cent of the Algerian population are berberphone, and so are perhaps as many as half of the population of Morocco. (Tunisia has about 1 per cent berberphones.) Some unofficial use was made of Berber in Morocco, and a less stringent language policy also allowed for some use of Arabic. In the Maghreb, then, neither the majority Arabic language nor the minority Berber language was given any official recognition. The route to any kind of advancement was to lie through the acquisition of French. The French also reinforced their position by encouraging migration from France to the Maghreb, with Algeria a favourite place of settlement.

The French policy of assimilation and neglect of Arabic had profound consequences. When the French eventually left the Maghreb, they left behind a well entrenched French language, particularly among the Arab élite. They also left behind an Arabic-speaking population but one that had little or no experience with that language as a medium for literacy or learning. Furthermore, the French had made no attempt to standardize Arabic, so that no common Arabic language existed for the area. The dialects of Arabic that were spoken in the Maghreb also differed considerably from those spoken in Egypt, Saudi Arabia, and Lebanon. These differences cut off the Arab peoples from one another. (Some Arabic 'dialects' are more different from one another than various Slavic 'languages'.) Arabs were forced to resort to the antiquated written form of the language, the Classical Arabic of the Koran, in attempts to communicate among themselves and to deal with the phenomena of modern life.

One estimate of the linguistic situation in the Maghreb in 1964 (Gallagher, 1966) produces some very interesting figures concerning the penetration of French into the Maghreb. In Morocco's population of 13 million at that date (1981, 20.9 million), 11 million spoke Arabic, 4 million spoke Berber, and 4 million spoke French. Of the 4 million who spoke French about 800,000 could also read the language; however, only about one Moroccan in thirteen could read Classical Arabic. Tunisia's 4.5 million population (1981, 6.5 million) were almost entirely Arabic-speaking but 2 million also spoke French. Of these 700,000 could also read the language, but only 700,000 of those who spoke Arabic could read Classical Arabic. The figures from Algeria show an even greater imbalance toward French. Out of Algeria's 11.5 million (1981, 19.6 million) 10 million spoke Arabic and 2.5 million Berber. However, there were 6 million speakers of French of whom only one in six could also read the language. In contrast, only 300,000 Algerians could read Classical Arabic.

From the above figures we can see that the spread of French and the suppression of Arabic appear to have been greatest in Algeria, the most French of the overseas possessions and the one that the French fought hardest to keep. Algeria had been a possession of France since 1830 when the first parts of it were conquered. French control was gradually extended with the military playing an important role in the administration from the very beginning, a role that it would be reluctant to abandon more than a century later. The army did encourage the settlement of people from France right from the beginning. But the French who came to Algeria did not understand North African ways and made little effort to do so. They were intent on their *mission civilisatrice*, on pacifying the area, and on extending French institutions to Algeria. To the very end of French rule, French settlers, the *pieds noirs*, were also intent on keeping Arabs 'in their place'. When independence finally came to Algeria, many of the French could actually trace their family histories in Algeria back through several generations. It was partly this policy of encouraging a strong identity with France through settlement that was to make independence such a bloody struggle: many French Algerians considered that they were being dispossessed of their birthright. It was also this policy that had such disastrous consequences for the Arabic language and Arabic education. If Algeria was an integral part of France, then the people should learn French. If they did not learn French, then no public support should be given to the teaching of any other language.

From the very first the teaching of French was regarded as the most efficacious means to help the progress of French domination in Algeria. For example, a decree of 13 February 1883, passed under the new educational policies instituted by Jules Ferry, specified that in the French schools of the Maghreb '*l'arabe ne pourrait être enseigné qu'en dehors des heures de classe*' (Arabic may be taught only outside of class hours').

French was to be used exclusively in the state-supported schools in those areas fortunate enough to have them. The Algerians already had schools – religious institutions in which the students were educated in the Koran. Koranic education consisted of teaching pupils to read, write, and memorize passages from the Koran. Later there would be formal instruction in Classical Arabic and the reading of commentaries on the Koran. Finally, there would be instruction in Islamic law and theology as well as the study of geography, history, mathematics, astronomy, and perhaps some natural science and medicine. At the highest level, at the best Arab universities, an inseparable union still existed between learning and religion, all these universities being attached to mosques, e.g., al-Azhar in Cairo, al-Zaituna in Tunisia, and al-Quarawiyyin in Fez.

Koranic education was also free education, the notion of state support for education being foreign to Arab culture. State-run, tax-supported, secular French schools were alien institutions which were in complete opposition to the beliefs of the indigenous population. French policies of land expropriation also resulted in the closing of many of the Koranic schools because they lost the financial base on which they depended. Arabs also rejected the few schools the French tried to promote in their place as alien, godless institutions of no relevance. Interference by the French did not stop there: they also exerted control over those officials who were to administer in Islamic affairs, insisting that they speak French and that the French authorities control the system of appointments. The French destroyed the Algerian system of education that they had found, and the mass of Algerians rejected the one the French tried to establish in its place.

In the late nineteenth and early twentieth centuries few Arabs received any education at all and those who did received that education in French. In 1900, after seventy years of occupation, there were only 88 Algerian students in all the French secondary schools in Algeria. It is estimated that when the French seized Algeria in 1830 there was something in the order of 40–50 per cent literacy in Arabic, but when they left three-quarters of the population were completely illiterate and there was only minimal literacy in Arabic and not much more in French. This policy found wide support from the French settlers, who saw no merit at all in educating the local Arabs. Such education could only threaten them. It would weaken the settlers' political and economic power because educated Algerians would hardly be likely to tolerate the position into which they had been forced in their own land: 'on the day when all the natives will have been educated, the *colons* will no longer have workers'.

It can be argued that the French missed the opportunity they had in the late nineteenth and early twentieth centuries to replace Arabic with

French in the Maghreb. French settlers at one time comprised about 7 per cent of the population and at the peak of the French occupation of Algeria the French proportion of the total population was probably as great as the Arab proportion in a previous era of Arab conquest and their resources were greater. But, whereas the Arabs succeeded in arabizing the indigenous populations and converting them to Islam, the French failed to impose either their language or their religion. They controlled both the power and the resources they would have needed, but they failed to develop any kind of sound policy for education of the local populations. By the mid-twentieth century the great increase in the Arab population combined with increasing aspirations made the French hold on the area increasingly tenuous and reduced possibilities for compromise. The policies the French adopted had proved to be quite ineffective either in combating illiteracy or satisfying the minimal needs of the people, and what educational reforms they did try to introduce proved to be far too little offered far too late.

The situation changed somewhat after World War I. By the end of that war some 173,000 native Algerians had served in the French army. There was a growing realization too that the key to advancement lay in learning French, and that the refusal to attend French schools was working to the disadvantage of Algerians. The demand for schooling in French increased, and more and more Algerians learned the language and became literate in it. Algerians also moved fairly freely between Algeria and France to meet a French need for cheap labour. In this way many Algerians acquired considerable familiarity with French language and customs. But very few passed over to the other side and took on French citizenship – in fact only 2,500 between 1865 and 1935. Those who visited France were also exposed to other political beliefs than the ones to which they were accustomed in North Africa, and these often caused them to become opponents of colonialism. For their part, however, the French settlers continued to resist all moves to extend knowledge of French among the Arab population fearing that such moves would jeopardize their own position.

When the French were eventually forced to leave Algeria in 1962 they left behind a school system that employed French as the language of instruction. There had been some recognition given to Arabic during the last few bitter years of French occupation: it could be taught as a foreign language! The French also left a country that had of necessity to run its affairs through the French language because Arabic lacked the resources and the personnel trained in its use that would be necessary if Arabic were to replace French. The school system was impoverished and in disarray but then so was much of the rest of the new country's infrastructure. If Arabic were ever to regain what many thought was its rightful place, then a process of arabization was called for, a process of deliberately recapturing the country from French. Both Tunisia and Morocco were also experiencing similar problems.

ARABIZATION

At independence each of the three Maghreb states was firmly committed to promoting Arabic as its national language but each faced a multitude of problems and has moved only very slowly to arabize. As we will see, each country now has an education system in which after an initial period of instruction in Arabic children are exposed to both French and Arabic. French still retains its supremacy in science and technology, in commerce, and in large industrial enterprises. It is still the language of large areas of government, in fact just about every area except justice and internal affairs, and even in much of education. However, in each country the only politically acceptable position for leaders to take is that it will be arabized. The actual process may be slow, and those in charge may seem somewhat unenthusiastic, but the goal itself cannot be challenged.

To be successful, arabization requires solutions to a number of urgent problems. One of the first is the fact that the Arabic of the Maghreb is spoken in numerous dialects, and each of the new countries lacks a standardized form. In each country the dialect of the capital has assumed the most important position, being, among other things, the dialect that most of the media employ. Today, the dialects of the capital cities are taking on the characteristics of standard varieties for each of the countries, and other dialects are being unified around each of these. But language reform or modernization of this kind has had to be carried even further. The writing system for Classical Arabic is not one conducive to achieving mass literacy: it fails to represent vowels, and it makes use of several letter variants to represent the same sound, depending on its position in a word. Consequently, much attention has to be given to improving the way any variety of Modern Arabic is written, if literacy is to become a more achievable goal. The adoption of a romanized writing system is also nowhere acceptable.

Just as in the rest of the Arab world, different varieties of Arabic are found in the Maghreb. There is the Classical Arabic of the Koran, the various developing local standards of Modern Arabic, and the large numbers of local dialects. Not surprisingly, considerable controversy exists concerning the desirability of the resulting situation. There are those who revere Classical Arabic and who deplore the new standard varieties because of the separation of language and religion that they imply. They may also go so far as to reject 'modern' vocabulary and recent syntactic developments in the language. Those who wish to promote Modern Arabic are concerned that so many local dialects continue to exist, and that there are competing forms of Modern Arabic. The continued existence of the dialects is seen as a threat to the modernization that standardization is designed to achieve, and the existence of various regional standards also makes more difficult the spread of pan-Arab feeling. To many millions of Arabs, however, the local dialects are the only forms of Arabic with which they are entirely comfortable. There is not even agreement that the most widespread variety of Modern Arabic, Egyptian Arabic, with its clear leadership in the media, literature, and movies, should be given some privileged position, Egypt's politics not meeting with the approval of most other Arab states.

Much of the infrastructure of the countries of the Maghreb still employs French. The more remote a particular branch of government from the people the less likely it is to employ Arabic as a language of work. External trade matters, therefore, are likely to be in the exclusive domain of French. At the other extreme are those agencies that concern themselves with mass primary education; these are likely to be entirely arabized. But even though they may be arabized they may still lack many of the means to promote the kind of Arabic education that they might prefer. There are grave shortages of materials in Arabic and French views about the nature of education are still influential. France has also continued to supply teachers to the area, as many as 20,000 each year in the mid-1960s. Most of the educated people in the Maghreb were educated in French, which was often the only language that they learned to write. Today, French is still the language in which many people feel most comfortable when they engage in formal activities that involve writing or any kind of documentation. The language still has a powerful hold. Grandguillaume (1983, p. 9) observes that:

la profondeur de l'implication du français dans la société maghrebine était telle que le changement de langue ne se réduisait pas à une opération linguistique, mais entraînait des conséquences sociales, politiques, culturelles, qui ont contribué à faire de cette question un problème conflictuel.

Arabization has proceeded at different paces in these three countries. In each, though, an attempt has been made to develop an educational system that employs Arabic in the first few years of schooling before education becomes bilingual in Arabic and French. Governments have also tried to insist that more Arabic be used in their internal workings. Consequently, Arabic is now used almost exclusively in each country in such ministries as Justice and Interior and very widely in Education.

But elsewhere French is in wide use, just as it is in the newspapers and on radio and television. Algeria, the country that was longest colonized and the one most cut off during the period of colonization from its Arab roots, seems to have tried harder than either Tunisia or Morocco to undo French influence, but the French language remains strong in Tunisia by choice and in Morocco by inertia.

Tunisia decided to move very slowly in its programme of arabization. The government saw the need to develop Arabic as an effective language and with this end in view strove to promote the dialect of Tunis as the model. As a result, Tunisia has made more progress than either of the other two countries in developing a local standardized Arabic based on the language and culture of Tunis. Tunisian Arabic may not have great prestige in the Arab world as a whole, but Tunisians hold it in fairly high regard while still continuing to revere Classical Arabic, the variety used in education. Tunisia also decided to retain French as a language of instruction and adopt a policy of bilingual education. To quote its own words, the government of Tunisia felt:

After the almost complete neglect of Arabic during the Protectorate, it was almost impossible to raise Arabic to being the sole vehicle of instruction immediately. A shortage of qualified teachers and the absence of adequate textbooks forbade such action as much as it might have been desired. Gradual well-timed progress was in order to avoid confusion and harm to the students in their various stages of education.

The results have been somewhat ambivalent. After the first three school years in Arabic, French becomes well entrenched in the years of bilingual education that follow so that most of secondary education is conducted in French. French is also used by those who wish to modernize the country or to appear modern. They may even go so far as to claim that Arabic cannot possibly serve as a language of modernization, not even the variety that the government has sought to promote. This ambivalence is further increased by the fact that French today retains little of its colonial stigma. However, Tunisia is still very conscious of its relationship with the Arab world; in 1979, for example, the Arab League moved its headquarters from Cairo to Tunis. Although it is still perhaps too early to gauge the full consequences of such a move, it would appear to give Arabic a further much-needed boost in Tunisia.

Morocco expresses a commitment to both arabization and islamization. But it has had to move cautiously with the former because of its large Berber minority. Under the colonial regime Berber received as little – or as much – official recognition as Arabic. The French tended to leave the Berbers alone, not wishing to add to their problems. The Berbers fear an energetic policy of arabization because of the harm it could do them. They support Arabic as the language of the Koran, but regard arabization as a serious threat to Berber identity. In this belief they find support from the King of Morocco, who is aware that an energetic policy of arabization will increase internal divisiveness.

The government has proceeded slowly to arabize the educational system. It tried to arabize the first year of primary education immediately after achieving independence and intended to arabize the higher years in rapid succession. However, it was forced to slow down this policy when it became obvious that standards were falling. In recent years considerable effort has gone into developing materials and training teachers. Today, the first four years of education have been arabized. These four years are followed by three in which instruction is divided between Arabic and French, and from then on instruction is mainly in French. French continues to play a considerable role in the country; it is still a language strongly associated with power and prestige in Morocco.

Algeria was in the worst position of the three countries when it gained independence in 1962. In fact, many members of the new Algerian Constituent Assembly were incapable of addressing their colleagues in Arabic. It was also necessary that Algerians should agree on what kind of future they wanted for their country. There were those who sought a rejection of all things French and wanted the state to return completely to Islam. Opposed to them were the modernizers who regarded the maintenance of the French language in Algeria as extremely important if the country were not to turn its back on the future. What we see today is a kind of accommodation between these two extreme views, but not at times a very comfortable one.

At independence very little Arabic was taught in what schools there were in Algeria and no ready supply of teachers and materials existed. The government declared Arabic to be the national language and decided to bring in about a thousand teachers of Arabic from Egypt to help arabize the system. This experiment was a disaster: dialect differences were too great and the traditional Arabic pedagogy these teachers brought with them compounded the difficulties. It was agreed that the immediate need was to get children into schools and introduce Arabic gradually, but progress has been slow and not without conflict. It was only in 1965 that the first year of schooling was arabized. By 1974 education had been made compulsory for all children, with the first two years to be exclusively in Arabic. French was introduced in the third year as a second or foreign language but was given increasing attention the higher a student progressed through the system. In its slow pursuit of arabization the government of Algeria has tried to extend this pattern to allow for more and more teaching of Arabic and through Arabic for older students in order to emphasize that French is a second or foreign language in an Arabic-speaking country,

Some Algerians thought that arabization would block the modernization that they sought for their country. In particular, it would not work to the benefit of the important oil industry. It is not surprising therefore that declarations such as one in 1967 that the civil service would be arabized, and another in 1969 that government documents would be first published in Arabic and then translated into French have proved to be ineffective. French is still the language of opportunity in Algeria and it is still maintained as such by those who control most of the opportunities. Opposed to them are those who see Arabic as the instrument for achieving a strong national identity which acknowledges the Islamic foundation of the state. For example, student strikes in 1978 and 1979 were directed against the government for its failure to proceed energetically with both arabization and islamization. Berbers too joined the discontented but this time in opposition to arabization: in 1980 there were student strikes and riots in Tizi-Ouzou and Algiers against the government clamp-down on Berber.

The 1970s were a period of conflict among the various factions. The civil service resisted arabization and outside such ministries as Justice and Interior French continues to be the preferred language. It is said that an Arab inspector in Algerian schools is likely to insist on speaking French to teachers whose French may not be very good because the prestige of his position requires that he use French. *Le Monde* also continues to be Algeria's most important newspaper. Even the National Commission on Arabization established in1973 had become moribund only five years later. One less than optimistic observer (Grandguillaume, 1983, p. 134) has commented that by 1980 while arabization was proclaimed as the policy of Algeria, it applied only as necessary. Like its neighbours in the Maghreb, Algeria is torn between the 'authenticity' that Arabic confers and the 'modernity' that French offers. Strong insistence on Arabic also leads to demands for islamization and protests from Berber minorities, while strong insistence on French encourages neo-colonial dependency. That compromises and indecision have been the major result of competition between Arabic and French for dominance in the Maghreb is not at all surprising.

ENGLISH AND SWAHILI IN EAST AFRICA

Outside the Maghreb there are a number of languages that are widely spoken in Africa in addition to the former colonial languages, English, French, and Portuguese. These include Swahili in East Africa, Mandingo, with its three main mutually comprehensible dialects, Malinke, Bambara, and Diola, in West Africa; Amharic in Ethiopia; Sango in the Central African Republic; and Wolof in Senegal. Most African countries have chosen to retain the former colonial language as the official language even though this language is usually known only to the members of a very small élite or within larger towns where there may be more general knowledge. The exceptions are few: Swahili in Tanzania, Kenya (where it is co-official with English), and Uganda (where it is co-official with Swahili and Luganda), Amharic in Ethiopia, and Somali in Somalia.

For the individual who lives in a state where there is an official language such as English or French, a local lingua franca (possibly Swahili or Wolof), and one or more languages of the home and community, there exists a wide choice of languages. What choice is made will likely depend on such factors as the age of the individual, his or her social position, and the particular situation involved. Older urban workers with little or no education may use only the language of the home and a little Swahili or Wolof, if these are known and appropriate. Younger, better-educated urban workers may use a considerable amount of either English or French and less Swahili or Wolof; they may even try to extend their use of one of the first pair into certain domestic activities. However, the general social pressure is to extend the use of the offical language or of a lingua franca that might be replacing it. Sometimes the lingua franca may meet the needs of those who seek to add another language much better than the official language.

In Senegal, for example, Wolof is spreading much faster than French even though it remains largely unwritten and French is the official language. Wolof is just too useful a language to be ignored by those who have another mother tongue. Even the French-speaking élite find it useful because it allows them to be understood almost everywhere. In Senegal, Wolof has become the language of the capital, Dakar, where it is almost universally the language of the home. If not, it is every child's second language. It as also the language of officialdom and of business. Only a very few know the official language or try to use it exclusively. So Wolof has become the de facto language of Senegal, the language that is spreading at the expense of both French and other indigenous languages, e.g., Peul, Bambara, and Diola, which are increasingly confined to the peripheries of the state and then to the rural parts of these as Wolof takes over the towns there.

In many parts of Africa there appears to be similar competition between an official language and a lingua franca. When such competition does exist, the lingua franca may well have greater appeal than the official language, even though that language is a European one and finds favour among the country's élite. An African moving to an urban environment – and Africa is urbanizing just as is much of the rest of the world – may well find it more useful to learn the local lingua franca than the country's official language. Learning the lingua franca is likely to provide access to jobs and social contacts; learning the official language is far less likely to open doors to employment, particularly, as is usually the case, when there is considerable socioeconomic or ethnic stratification. Consequently, the urbanizing African is more likely to learn Swahili than English in Uganda and Kenya, Pidgin English than Standard Nigerian English in Nigeria, and Diola than French in Ivory Coast. Being able to speak English or French is a sign of education but it is not easy to acquire that education; being able to speak a lingua franca is a sign of a willingness to participate in a modernizing society. A lingua franca is also much easier to learn. Moreover, an African lingua franca is an indigenous language, and for many people who learn a lingua franca or wish to promote one that is an additional important consideration.

While there is still some uncertainty concerning the precise origin of Swahili, there is no doubt that in its phonological and grammatical structure it is a distinctly Bantu language, but that its vocabulary owes a great deal to Arabic and English with also some words from Portuguese and a number of languages of India. It may have appeared on the coast 1,000 years ago as a Bantu language brought from the interior. There, it came into contact with Arabic and the Islamic faith and remained a coastal language until the early nineteenth century, because until that time trade proceeded along traditional routes from the interior to the coast rather than vice versa. It was only when trading patterns developed that required caravans to proceed into the interior that the need for a lingua franca became acute and Swahili was pressed into service. These caravans carried goods into the interior – often cotton goods originating in the United States – and sought ivory in return. They penetrated the interior from various points on the coast, but access to present-day Kenya was largely denied because of Masai resistance. This resistance also forced trade with Buganda to be conducted around the west of Lake Victoria and further restricted the spread of Swahili in the area.

Swahili is now a mother tongue only among the coastal population from southern Tanzania to southern Somalia, including the islands of Mafia, Pemba, and Zanzibar ('the coast of the blacks'). But it is a second language in a much greater area, being the major lingua franca of the whole of East Africa with English as its only serious competitor there. Swahili has never been a unified language; it has also been written in both Arabic and Roman scripts. Only in quite recent times has any attention been given to standardizing the language, so it is not surprising that considerable controversy surrounds this task.

By the time Europeans colonized this part of the world Swahili was widely used for trade and intertribal communication. Although very few people spoke the language natively, many in the area were familiar with it. The European colonizers were forced to give some attention to language matters in their new possessions. Each colony required the development of an infrastructure which depended heavily on language. So choices had to be made concerning which language or languages would be encouraged, and opportunities had to be created for their use and for people to be educated in them. Choosing who would be educated also became an important issue, since education conferred power and prestige on those who were educated. In deciding what to do in East Africa, each colonial power was therefore forced to come to terms with the position that Swahili already held in the area.

Because of the widespread familiarity with the language, the Germans found Swahili particularly useful in German East Africa (now Tanzania) and gave it their support. They took a coastal language used for trade and by missionaries and turned it into a language of power, employing Swahili-speaking Africans as political agents, teachers, and civil servants. Tribal authorities, when and if they became integrated with the administration, also had to use the language, and German officials generally took pride in their competence in the language. A demand grew for Swahili education and for materials in Swahili. Word lists, dictionaries, and grammars began to appear and the language became one that could be studied and promoted. The Germans also created a Chair of Swahili at the University of Berlin in 1887, produced textbooks for use in the schools, and ensured that Swahili became the lingua franca of the administration and military. Because of its association with Islam, Swahili possessed a religious vocabulary that Christian missionaries were able to make use of, and, since its distribution also far exceeded that of any of the vernaculars of East Africa, many missionaries were often tempted to use it exclusively in their work.

By the outbreak of World War I Swahili had become the lingua franca of much of East Africa. It was well established in Tanganyika and Zanzibar and to a lesser extent in Kenya. However, it met with considerable resistance in Uganda where it continued to be associated with the Muslim slave trade that had penetrated from the coast. When the Germans were removed from German East Africa after their defeat in 1918, Swahili was able to maintain its position there because it had become indispensable. The British took over German East Africa but left the language policies of the previous administration largely intact, merely substituting English for German and doing a little more than the Germans did to promote their own language. Swahili remained the language of internal communication in the renamed Tanganyika.

Swahili has continued its spread in East Africa for economic, administrative, and even religious purposes. It is the paramount language of internal trade, the common language of groups like railway workers and miners, who spread it wherever they go, and armies and police forces use it as the language of command at the lower levels. Swahili has also become a more secularized language as its connection with Islam has become increasingly tenuous. But it still retains its connection with Islam, just as English is associated with Christianity, and there are those who seek to strengthen this historic bond between Swahili and Islam.

As we have indicated, Swahili is spoken in a number of varieties some of which are not even mutually intelligible. Each variety is spreading as part of the general phenomenon of the diffusion of the language with the spread ,of the most standard form – that spoken in Zanzibar – more noticeable than that of any other variety. According to Whiteley (1969, p. 3), there are four major groups of speakers of Swahili. There are those who speak Swahili as a native language. These people are located on the coast, on the islands of Pemba, Zanzibar, Mafia, and further afield in the Comores, and in some interior towns such as Tabora and Ujiji. A second group are those who use the language every day but for whom it is a second language. Such speakers are found in Tanzania and Kenya. A third group of speakers of Swahili, also located in Tanzania and Kenya but also in Uganda, have only a very limited knowledge of Swahili. Finally, there are many people who use the language infrequently and only as a vehicular language in countries such as Somalia, Mozambique, Rwanda, Burundi, and Zaire (around Kinshasa). These different degrees of knowledge of Swahili also clearly reflect the way the language has spread from the coast into the interior.

One of the problems that the British faced in East Africa if they were to make widespread use of Swahili was that of deciding on a standard form of the language. Swahili was spoken everywhere in East Africa and it was the language of the common military force of the area. There was, however, a growing realization that a standard form of Swahili would be helpful in the further spread of the language, particularly through formal education and the development of written materials. An attempt was therefore made in 1925 to decide on a standard variety, but this attempt ended in failure. In that year a Committee for the Standardisation of the Swahili Language met at Dar es Salaam, but its recommendation that the Zanzibar dialect be preferred over the Mombasa dialect led to supporters of the latter dialect walking out in protest. Consequently, in 1930, the Inter-Territorial Language (Swahili) Committee (later known as the East African Swahili Committee until 1964 when it was incorporated into the Institute of Swahili Research at the University of Dar es Salaam) came into existence in order 'to promote the standardisation and development of the Swahili language'. It had representatives from Kenya, Uganda, Tanganyika, and Zanzibar. This committee set out to standardize the orthography and secure uniformity in vocabulary and grammar. It also sought to stimulate works to be written in Swahili, to encourage translations into Swahili, and to monitor the standards of all works written in the language. Once again a committee appointed to deal with the matter chose to standardize on the Zanzibar dialect rather than on the Mombasa dialect, favouring exploiting the widespread distribution of the first over the much more localized distribution of the second, even though the latter enjoyed a historical and literary tradition denied to the former.

In all of this activity Europeans controlled the decision making, not Africans, and this control did not escape criticism. Many Africans regard the written form of Swahili that the committee developed as extremely artificial and stilted and not at all a genuine expression of African-ness. They sometimes describe it pejoratively as *Kizungu* ('European language') or *Kiserikali* ('Government language'). Not surprisingly, Mombasans are particularly critical. It was not until after independence that Africans themselves took charge of the language with Tanzania in the vanguard.

Swahili and English found themselves in direct competition in East Africa until the end of World War II. As late as the 1950s the British in East Africa tended to regard Swahili as an obstacle to education, standing in the way of both the vernaculars and English, and they failed to appreciate its unique position. They saw little use for it in the schools of the area. For a while English even began to make some headway against Swahili as educational systems were developed in the final years of the colonial era. In Kenya, for example, there was a growing demand for education in English as more and more people from England settled the colony and English became more influential. Several tribal languages also gained some recognition because of their importance and, for a while, Swahili seemed to impose itself as an obstacle between those tribal languages and English. In Uganda the policy was to exclude Swahili in favour of English and the important local languages: only in those few areas in which it was a mother tongue was any recognition given to Swahili. While there was also a demand for education in English in Tanganyika, Swahili managed to preserve the place it had gained as the language of administration under the earlier German regime. It further continued its spread among the population to become the only language known throughout the colony.

Independence has not resulted in any drastic shifts in language policy in the new countries of East Africa. Swahili and English remain the two most important languages in the area. Swahili is the political language of the area but English is the language that appeals to those with either educational or economic ambitions. Swahili has become the most important language of Tanzania, and it is important, but to a much lesser degree, in both Kenya and Uganda. In the last two cases, however, English remains very important, since one country still lacks a broad leadership thoroughly in command of Swahili, and the other was for a time under the control of a leader who used the language but was eventually deposed. Speaking of the linguistic situation that existed in the 1960s, Ansre observed (1974, p. 387) that 'there is no feeling of rivalry between English and Swahili. In fact, multilingualism is the obvious trend'. Numerous others have confirmed Ansre's observation in the years since.

Swahili has made most progress in Tanzania, a country that resulted from the union of Tanganyika and Zanzibar in 1964. It was the language of the Tanganyika African National Union (TANU), the African group that led the movement for independence, within which it was regarded as an important ideological resource. It was also the favoured language of the head of that movement, Julius Nyerere, the first President of Tanzania, who had himself translated both *Julius Caesar* (*Juliasi Kaizari*) and *The Merchant of Venice* (*Mabepari wa Venisi*) into Swahili.

By the time of independence Swahili was the most obvious choice as the language of Tanzania, a country estimated to have well over a 100 indigenous languages of which it was one. In Tanzania Swahili was not a language associated with a particular ethnic group; it was widely spoken as both a first language and a second language; it was an African language connected to many of the other indigenous languages, well over 90 per cent of which are Bantu; it had been used successfully for generations under both German and British administrations in both government and education, although with considerably less enthusiasm by the British than the Germans; and it was a clear marker of independence in contrast to English, the choice of which might have been seen to perpetuate the former dependence indirectly if not directly. Some of Nyerere's first moves after independence were to make all his speeches in Swahili, to declare Swahili as the national language in 1961, to promote the formation of a Tanzanian culture that would be heavily dependent on the language, and to appoint a Promoter for Swahili in the Ministry of Community Development and National Culture. In 1967 he made Swahili the official language as well.

Swahili is now the language of primary education in Tanzania. Tanzanians have opted to develop a comprehensive, self-contained system of primary education rather than one of more limited ambitions but from which the 'best' would be selected for further study, and much of the country's resources would go toward the education of the resulting élite. This choice is in accord with the particular brand of socialism (*Ujamaa*) that the leadership has chosen to pursue. Swahili is also gradually replacing English in the secondary schools. Its progress there is delayed through the lack of suitable teaching materials, and the need to retrain teachers to teach subjects in Swahili that they themselves have learned through the medium of English. The University of Dar es Salaam still continues to use English as its language of instruction with Swahili confined to language courses. Tanzanians acknowledge that there has been a decline in recent years in the ability of students to use the English language: this decline is part of the price that has had to be paid for promoting Swahili in the cause of achieving national unity and improving the general level of education.

In 1967 Tanzania established a National Swahili Council. Its objectives were to promote the development and use of Swahili in the country; to coordinate various promotional activities; to encourage use of the language in business and public life; to encourage high standards of use; to develop technical terminology; to publish works on Swahili language and literature; and to provide services to the government, the public, and to individuals who chose to write in Swahili. Today, partly as a result of the work of the council, Swahili is a highly favoured language of publication in Tanzania, in contrast, for example, to Kenya where English has far greater cultural prestige.

In Tanzania Swahili is now the language in which the government, the courts, and the internal administration work. It is also the common language of the people although the native language of possibly as few as 10 per cent. Some English is still used, for example in the higher levels of the judicial system, but among the various former British colonies of East Africa none today is less reliant on English. Some use is also made of the vernacular languages at the lower levels of internal administration because not everyone speaks Swahili.

The pattern of language use in Tanzania is a triglossic one. That is, many people use three (or even more) different languages depending on circumstances. There is also no great pressure to eliminate one or more of these. There is one place for English, for example in international dealings and in scientific and technological matters, another place for Swahili, and still another place for the vernaculars. To participate in supranational affairs, as, for example, in the Organization of African Unity or the United Nations, one uses the supranational language, English. To establish a national identity for political or cultural reasons, one uses the national language, Swahili. To reinforce local ties and a sense of continuity with the past or to affirm the values of a local group, one uses a local language. Tanzanians find value in their various languages but the one language that symbolizes their common identity as Tanzanians is their national language, Swahili. One may even argue that Swahili language and culture have been so successfully superimposed on Tanzania that a new Tanzanian identity has been achieved. Even though Swahili is not spoken uniformly in Tanzania, it is spoken almost universally. People share the common experience of the language and the associated culture. Through these they have achieved a common political and social consciousness that provides a countervailing force to local differences. Swahili also serves as a symbol of modernity without the associations that adhere to English. Its prestige may still be limited but it is authentically African.

In neighbouring Kenya, Swahili has made much less progress. During colonial times Swahili had a much smaller place in the life of the colony than it had in Tanganyika. The British favoured the vernaculars more than they did Swahili and, with few exceptions, the missions also preferred to use these local languages in their work. The vernaculars were few in number, Swahili did not have a wide distribution, and the variety of Swahili that was spoken was somewhat different from the variety spoken on the coast. Repeatedly between the wars the British rejected any other type of education than beginning instruction in the vernaculars and introducing English in the later stages. Gradually, however, Swahili crept into use into various schools, finding recognition as a vernacular in some and as a subject of instruction in others. English was also extended downward in the curriculum so that more and more pupils were introduced to it at earlier and earlier ages. Eventually Swahili and English found themselves in competition but English always had the upper hand, particularly after World War II when, in the last years of colonial rule, the British did their utmost to promote English at the expense of Swahili. This was the situation that existed at independence.

At independence English was clearly the prestige language of Kenya. Swahili was also in use as a lingua franca but it lacked the prestige of English. Among the vernaculars that were spoken, two – Kikuyu and Luo – were particularly important because of the number of people who spoke them and their geographical locations. However, the new country lacked any kind of unifying language. English was clearly a foreign language; Swahili was not at all well established and was only a regional language; and the choice of one of the vernaculars over all others would not encourage national unity. So far as education was concerned the initial policy proposed in 1964 was that English would be the language of instruction in the primary schools and Swahili would be taught as a compulsory subject because of its 'unifying national influence'.

English is still the official language of Kenya even though the country's only political party, the Kenya African National Union (KANU), has long maintained that Swahili should be the country's national language.

President Kenyatta saw more and more use being made of English, particularly in the capital of Nairobi and determined to give Swahili the boost it appeared to need. Kenyatta, a Kikuyu himself, was also opposed to favouring any one vernacular over another. He therefore proclaimed Swahili to be Kenya's national language, but he made no attempt to develop some kind of rational plan to foster its use. Instead, the government proceeded by saying where and when Swahili would be used and English banned. In 1974, for example, Swahili was declared to be the sole language of the country's parliament, an announcement that led to a storm of protest in that institution and its temporary closure. English had to be restored for use there in 1979: it proved to be impossible to do without it. English is still the language of daily government activity, of business, and of much instruction in the schools, and Swahili is far from being accepted as the national language of the country.

Kenya is a far less egalitarian state than Tanzania, and the roles that English and Swahili play in the lives of the two countries are highly indicative of the differences. English still symbolizes power and prestige in Kenya and that gives it a great advantage over Swahili, which has none of these associations. In Tanzania power and prestige are now associated with the country's national language, Swahili. Kenyans are also cut off from Tanzanians in the variety of Swahili they favour, a factor that increases to some extent the difficulties of developing a widespread 'Swahili' consciousness. The Kenya variety of Swahili is based on the dialect of Mombasa, the dialect that was not chosen as the basis for the standard in Tanzania but which many Kenyans who do not speak the standard variety regard as just as legitimate. Another point of some importance is that the capital city of Kenya, Nairobi, is located in the Kikuyu-dominated part of the country. Swahili has no great prestige among the Kikuyu, but English does, because of the language's long association with political power.

There is also less incentive in Kenya than in Tanzania for speakers of the local vernaculars to add a second language or to submerge their differences under a common language. Kenya has far fewer ethnic groups and languages within its borders than does Tanzania. A number of these are also quite large with four each comprising over 10 per cent of the population: Kikuyu (19.8 per cent), Luo (13.8 per cent), who are also a non-Bantu people, Luyia (13.1 per cent), and Kamba (11.2 per cent). There is little reason for speakers of these languages to add Swahili when English still offers great attractions, and when there is still a considerable amount of jockeying for power among the various ethnic groups within the country and some concern that the Kikuyu will seek to dominate the rest. In spite of all such factors Swahili is nevertheless widely used in Kenya. A knowledge of Swahili is also more prevalent among the two-thirds of Kenyans who speak a Bantu language than among the remaining non-Bantu, among those who live in :owns rather than in villages, and among lower-income people than those who hold white-collar positions.

The government of Kenya itself has shown little of the enthusiasm for Swahili that the government of Tanzania has displayed. Swahili is not the obvious choice in Kenya for the national language. English is still strongly entrenched. Several other languages are spoken by relatively large minorities, and ethnic tension is an important component in the political life of the country. It is not surprising therefore that Kenya is still very much a multilingual state in which languages compete for influence in a way that they do not in Tanzania. Nor is it surprising that the government of Kenya has failed to establish either a comprehensive language policy or implement any changes in the school system that might result in the replacement of English by Swahili. The country still favours an educational system which promotes English as the language of advancement, but only a small minority survive the competition that the system fosters. More and more use is made of the vernaculars and of Swahili at the beginning levels of instruction, but the vernaculars continue to be associated with factionalism and Swahili with low prestige. While Swahili remains the symbolic national language of Kenya, overall language policy there is quite clearly marked by ambiguity and uncertainty.

The linguistic situation in Uganda is also ambivalent. About 30 different languages are spoken in Uganda with about two-thirds of the population, mainly in the south, speaking a Bantu language, among which Luganda is most important, and most of the rest, in the north, speaking either a Nilotic language (e.g., Lango spoken by Milton Obote, or Kakwa spoken by Idi Amin) or a Sudanic language. Under the British administration of Uganda, the Baganda and their language, Luganda, were given privileged status over other groups and their languages, particularly in the administration of the country. Some of the other vernaculars were used in addition to Luganda as languages of instruction. English was also used, and for a time Swahili too, but the latter was often resisted by those who saw it as an instrument of Islam. Swahili did, however, become a useful lingua franca in the towns, particularly in the capital, Kampala, and it also found its way into use in military and police work.

Luganda, the langauge of about one-sixth of Uganda's population, was not a possible national language or even lingua franca of the Bantu-speaking area of the country. Other Ugandans tended to view the Baganda as imperialists within the country. Luganda was never a possibility for the north of Uganda. The two possible languages for the country were English and Swahili. English had never been in widespread use outside the highest levels of administration, law, and education and it was thoroughly élitist. Swahili had limited uses but low prestige and the Baganda were opposed to it, preferring their own language and regarding any extension of Swahili as a direct threat to their own prestige. They had even managed to have the teaching of Swahili ended in the schools during colonial times, and immediately after independence succeeded in keeping the language off the radio. English therefore remained the official language of Uganda after independence largely by default.

The privileged status of Luganda did, however, carry over after independence until 1966, when Obote deposed the Kabaka of Buganda. He then tried to find ways of reducing ethnic conflict. To do so he maintained English as the language of administration, believing it to be the most neutral choice in the circumstances. When Amin deposed him, Swahili, the language of the army, suddenly became important and its importance grew as Amin became increasingly dictatorial and indulged in ethnic conflict with a view to subduing the Bantu peoples in Uganda. Swahili came into more widespread use as the English-speaking élites were either reduced or eliminated, and Amin named it the national language of Uganda in 1973. Even when Amin was removed from power, the invasion by the Tanzanian army in 1979 gave Swahili a boost.

Today, Swahili is still the national language of Uganda but each of English, Swahili, and Luganda is an official language. Each has its own functions. English is found in use in the higher levels of administration, justice, and what advanced education remains. Swahili is widely used in business matters, among the lower classes in the towns, and in the army and police. Luganda is still the preferred language of the Baganda and is widely used in the capital itself. Of necessity such ministries as Culture, Education, and Agriculture find they must use some of the other vernaculars in their work. With the devastation of the last decade or more, it is difficult to predict what the future will bring to Uganda. Swahili is associated with the army and its tarnished reputation, and also with the 'liberating' Tanzanians, who outstayed their welcome. It is the prestige-less language of the streets with no ready appeal to those who aspire to learning or anything that extends their visions beyond the merely local. The vernacular languages are associated with the ethnic infighting that has bedeviled the country. Only English has emerged unscathed from recent conflicts, but the ranks of those who speak English and the resources for teaching and using it have been severely depleted.

Zaire also makes some use of Swahili. Zaire is a former Belgian colony in which French was, and continues to be, the language of the central administration. But Swahili is an important regional lingua franca. The variety of Swahili used in Zaire today in the industrialized Katanga province is different from the east coast variety. The difference arises from the rapid development of Swahili among a labour force that was brought in to work the mines in the early twentieth century. At that time the Belgian authorities wanted to make sure that an English-speaking labour force of mainly South African origin did not develop. They restricted the recruitment of anglophones and brought in black workers from elsewhere in Africa, and they encouraged the use of Swahili as the lingua franca of the mining towns that developed. By the time the Belgians left the Congo both French and Swahili were in widespread use there. The Belgians found it necessary to use Swahili in signs, notices, the conduct of business, the market place, and even to teach French. Swahili was the lingua franca of all and it became the native language of the children of many exogamous marriages in the working population. Tribal languages were also sometimes abandoned for the advantages that accrued from speaking Swahili.

The Belgians found this use of Swahili worked against their interests to some extent, in that it allowed those who spoke the language to maintain contact with Swahili speakers elsewhere. They often tried to promote Lingala in its place in their attempt to cut off the Congo from the outside world, just as they severely limited access to education in French for the same reason. After independence, Swahili became along with Lingala one of the important national languages of Zaire, the others being Kikongo and Ciluba. Swahili is also not spoken uniformly in Zaire and, while most of those who do speak it hold it in high regard, it has none of the standardized characteristics of either the Zanzibar or Mombasa varieties. Furthermore, when it competes with a European language, that language is French not English.

FURTHER READING

Arabs: Lewis 1966; Islam: Merad 1984; the Maghreb: Toumi 1982; arabization: Grandguillaume 1983, Heggoy 1984, Stevens 1983, Young 1976; the spread of English in Africa: Mazrui 1975; Swahili: Fabian 1986, Whiteley 1969; language issues in East Africa: Scotton 1982, Whiteley 1971, Young 1976; Tanzania: Abdulaziz-Mkilifi 1978, O'Barr and O'Barr 1976, Polomé and Hill 1980; Kenya: Whiteley 1974; Uganda: Ladefoged et al. 1972, Scotton 1972; Zambia: Ohannessian and Kashoki 1978.

9

Belgium, Switzerland, and Canada

Belgium and Switzerland are the two countries of Western Europe that always receive considerable attention in discussions of minority-language arrangements. Belgium is often cited as an example of a country which may fall apart at any time because of its precarious linguistic balance. On the other hand, Switzerland appears to be the best example one can find of a state in which groups speaking different languages have come to an arrangement, in which no group feels threatened, and in which all groups work together to continue the system that has evolved and to solve the problems that inevitably arise from time to time. Canada is a third country in which there is a sharp linguistic cleavage. It is also a country that has experienced some very recent linguistic turmoil as the French minority has sought to 'recapture' a territory that it felt it was losing to the English majority. Canadians have found it necessary in recent years once again to grapple with the issue of 'bilingualism' in Canada and to try to work out an arrangement between the English and French languages and peoples that is acceptable to all.

BELGIUM

Belgium is a state with a population of nearly 10 million but with no natural boundaries. In one sense it is a historic state in that it can trace its history back to the *Belgae* of Caesar's time. However, its modern history really dates from 1830, when it was quite clearly separated from the Netherlands, after its earlier separation from France in 1815. There is a fundamental linguistic cleavage in the state: the historic border for at least 1,000 years between the Romance and Germanic languages in Europe runs through the middle of Belgium in an east-west direction just south of Brussels. Like the borders of the country itself this border has no natural markers. In the French or Walloon area south of this line, the population uses French, just as do their neighbours to the south in France itself. The French area comprises the provinces of Hainaut, Namur, Luxembourg, and Liège. In the Dutch or Flemish area north of this line, the population uses a variety of Dutch just as do their neighbours to the north, the people of The Netherlands. The Dutch area comprises the provinces of West Flanders, East Flanders, Antwerp, Brabant (which includes Brussels), and Limburg. But the border is not as 'clean' as this: along this language border, particularly at its western extremity, are pockets of Dutch speakers in the French area and of French speakers in the Dutch area. On the eastern border of what is the French-speaking part of Belgium there are also small pockets of speakers of German along the borders with West Germany and Luxembourg. brussels itself is now officially bilingual but it is in the Dutch area and is surrounded by small pockets which are French-speaking.

Both the Dutch and French in Belgium look outside the country for standards for their languages. This is a little more difficult for the Dutch than for the French since the variety of Dutch that is spoken in Belgium is somewhat divergent from Standard Dutch. Some speakers of Dutch in Belgium seek to maintain the differences that exist so that they can continue to distinguish themselves from their neighbours in The Netherlands but the pressure exerted in education and in the media tends to reduce the differences that do exist. In contrast, Belgian French is quite close to the Standard French of France, and francophone Belgians are language purists at heart. Unlike the German Swiss they take no pride in speaking a clearly regional variety of a European language that has its centre in a neighbouring country, so Belgian French holds none of the attraction to its speakers that Swiss German has for those who use it. Both the Dutch and the French in Belgium are also encouraged to look to standards set elsewhere since neither wants to be contaminated by the other.

Although precise figures are not available about how many people speak each of the languages, it is estimated that about 56 per cent of the total population reside in the Dutch area of Belgium. The French area has about 32 per cent of the population. However, the capital city of Brussels with its 11 per cent of the total population and a population of over one million is located in the Dutch area. Although Brussels is officially bilingual, in actual fact it is a French-speaking city, second only to Paris in the world in importance in this respect. The German-speaking proportion of the population is minuscule, comprising less than 1 per cent of the total. Belgium now cleaves along language lines. Religion used to be an issue but the school settlement of 1958 which allowed public money to be used to support Roman Catholic education effectively removed religion as an issue in the political life of the country. There are now Roman Catholics and Protestants on both sides of any language issue that arises. Parties too are likely to split by language affiliation whenever language becomes an issue. In Belgium, groups form and compete along linguistic lines; other issues are far less important. Consequently, most of the political crises in recent decades can be traced directly to a failure to reach accommodation on linguistic issues.

Language has become such a divisive issue in Belgian political life that no longer does the Belgian government try to find out who speaks what language. The last census to seek such information was that of 1947 but the way the question was phrased and the uses to which the answers were put aroused so much hostility that Belgian censuses no longer seek to establish who actually speaks what language where. Instead the fiction prevails that in the area which is described as Dutch-speaking everyone speaks Dutch, and in the area which is described as French-speaking everyone speaks French. There are also German-speaking areas and 'protected' areas in which minorities are guaranteed certain linguistic rights, e.g., to use French in a German-speaking area or German in a French-speaking area. Brussels itself is designated as a bilingual area, and although only about 11 per cent of the population lives in this area, it has become the key battleground for the two major competing languages of Belgium. What is particularly interesting is that it is quite possible to argue that in Belgium both French and Dutch are minority languages but at the same time are also majority languages.

When the modern Belgian state came into existence in 1830, the language of the state was French even though the Dutch outnumbered the French. The first census of 1846 showed that, whereas 2.4 million were Dutch, only 1.8 million were French. Brussels was also a Dutch city dominated by the third of its population who used French. French was an important European language, French culture was highly regarded, and French was the language of opportunity. Dutch had none of the same attractions. It had not been standardized, and that fact alone made it unsuitable for the affairs of state. During the first part of the nineteenth century Dutch did indeed undergo standardization because the Netherlands found it necessary to have such a standardized language. The result is that the various dialects spoken in Belgium fell into disfavour as this standard variety became more and more available. But this disfavour simply mirrored the same disfavoured position of the Dutch themselves in Belgium.

In the nineteenth century the francophone élite of Belgium succeeded in constructing a unified and centralized state on the French model, one in which the French language had a clear ascendancy and in which

Brussels became an increasingly francophone city. The Dutch in Belgium found themselves in a strange situation: they were numerically a majority but linguistically a minority. Much of the modern internal history of Belgium can be explained as the attempt of this numerical majority to lose that minority status and to achieve some kind of parity in influence with the numerically smaller group. During the last hundred years we can see the fruits of this struggle in the gains that the Dutch have made.

In 1883 the Dutch won the right to have bilingual secondary schools in Flanders. The following year the country issued bilingual postage stamps for the first time. In 1886 it became possible to use Dutch in the Belgian Parliament and in 1898 Dutch became one of two official languages with laws to be written from that date in both languages. In 1921 the principle of territoriality was established under which certain parts of the country were to be administered in French and other parts in Dutch. In 1930 the University of Ghent received a new charter which made its language of instruction Dutch. In 1935 Dutch was recognized in the courts and in 1938 in the army. The last language census occurred in 1947 with the results not released until 1950. It showed almost no Dutch-speaking minorities in the French-speaking area, but numerous French-speaking minorities in the Dutch-speaking area, particularly around Brussels and in and around various other cities in the Dutch-speaking area. The census did lead to an agreement to maintain the existing language arrangements for a further ten years. By 1962 the principle that education in Dutch-speaking Belgium would be entirely in Dutch and in French-speaking Belgium entirely in French was firmly established. (The overriding principle that established such territorial unilingualism in education within Belgium was later upheld in 1968 by the European Court of Human Rights and accepted by the Council of Europe.) In 1967 the 1830 Belgian Constitution was finally translated into Dutch. Today, there is even a movement with the aim of dividing the nation in two because some Flemish nationalists in Belgium believe that only separation can guarantee those who speak Dutch all the rights they should have.

A key issue all along has been the linguistic situation in Brussels. Brussels lies in the Dutch-speaking part of Belgium, the most populous part of Belgium and in the last few decades also the most prosperous part. The Dutch in Belgium are not economically disadvantaged: they have prospered while the French have declined. However, the 1947 Census which created so much controversy showed that only one in four residents of Brussels spoke 'Dutch only or mainly'. French had become the language of Brussels. Speakers of Dutch who moved to Brussels quickly learned to speak French and their children generally were brought up as francophones. If anything this tendency has increased in recent decades, for today possibly as few as 20 per cent of the inhabitants of Brussels are Dutch or declare themselves to be so, and as many as 85 per cent are francophone. Moreover, the French area around Brussels has always been an expanding one. The language settlement that promised a kind of linguistic peace for the country required that Dutch be given equal influence within Brussels and that the spread of French beyond its borders be contained. Furthermore, the formula for allocating seats according to the populations of the variously designated linguistic areas favoured the Dutch only if Brussels were treated as a genuinely bilingual area in which parity existed between speakers of the two languages.

The 1960 Census, postponed to 1961, was to have included a question about language. The final census did not include such a question because of Dutch opposition. They preferred to live with the fiction of parity within Brussels which, along with their numerical superiority outside, would guarantee them majority representation in government. If Brussels had been treated as the francophone city it actually was, the French would have been able to claim a total superiority instead. The major important linguistic outcome of the discussions of this time was some minor territorial adjustments in 1962–3 to settle some of the problems that remained from the original language assignments. Among these were some adjustments to the bilingual area of Brussels itself. It is from this era that comes the linguistic settlement that now prevails in Belgium because only very minor tinkering has been allowed since that date.

It was a language issue that brought down the Belgian government in 1968, that of the future of the French-speaking University of Louvain. It became necessary to split both the University of Louvain and the Free University of Brussels into two institutions each, with one in each pair becoming a French university and the other Dutch. The new government also undertook to revise the Constitution to see if that would alleviate the difficulties the two major linguistic groups were experiencing in their relationships with each other. The revised Constitution transformed the unitary Belgian state into a community state. It guaranteed parity between the major linguistic communities, a process of adjusting the number of seats held by each linguistic area as the population varied, the protection of minorities, some cultural devolution, and the recognition of Brussels as a special region. It was a major step in turning what had been a unitary state into a quasi-federal one organized along language lines. In 1977 the various political parties in Belgium agreed to a further development in the same direction. Each of the three regions (Flanders, Wallonia, and Brussels) would gain considerable autonomy and have its own assembly. Brussels would also be limited in size to the existing 19 communes, but the French living on its periphery would have the same rights and facilities as the Dutch living within the city itself.

Belgium is now divided into four linguistic regions and each is a separate territorial entity: the Dutch, French, and German regions, and the bilingual area of Brussels. There are also three recognized cultural communities, the Dutch, French, and German, each now with its own community council. There are also three political and administrative regions: Flanders, Wallonia, and Brussels. Brussels has its own regional government with prescribed checks and balances. It also has three cultural commissions, one to look after French interests, another to look after Dutch interests, and the third to look after common interests. Linguistic parity between the languages is required in Cabinet appointments, although the prime minister may be of any linguistic background, and is not counted in decisions as to whether or not parity has been achieved. There is also a scheme of voting which requires double majorities so that one linguistic group cannot force its will on the other by a simple majority vote. There are virtually separate French and Dutch ministries for Education, Justice, and Interior, and among civil servants 40 per cent are required to be French-speaking, 40 per cent to be Dutch-speaking, and the remainder to be bilingual with the two language communities each supplying half of these. Minorities are also assured protection under the terms of the amended Constitution.

The result is a kind of linguistic balancing act. The French saw their overall numerical decline in spite of the control they had over Brussels. The new arrangements guaranteed that they would remain equal in political power in the country. The Dutch were willing to sacrifice their numerical superiority to contain the spread of French outward from Brussels and stop any further encroachment of French into Dutch territory. Even if they could do litle or nothing to increase the amount of Dutch used in Brussels (and every study shows that the various attempts to do this have been quite fruitless and that French still dominates at the very centre of the Belgian state), they received a guarantee that the fiction of a bilingual Brussels would be maintained. For the residents of bilingual Brussels the settlement meant that parents were guaranteed education for their children in the language of their choice, which was, of course, a guarantee to the large majority who sought it that French-language education would be available to their children.

Just under 1 per cent of the Belgian population is German-speaking. These people reside either in the province of Luxembourg, and have been citizens of Belgium since 1830, or in the province of Liège, and have been citizens of Belgium only since 1919. They live in the French-speaking part of Belgium and feel that, although they have certain linguistic privileges and protections, their language and identity are threatened because they lack the power to regulate their own affairs. In World War II some of the German-speaking Belgians supported the invading Germans, who actively courted them just as they courted dissident Flemish, and it has taken other Belgians a long time to forgive them for this. Today, however, there is a growing movement in this German-speaking area to preserve the language and to give German the same rights in Belgium as both French and Dutch enjoy. The German situation is made worse by the fact that the group resides in the French part of Belgium, a region that is in decline both economically and demographically. The French have nothing to gain by encouraging a separate German identity in their own midst.

Most observers agree that the Belgian state has a considerable potential for disintegration over language issues. The twentieth century has seen a hardening of the linguistic boundary within Belgium. The boundary that marks the linguistic division between the French and the Dutch and the anomalous position of Brussels have created a cleavage within Belgium that has replaced almost all other cleavages. Previous cross-cutting cleavages actually served to unite Belgians across linguistic lines: French Catholics could unite with Dutch Catholics against French Protestants united with Dutch Protestants over such issues as religion in the schools, independently of their language differences. Much of the dispute in Belgium's political life in the late nineteenth century focused on just this issue of religion. Later, socioeconomic issues became the focus of Belgium's political divisions. Again though, the issues cut across linguistic divisions. Governments and political oppositions could draw on both the French and the Dutch in support of particular religious or economic positions. In fact, Belgium is often cited as a prime example of the consociational model of democratic government because of its success in resolving internal conflicts in this way. Issues which threatened national peace could be resolved through the accommodations that the political élites would arrange, accommmodations that would leave the political balance unchanged. No particular issue was allowed to get out of control because all interest groups would be involved in the decision making and no issue was allowed to become a 'single issue', i.e., one that would override all others.

What disrupted the consociational system was the growth of Flemish nationalism, Walloon resistance to this, and the uncertainty created by the position of Brussels in any resulting settlement of the linguistic dispute that arose. Accommodation gave way to confrontation on a single issue, that of language. Other loyalties and interests were forgotten. Parties restructured themselves along linguistic and regional lines. Extremist positions became easy to adopt, and, as extremism flourished, compromise became less and less possible. The two world wars also hardened attitudes since during both wars the Flemish profited from the anti-French position of the occupying Germans. However, their gains were turned to losses when the wars ended as on both occasions the French took the opportunity of victory to suppress Flemish nationalism. The period after World War II, with its disputes about the position of the royal family, the schools of the country, and its general strike, further exacerbated linguistic tension.

One response was a growth of federalism, even among the French. But Belgium is still nominally a unitary state. Its success had depended on a series of internal political compromises over religious and economic issues and the avoidance of ethnic conflict on a regional basis. In recent decades, however, that unitary state has been rapidly turning into a federalist one, in spirit if not in fact, a federalist state of three parts – a Flemish north, a Walloon south, and Brussels, the anomaly. Even the national political parties have been forced to reorganize along 'federal' lines. It was the linguistic arrangements negotiated in the 1960s that thoroughly undergirded this kind of quasi-federalist solution to Belgium's problem.

Linguistic conflict strikes at the heart of the present state. Of the two major groups the Dutch are the more language-conscious since they have traditionally been the disadvantaged group in Belgium. But the French too are beginning to discover how much their position has eroded as they see their status reduced, their economic power decline, and their numerical superiority in Brussels effectively denied. Brussels is, of course, a 'hot spot' for both language groups. The 1970 Constitution tried to resolve many of the issues through a thorough separation of the two languages and stabilization of the linguistic boundary in and around Brussels. The system arrived at in the 1970s can work only if the two languages can achieve equality in some kind of dual system within a unitary state. However, if both groups within the state continue to feel threatened, if economic differences between the regions continue to increase, if the issue of Brussels comes to the fore again, and if boundary disputes between the two languages cannot be resolved, then it is hard to see how Belgium can continue as a unitary state. Various 'language' incidents in the 1970s and 1980s have led to riots, ministerial resignations and attempts to resign, and the inability to form a national government for a protracted period. There is no indication either that we have seen the last of such incidents.

Lijphart (1981, p. 1) has said: 'Belgium can legitimately claim to be the most thorough example of consociational democracy, the type of democracy that is most suitable for deeply divided societies'. It *is* deeply divided, and there is a further potential division that we should note. Nearly one in ten of Belgium's population is an immigrant worker or is a family member of such a worker. One worker in three in Brussels is actually a foreigner. Most such workers and their families claim that they will be returning to their countries of origin, but many will not return. Belgians themselves have not been particularly eager to assimilate such people or to deal with them in some kind of pluralistic system. They see them as a 'problem', in the same way that citizens of other Western European countries view equivalent groups. As these migrants become an increasingly permanent feature of Belgian society by deciding to stay rather than to leave, they will affect the delicate linguistic balance that has been achieved, particularly in Brussels to which they are attracted. They will also introduce further linguistic and cultural differences into an already divided society. It remains to be seen how Belgians will adapt to these new circumstances

Accommodation between the two major groups in Belgium is possible only if each has something to gain; at present it is not clear what either has to gain, except remaining somehow 'Belgian' in the world. That may not be enough. It may be better to be a 'Walloon' rather than a French-speaking Belgian or a 'Flamand' rather than a Dutch-speaking one. More and more Belgians have begun to entertain such a future for themselves, perhaps within a United States of Europe. But we must remember how extraordinarily difficult it is in the modern world to bring about such a rearrangement. Although separatism may be fashionable in some quarters, it can point to only a single success story, Bangladesh, and that was undoubtedly a fluke.

SWITZERLAND

Switzerland is often cited as a model for those states that contain more than one language. In fact, Switzerland is a state in which there is more than one minority language and in which those who speak the majority language, German, do not seek to exert their linguistic superiority over those who do not speak that language, preferring instead to share power and influence with them. The linguistic harmony that exists in Switzerland stems from a combination of keeping the languages apart and a system of government that is highly decentralized. Each of the Swiss cantons has full cultural and political autonomy as well as absolute control of the language that is to be used within its borders. Moreover, there is a well-established nationwide system of checks and balances for settling internal disputes, which, together with a strong feeling of Swiss identity and a posture of international neutrality, enables the Swiss people both to solve problems as they occur and to maintain their prosperity. Only the controversy over the Jura has seriously marred the internal linguistic peace of Switzerland in recent years. It was a kind of aberration in Swiss life, but one that the Swiss succeeded in correcting.

The present language distribution in Switzerland dates fom the Middle Ages, when part of the Alpine region was germanized, and the four linguistic regions of modern Switzerland were established. This process occurred before any kind of Swiss state came into being. In fact, at this time members of each of the language groups had more in common with those who spoke their language elsewhere than they had with one another. A loose confederation of Swiss states was formed in the Middle Ages; it was a military defensive alliance of 13 cantons originating in 1291. As early as 1515 it adopted a policy of neutrality toward other states. The working language of this confederation was German. During the revolutionary period at the end of the eighteenth century this loosely organized federation was succeeded briefly by a highly centralized Helvetic Republic which lasted until 1803, with its Constitution made in Paris. It was the Constitution of this republic that for the first time guaranteed the linguistic equality of German, French, and Italian in Switzerland. Between 1798 and 1848 the Swiss experimented with a variety of linguistic arrangements as the political climate of the times changed, until finally in the latter year the modern federation came into being with its three equal official languages, German, French, and Italian, to which a fourth, Romansch, was added as a national language much later.

We should note that the cantons form the basic building blocks of the Swiss state. It has been said that before 1848 Swiss federal politics was more like international relations than national politics. Only after 1848 did a federal government with any kind of power materialize with control over an army, a bureaucracy, a federal capital, etc. Federal political parties in Switzerland have always eschewed a 'winner take all' philosophy. They see themselves as groups that must necessarily exist in order to provide the state with a central government, the members of which must serve all interests in Switzerland not just those who happened to elect them.

The 1980 Census showed that among all the residents of Switzerland 65 per cent were German-speaking, 18.4 per cent were French-speaking, 9.8 per cent were Italian-speaking, 0.8 per cent were Romansch-speaking, and the remaining 6 per cent spoke other languages. Among the 5.2 million Swiss citizens 73.6 per cent spoke German, 20 per cent spoke French, 4.5 per cent spoke Italian, and 0.9 per cent spoke Romansch. Over a 40-year period these percentages have remained fairly stable in the case of German, but have showed a rise from the 3.9 per cent of 1941 in Italian and slow declines in French and Romansch. Well over 90 per cent of those who speak German and French live in cantons in which their languages are completely protected. The percentage is lower – about 80 per cent – for those who speak Italian.

Numerically, the Germans dominate the Swiss state but the cantonal structure guarantees other groups rights in their own territories. The Germans of Switzerland are now quite proud of the fact that they are different from the other German-speaking peoples of Europe. They even take pride in their variety of German, known as *Schwyzertütsch* (Swiss German) in contrast to *Hochdeutsch* (High German). They continue to speak their local variety but write the standard variety. This diglossic situation seems to be an entirely twentieth-century phenomenon, because at the beginning of the century it appeared that the spoken variety of Standard German was about to make huge inroads into Switzerland. However, insistence on Swiss neutrality reinforced resistance to Standard German and the twentieth century has actually witnessed an ever-increasing use of the Swiss variety of spoken German. Today, less and less use is made of spoken Standard German in the media, religious worship, political debate, and even in higher education. When the Swiss speak Standard German, they are also likely to sound formal and bookish because of their unfamiliarity with its nuances.

Currently, Switzerland has three official languages – German, French, and Italian – and since 1938 a fourth language – Romansch – has been recognized as a national language. Any of the official languages can be used in parliament, and all federal laws are published in the official languages. While laws are introduced and passed in all three official languages – and no language has legal precedent over any other when there is any conflict over interpretation – only certain laws have been translated into Romansch, e.g., the Civil Code, the Penal Code, and the Bankruptcy Law. The federal government must also deal with individual citizens in an official language of the citizen's choice. Moreover, each of these languages must be represented in the highest court in the land, the Federal Tribunal.

The federal system in Switzerland holds the three official languages as equal to one another and none is a 'minority' language. The national language, Romansch, also has the same status of equality whenever it is used. With the exception of matters under the jurisdiction of the federal government, cantons have complete sovereignty within their borders, including over language matters. The territorial linguistic integrity of each canton is assumed as a basic principle. A canton has no obligation to provide services in any language but its official language; moreover, residents of the canton are obliged to use that language in dealing with cantonal matters and their children must be educated in it. Only in officially designated bilingual cantons and municipalities are exceptions made to this principle.

In the seat of the federal government, Bern, the language of work is almost exclusively German, sometimes French, and only very rarely Italian. Most documents originate in German and German is regarded as the language in which work gets done most promptly and efficiently. French-speaking civil servants see few career prospects in the federal civil service and it was not until 1981, in an exception to the territorial principle of language distribution, that French-speaking civil servants in Bern were allowed to send their children to schools in the city which were specially opened for them and in which French would be the language of instruction. In spite of such difficulties French remains a language of prestige in Switzerland: the German Swiss have shown no reluctance to learn French or to use it in cross-language contacts.

The major language dispute in Switzerland has been over the Jura where French-speaking Jurassians sought political autonomy. This desire for autonomy was a long-standing one. The Jurassians objected to the settlement arranged under the Treaty of Vienna that placed them within the German canton of Bern, and as a result during the nineteenth century French–German relationships in the canton were sometimes quite stormy. In its modern phase the problem of the Jura goes back to 1947, for it is from that year that we can date the most recent attempt of this French-speaking minority of the German-speaking canton of Bern to gain linguistic autonomy. Not all the French-speaking Jurassians were in favour of some separate status because the issue was not simply a linguistic one. Bern was mainly Protestant and, while most of the French were Catholics, a significant minority in the South Jura were not, and these accepted the status quo, fearing that they would be submerged in a Catholic canton if complete separation were successful. The separatist movement therefore developed in the three most northern districts of the canton where French-speaking Catholics sought separate cantonal status for themselves.

The 1947 crisis over the refusal of the cantonal government to approve a speaker of French to a government portfolio led to certain constitutional changes within the canton by 1950. These changes recognized that the canton contained two peoples, and allowed for the Jurassian flag to be flown alongside the Bernese flag. It granted full equality to the French language and even required that French alone should be used in the six French-speaking districts of the Jura. The Jurassians were also assured of two seats in the cantonal government. However, they were not given the separate electoral districts and chamber which a number of them had sought. The separatists were not satisfied. They rallied behind their organization, the Rassemblement Jurassien, and the French Protestants of the south formed the Union des Patriotes Jurassiens to oppose them. The lines of battle were drawn.

It took 25 years to resolve most of the issues. During these years there was a certain amount of violence but there were also constant efforts to resolve the various issues through the ballot box in a series of plebiscites in 1959, 1974, and 1975. The 1959 plebiscite was designed to settle the issue of whether the French-speaking area would become a separate canton, although that was not how the actual issue was phrased. When all the votes were tallied, the proposal was very narrowly defeated, the wishes of the Protestant south having prevailed over those of the Catholic north. The French-speakers of the northern Jura were dissatisfied with the results and resolved to continue their struggle for their own canton. However, the Bernese government considered that the plebiscite had settled the issue and refused to negotiate any further.

The issue would not go away, and by the late 1960s it became apparent that some new arrangement would have to be worked out if there was to be peace in the Jura. Consequently, the cantonal constitution was amended to allow for a series of plebiscites which would allow the various communities in the Jura to determine their future. The 1974 plebiscite which asked whether the people of the Jura wanted a separate canton showed that the Catholic French were strongly in favour of this separate status but that the Protestant French were just as strongly opposed. Overall though, the vote was for a separate Jura. The next issue became that of deciding which communities would form that separate Jura. Further plebiscites in 1974 and 1975 decided that issue, but not without arousing considerable animosity between those who wanted to separate and those who did not. A new Jura canton emerged; all the communities with a Catholic majority joined it, and all those with a Protestant majority stayed with the canton of Bern.

The separatists were not at all happy with this result. They wanted to see all the speakers of French united in a single canton. They were of the opinion that the vote had resulted the way it had because many immigrants to the French-speaking areas from the German-speaking part of Switzerland had voted against separation, and these people were not really native to the area. It was the opinion of the separatists that their right to vote on this issue could only be exercised at the expense of the rights of the French-speaking residents of the area. Many of those of German-Swiss background actually now speak French in this part of Switzerland, so this argument was not a very strong one. Moreover, the Swiss Constitution gave them the right to vote, since it does not distinguish within any particular area on the basis of language, and insists that all residents of a particular area have a right to be consulted on matters that affect them.

The constitution proposed for the new canton of Jura contained a provision that it would accept any territory that was the subject to the

1974 plebiscite should that territory decide to secede from its current arrangements with both the federal government and its cantonal government. However, the Swiss federal government disallowed this part of the proposed constitution, and when the new Jura canton came into existence in 1979, after the 1978 plebiscite in which 82 per cent of the Swiss voters approved the new constitution for the Jura, it was without such a provision. The new arrangement has not satisfied the more militant French of the north who wish to see the Jura extend to the south. There are certain localities which could easily be added to the French-speaking Jura but there is little likelihood that this will happen while the rhetoric remains heated.

The plebiscite of 1978 fixed the present boundary between Bern and Jura. How long it will stay fixed is a matter of conjecture. Religion seems to be less and less a force to be reckoned with so it is quite possible that the Protestant–Catholic division that split the French will not be as important in the future as it was in the past. Those of German ancestry in the French-speaking area of what has remained part of Bern also learn French and sometimes even identify themselves as French. If this tendency to assume a French identity continues to strengthen as religious distinctions continue to weaken, much of the area that borders on the Jura may find it has a greater identity with the Jura than with Bern. Since there are no large towns along the border or large cities involved in the basic dispute and the linguistic boundaries are no stronger than recently established cantonal ones, there also appears to be plenty of room for linguistic gains and losses along the border that emerged in the late 1970s.

The resolution of the Jura problem was 'typically' Swiss. A way was found to defuse what almost anywhere else would have been a state-threatening crisis. The Swiss have a long history of trying to resolve differences at the level where they affect people directly. In this case the issue was that of the future of the Jura. Even the citizens of the old canton of Bern came to recognize that the people of the Jura, not of Bern as a whole, had to decide the issue. A century or more of Bernese control of the Jura had ended in failure; it was time for the Jura to find a solution for its future. All that was necessary was to work out an appropriate procedure, one that would involve all those who would be affected. The series of plebiscites was the result. Unlike similar disputes in Canada and Belgium, local disputes of this kind do not pit one part of the whole country against the other part. Instead, the dispute is localized between neighbouring cantons and others keep out. Moreover, the dispute occurs within a constitutional and linguistic arrangement which favours solutions rather than one which tends to exacerbate conflict. As we have noted, though, whether or not the solution arrived at will be ultimately successful is still of some interest, since it is still too early yet to appraise the full consequences of the divisions created by the votes of the 1970s.

Italian speakers comprise only a small fraction of the Swiss population, but once again they form a clear majority in the part of Switzerland they occupy, the canton of Ticino. However, it is a part of Switzerland that is becoming increasingly attractive to other Swiss and even to Italians from Italy. In the major economic and cultural centres such as Locarno and Lugano, over 80 per cent of the population speak Italian, and the language is secure there. But in some of the remoter valleys of Ticino the Italian-speaking population has fallen to close to 50 per cent, as outsiders buy up property and weaken the indigenous Italian language and culture. The pressure the Italians feel in Ticino is from the increasing numbers of German-speaking Swiss who have come to prefer to live or retire in that part of Switzerland. They bring with them their language, and make it all that more difficult for the Italians of Ticino to maintain an Italian-Swiss identity, particularly at a time when Italians in Switzerland enjoy none of the status of the Germans or French. Switzerland also has a policy of recruiting low-paid 'guestworker' help from countries such as Italy, and, in particular, from the poorest parts of those countries. These guestworkers have boosted the use of Italian in Switzerland, and Italian has even become the lingua franca of guestworkers from such countries as Yugoslavia, Turkey, and Greece. But this is a mixed blessing, for it does nothing to enhance the status of Italian within Switzerland as a whole.

The one truly endangered language of Switzerland is Romansch (or Rhaeto-Romance, or Ladin), a language spoken in a variety of dialects by about 40,000 residents of the canton of Graubünden (or Grisons). All speakers of Romansch also speak Swiss German, although not always very well. Speakers of Romansch are also likely to have mixed feelings about their language, and will often readily acknowledge the 'superiority' of German. Although in recent years more and more young people have been taking pride in the fact that they can speak Romansch, nevertheless it is difficult for them to resist the proces of germanization and to hold on to whatever Romansch–German bilingualism they have. Romansch controls no cities or towns and the largest urban concentration in Graubünden is in Chur, where 11 per cent of the city's population of 30,000 speak the language. The next largest urban concentration is actually in Zürich, where there are 2,500 speakers of Romansch but these comprise less than 1 per cent of that city's population. Romansch is also increasingly limited in its functions: it is used in the home and still sometimes in agriculture, but less and less in both.

Romansch has been a language in steady decline over the last half millenium That it has lasted so long may be attributable to the fact that it was spoken in a region of isolated valleys and also to the fact that it was long supported by the cantonal authorities in keeping with the Swiss spirit of linguistic tolerance. Today, the isolated valleys where Romansch survives are no longer isolated. They are popular with tourists and many Swiss of German-speaking and Italian-speaking backgrounds have chosen to live there. They are also dominated by mass media in which there is almost no place for Romansch, since there are no daily newspapers published in the language and it is used on radio and television only a very few hours a week. Consequently, German now predominates in much of the northern area of the canton and Italian in the south.

By a referendum in 1938 Romansch became a national language of Switzerland but not an official one. The referendum itself was held at the instigation of the Romansch speakers. Italy was trying to make a claim for this part of Switzerland and for the loyalty of speakers of Romansch, going so far as attempting to establish that Romansch was a dialect of Italian. Status as a national language gives Romansch some protection in the area in which it is spoken, that is, within Graubünden, enabling children, for example, to receive a bilingual education in Romansch and one of the official languages in their primary school years. Secondary education, however, is exclusively in German, but it is possible to study Romansch at certain of the Swiss universities and to take training in the teaching of Romansch. National-language status also enables those who speak Romansch to deal with the cantonal government in Romansch and to use that language in cantonal courts. The language cannot be used, however, in dealing with the federal government or in its courts.

In spite of the protection that has been traditionally afforded to Romansch each successive census shows that fewer and fewer Swiss as a proportion of the whole population speak the language. There are several reasons for this. One is that Romansch has only a very local appeal in comparison to German, French, and Italian. A second is that each of these languages has a neighbouring country in which many millions speak the language. A third is that each of these languages also has a highly standadized form and a flourishing literature. Romansch is lacking on all three of these counts. There are economic reasons too. In the high valleys in which Romansch is spoken there has been a decline in the farming industry. The young have often preferred emigration to other parts of Switzerland to staying and trying to make a living. When they do stay, they often have to make that living catering to the influx of tourists and other outsiders who see the high valleys as a desirable place to live or to pursue recreational activities. Such immigration further weakens any hold that Romansch might have.

Unlike the French of the Jura, the speakers of Romansch have not campaigned for any kind of separate status. No leadership with that aim has emerged. They have been content with what protection they have been given and with what they have achieved. However, this mutual tolerance is not likely to change the basic situation that exists. Quite simply, if the economic decline of the area in which Romansch is spoken continues and there is no change in the patterns of migration, it must inevitably happen that Romansch will continue its decline and begin to exhibit all the characteristics of a moribund language.

Language has not become a divisive issue in Switzerland the way it has in Belgium. The Jura is an isolated example. While it is true that the French and German Swiss may not view international issues in the same way, they tend to adopt a common view on internal matters. Linguistic issues are not allowed to threaten the state. The constitutional system encourages the local resolution of difficulties and the avoidance of disputes that might drag on over decades and even centuries. Even cantonal boundaries are not sacrosanct; they can be modified if the situation warrants, as in the Jura.

The Swiss could divide themselves internally in a number of different ways. The Germans could attempt to control all aspects of life in the country because they comprise an overwhelming majority of the population. Or there could be a Protestant–Catholic division since these two religious groups are roughly equal in numbers. However, in late twentieth-century Europe such a division by religion seems rather unlikely. Or an attempt could be made to structure political loyalties on the basis of socioeconomic interests, a much more likely scenario. Switzerland could develop a two-party system with one party 'winning' power periodically and then 'losing' it to the other. However, Swiss political life has not been framed in terms of such winning and losing. Moreover, the country is federal in nature, and national solutions and national political life depend on the consent of the cantonal units.

In the Swiss view majorities do not force their will on minorities, not even in the mild way this imposition is done in other systems in which political regimes change as a result of democratic elections. The Swiss prefer to use plebiscites to sound out mass opinion (e.g., on the issue of health insurance) and to form coalitions to work out solutions. Majorities even take in minorities when they form governments. This allows minorities to share in the power. The structure of the Swiss Federal Council itself is a good example of this sharing: it must mirror the composition of the Swiss electorate as that composition is revealed every four years in elections. So for five speakers of German there will be at least one, usually two, of French and one of Italian. This is one way of ensuring that all groups affected by decisions are consulted and that no group is left out of the decision-making process. Linguistic minorities not only have the constitutional guarantees afforded under the Swiss Constitution, but they also have the special guarantees in their cantons in which they form a majority, or in those in which they form part of a 'bilingual' community, and even some in those in which they are a genuine minority. They are consulted or co-opted and they are not rendered powerless. In this way the Swiss try to avoid any possibility that linguistic differences will tear apart the fabric of their federal state.

Switzerland has proved to be a remarkable success story for linguistic accommodation. McRae (1983, p. 240) says that Swiss linguistic coexistence 'has been built upon an intricate combination of historical, structural, attitudinal, and institutional factors skillfully and patiently woven into a reinforcing pattern by human effort and statesmanship'. A wide variety of differences has been dealt with in the system that has resulted, not just linguistic ones alone but religious, economic, and social issues too. Switzerland even survived the very severe test of World War I, when there were fundamental differences between the French and Germans in Switzerland over which side in that war deserved Swiss sympathy. Partly as a result of that experience a 'Swiss way' of resolving issues is firmly entrenched in the country. For example, Swiss Germans are proud of their own variety of German, and the Swiss French find little appeal in la Francophonie: neither Standard German nor la Francophonie are part of that 'Swiss way'.

There are, however, a few danger signals that cannot be ignored. There is considerable unilingualism in Switzerland, and often English is the second language that is learned rather than another of the country's official languages. The Swiss cannot always easily talk to one another but their efforts to localize problems reduce difficulties. Swiss German is also inward-looking rather than outward-looking, and cuts Swiss Germans off from other speakers of German elsewhere. It also makes the learning of German more difficult for the French and Italians of Switzerland since it is not at all easy to acquire a 'low' language in a diglossic situation except by living among those who use it. Finally, the 'guestworker' group within Switzerland has shifted the linguistic balance. The new balance seems to favour the Italians, but this may be only a temporary phenomenon. It certainly disfavours the French. However, the long-term winners are likely to be the Germans, as German is almost certainly the language that the second and third generations will come to use in most cases. However, the whole history of Switzerland would suggest that the country will find none of these issues intractable.

CANADA

Although constitutionally 'bilingual' in certain respects, Canada is predominantly an English-speaking country. There is a French presence in Canada, but in Canada as a whole and in the wider context of the entire North American continent that French presence is quite small. Quebec is a French island in an ocean of English. As we will see, the French have met with resistance in any efforts they have made to spread their language beyond that island. Moreover, they have constantly been assaulted by English within their own territory to the extent that in recent years they have had to adopt measures designed to stem any further incursion of English. Today, Quebec must be constantly on guard if it is to remain French-speaking. Regularly losing speakers to English, the province must find ways to replace these. What we see in Quebec then is a kind of organized rearguard action to preserve French, one which has had both successes and failures, but one from which the French themselves can seek no respite.

Canada is a federal state with a population of 24.3 million at the 1981 Census. It is a bilingual country in that it has two official languages, English and French, each with certain rights and protections. The two languages themselves exist in a fundamentally unequal relationship, historically and demographically. In that inequality lies the explanation of much of the linguistic discontent that has been behind the difficult relationship that has existed between the government of Quebec and the federal government in Ottawa since the 1960s.

The English and French competed in colonizing the northern part of North America. That competition was ended in 1759 when the English finally conquered the French in a decisive battle on the Plains of Abraham and captured the city of Quebec. Canada came into existence at that time; it was a British possession to the north of those colonies that were soon to break away from the Crown and unite to form a new country, the United States of America. Canada stayed loyal, and gradually expanded to include other British possessions in North America and to fill the prairies to the north of the United States.

Canada actually dates its origin as a virtually independent state to 1867, the year of the British North America Act. This Act of the British Parliament was the last of a series of constitutional arrangements made in London to provide some kind of governing structure for this British colonial possession in North America. The 1867 Constitution established a framework for self-government, but it was actually not until 1982 that the government of Canada and the government of the United Kingdom finally 'patriated' the Canadian Constitution, i.e., gave Canada complete charge of its own constitutional affairs.

Under the arrangement made in 1867 the French in Canada seemed assured of opportunities to spread their language and culture as the nation itself spread westward. They were guaranteed the right to use their language in their own province of Quebec, although a right to use English was also entrenched there, and they were encouraged to believe that as French settlers went west they would find adequate guarantees of their linguistic rights elsewhere in Canada. Since the French tended to have large families, natural population growth would also favour them. The French viewed the 1867 agreement as one between two 'founding peoples' and they looked forward to an era in which English and French would be in a position of perfect equality in the new country, particularly as it opened up the West for settlement.

Whatever hopes the French had for maintaining equality with the English were soon dashed. For example, in the last few years of the nineteenth century the newly (1870) created province of Manitoba abrogated what rights the French had to their language in that province, rights that were not restored until 1985. Increasingly the French in Canada found themselves confined to Quebec, itself dominated by the English of Montreal. Only the high birth rate in the province, the 'revenge of the cradles', kept the French relatively secure there, making up for both the considerable emigration of francophones to the United States, the 'fatal haemorrhage', and the increase in the anglophone population in the province. As the French found themselves more and more confined to Quebec and saw the progressive loss of French speakers outside that province to English, they became acutely conscious of the danger they faced, that of the extinction of their language in North America.

The French did have certain protections, both constitutionally and as a result of a variety of practices that had developed over the years. For example, Quebec was guaranteed a certain number of seats in the federal parliament, and the remaining non-Quebec seats had to be allocated in proportion to the non-Quebec population. There was always French representation on the Supreme Court of Canada and in the the federal cabinet. Royal commissions quite often had English and French co-chairpersons when these inquired into legal and cultural matters. The federal Liberal Party had a tradition of alternating anglophone and francophone leaders and, since it was the party most frequently in power during the twentieth century, the French segment of the population sometimes provided the country's prime minister. Francophones were also to be found in the civil service and armed forces but more frequently at the lower levels than in senior positions. The overall system, however, was one in which the English in Canada clearly had the ascendancy in a federal system of nine anglophone provinces and a solitary francophone one. The system was also one of majority rule, and this furthered competition and antagonism rather than any kind of consociationalism. The result was 'two solitudes' in Canada, two peoples largely cut off from each other, each with its own view of Canadian history and identity, with little chance of reconciliation.

By the 1960s it was evident that certain developments that had occurred required a rethinking of the relationship between the English and the French in Canada and of the two languages. By the 1960s it was apparent that about 80 per cent of the 30 per cent or so of Canadians who were of French origin were located in Quebec. Moreover that proportion was falling and still continues to fall, being 30.4 per cent in 1961, 28.7 per cent in 1971, and 26.8 per cent in 1981. The 20 per cent of the French who lived outside the province had either already given up their language or appeared well on the way to doing so. Only in areas adjacent to Quebec, in the so-called 'bilingual belt', i.e., parts of the province of New Brunswick to the east and parts of eastern and northern Ontario to the west, did the language have any degree of security. What was more threatening, though, were two factors within the province of Quebec. The first was that the birth rate there had fallen to become the lowest in Canada. The French in Canada could no longer be sure that they could maintain their historic proportion of the overall Canadian population, something in the proportion of 30 per cent. The second was that immigrants to Quebec from outside Canada were settling in Montreal and learning English, the language of the anglophone élite and of power in that city, not French. In this way the already strong English minority in the province was gaining converts from those who were of neither English nor French origin. Immigrants to Quebec saw the English language rather than the French language as offering a better future for themselves and their children. This choice was the obvious one everywhere else in Canada; it was particularly threatening to the French that it would also seem so obvious in Montreal.

In 1963 the government of Canada appointed a Royal Commission on Bilingualism and Biculturalism to look into the relationship between the English and French in Canada and make recommendations for changes. In its report to parliament the commission completely rejected any 'territorial' solution to the problems the country faced with regard to language. Its recommendations led to the Official Languages Act of 1969, which guaranteed the French everywhere in Canada certain basic rights in dealing with the federal government and its various agencies. The act also proposed a number of measures to guarantee support of the French language outside Quebec, measures that would in some way provide this minority with some of the support that the English minority in Quebec itself had enjoyed since 1867. Parliament's intention was to provide a measure of security for the French language outside Quebec by placing it on an equal footing with English so far as the federal government was concerned and, in doing so, appease those in Quebec itself who were beginning to seek a new deal for the province within the federal structure.

Parliament appointed a Commissioner of Official Languages, a kind of linguistic ombudsman, to report annually to it on the progress, or lack of progress, that had been made in carrying out the the numerous provisions of the Act. The Act itself created a considerable controversy, being regarded by many anglophones as a device to be used to 'push French down our throats'. Over the years since its passage the enforcement of its provisions has brought about much controversy and not a little strife, most notably a crisis over the language, or languages, of air traffic control in 1976. The Act has also been criticized by many who were of neither English nor French origin for giving French a status it appeared no longer to merit in certain parts of Canada, particularly those parts in which speakers of languages other than English or French outnumbered francophones, or in which the francophone population had become virtually extinct as a result of previous policies and attitudes.

But whatever the controversies and disagreements, when Canada finally patriated its Constitution in 1982 certain rights of the French to their language in Canada were enshrined in that document. In future, the language rights of the French in Canada can be changed only after a complicated process of constitutional amendment; they can no longer be changed merely by a simple majority vote in any parliamentary session. The government of Quebec refused to sign the constitutional document because it did not appear to go far enough to protect Quebec's interests and the interests of the French outside Quebec, so not even the new Constitution can be said to have resolved the major differences between the English and French at the federal level.

At the same time as the government of Canada was guaranteeing French rights throughout the country as a whole, the government of Quebec was taking measures to minimize the use of English within that province. Quebec had modernized during the 'Quiet Revolution' of the early 1960s and created a new sense of purpose, a national sentiment, an intelligentsia, and its own cultural outlets. Now it was time to put its linguistic house in order. While the federal government saw its mission as one of extending bilingualism into the rest of Canada, the provincial government of Quebec saw its task to be that of restoring French unilingualism within the province. Successive Quebec governments therefore passed a variety of bills designed to make French the language of work in Quebec and to require residents of Quebec to be educated in French except when they had a constitutional right to be educated in English. The last of these laws, Bill 101, the Charter of the French Language, was passed in 1977 by a Parti Québécois government that swept into power in 1976 on a separatist platform. Bill 101 established an Office de la Langue Française to promote the use of French in the workplace and English was even banned from signs in the province. However, it was the provisions in the bill that dealt with education that became a major issue between the federal and provincial governments, because Quebec opted for a very narrow interpretation of the constitutional right to education in English in the province. In 1984 the Supreme Court of Canada ruled that Quebec's interpretation was too narrow and voided those parts of Bill 101 that had restricted anglophone rights to an education in English in Quebec to those who could demonstrate that they had such rights because their parents had been educated in English in the province. The separatist ambitions of the Parti Québécois were also thwarted in a 1980 referendum when 59.5 per cent of the provincial electorate voted against seeking a separatist solution to Quebec's problems through 'sovereignty association'. The Parti Québécois finally lost power in 1985.

The 1982 Constitution and the willingness of the Supreme Court to enforce its provisions were not all detrimental to the French cause in Canada. For nearly a century the French in Manitoba had been denied certain rights that had been guaranteed to them under Section 23 of the Manitoba Act when that province was created in 1870. The Supreme Court ruled that these rights, which had been taken away in 1890, had to be restored even though the demographic composition of the province today is quite different from what it was when the rights were abrogated. There are very few francophones left in Manitoba – about five per cent of the province's population – so it is not surprising that this decision of the Supreme Court appears to some observers to be almost a classic case of 'closing the stable door after the horse has gone'. Restoring the rights will also be a costly process, one that many Manitobans feel is no longer appropriate, given the numbers of francophones in the province today and the likelihood that these numbers will continue to decline regardless of the court's decision.

Figures from the 1981 Census show clearly that the historic decline of French in Canada is still continuing in spite of efforts by both the government of Canada and the government of Quebec to prevent further erosion. (Census figures regarding language distributions and uses are very important in Canada: it would be unthinkable that a Canadian census could ignore language issues, or for the particular questions that are asked and the findings not to be subject to prolonged scrutiny.) The percentage of residents of Canada who gave French as their mother tongue was 28.1 per cent in 1961; it fell to 26.9 per cent in 1971 and to 25.7 per cent in 1981. However, during the same period there was an increase in Quebec of those who gave French as their mother tongue, an increase from 81.2 per cent in 1961 to 82.4 per cent in 1981, with the decline to 80.7 per cent in 1971 apparently having been reversed. But, whereas Quebec had become just a little more French-speaking over those two decades, Canada outside Quebec had become less French-speaking. The 6.6 per cent of the total Canadian population outside Quebec who gave French as their mother tongue in 1961 had declined to 6.0 per cent in 1971 and then to 5.3 per cent in 1981. Between 1971 and 1981 the French-speaking population of Canada actually grew by 8 per cent with 85.4 per cent of it concentrated in Quebec; however, the English-speaking population grew by 15 per cent in the same period, mainly as a result of language shifts and transfers toward English, which is the language of Canada that draws speakers everywhere outside Quebec, both francophones and allophones, i.e., those whose first language is neither English nor French.

This attraction of English is also seen in which language is preferred for use in the home. In Canada as a whole the most used language in the home is English. English was used by 68.2 per cent in 1981 in contrast to 67.0 per cent in 1971. French was so used by 24.6 per cent in contrast to an earlier 25.7 per cent. Inside Quebec there was an increase in the use of French as the language of the home between 1971 and 1981 (80.8 per cent to 82.5 per cent) and a decrease in the use of English (14.7 per cent to 12.7 per cent). This reduction in the use of English in Quebec apparently continues into the 1980s, partly as a result of the province losing about 10 per cent of its anglophone population in the first five years of the decade as these people choose to relocate themselves elsewhere in Canada. Outside Quebec, English use in the home increased between 1971 and 1981 from 87.2 per cent to 88.1 per cent, and French use declined from 4.4 per cent to 3.8 per cent. In Ontario, Canada's most populous province, there were in 1981 only 475,000 out of 7.2 million who claimed French as their mother tongue; this 5.5 per cent compares with 6.3 per cent in 1971. What is also of interest is that in 1981, 7.2 per cent of the population of Canada gave a language other than English or French as the language of the home. It is very likely that most of these will eventually convert to English. Even in Quebec itself, English has considerable attraction for many of those who responded this way.

One of the conclusions that Canada's Commissioner of Official Languages drew from the 1981 Census in his 1985 Report to the

Parliament of Canada was that official bilingualism in Canada was poised between an honest linguistic partnership and the distinct danger of linguistic territorialism on the Belgian model. Such a conclusion seems to be entirely warranted. The tendency of the two languages in Canada to divide on a territorial basis has been apparent throughout the twentieth century. It was certainly very obvious when the Royal Commission on Bilingualism and Biculturalism was doing its work in the middle and late 1960s. The commission deliberately set out to reverse the historic trend toward separation of the two languages. So far there has been no reversal, and no evidence exists to show English will not continue to gain at the expense of French outside Quebec. Moreover, the French within Quebec will likely have a difficult task in maintaining their language there in sufficient numbers to keep French close to its historic proportion of being the language of 30 per cent of the Canadian population. English is no less a threat to French in Canada than it has ever been.

A further disturbing fact for the French in Canada has been the growth in power of the federal government since the end of World War II. This growth threatens the French more than any group, since it puts them increasingly into a minority position. It makes them less and less equal with the English, and drives them further away from achieving parity as one of the 'two founding nations' of Canada. Quebec has become just one of ten equal provinces with which the federal government must deal, and when Quebec disagrees with either the federal government or with the other provinces, it finds itself in very much a minority situation. Recent emphasis on such matters as national unity, 'Canadian' identity, the choice of a flag and an anthem, and the patriation of the Constitution, have also tended to sharpen differences between Quebec and the rest of Canada. Such concerns have also caused the people of Quebec to look within toward their own identity, culture, symbols, and, of course, language.

The situation is further complicated by the fact that Canada is also a country of immigrants. There are large immigrant groups, such as the Italians, Germans, Ukrainians, Portuguese, and Chinese. Many of these groups also face severe language loss, and some of those who speak on behalf of these groups think that the French in Canada, particularly the French outside Quebec, should have no privileges, so far as language is concerned, that they themselves do not enjoy. This feeling is particularly strong in parts of western Canada. The importance of such claims is better understood if one realizes that Canadians of ethnic origins other than English or French now comprise almost the same proportion of the Canadian population as those of French origin – English origin 45 per cent, French origin 28 per cent, and other origins 27 per cent.

Outside Quebec those of other origins vastly outnumber those of French origin, and the language that is predominant is English. The 1981 Census figures show that in the four western provinces of British Columbia, Alberta, Saskatchewan, and Manitoba 79.8 per cent are of English mother tongue but only 2.7 per cent are of French mother tongue, with the remaining 17.5 per cent, of course, neither. This then is a further pressure on French outside Quebec, but one too that has consequences even within that province.

It is possible to compare the retreat of French in Canada with that of the advance of Spanish in the United States. French has no neighbouring francophone territory from which it can draw strength, either culturally or through migration. There is also virtually no immigration to Quebec from France. Nor is there replenishment of the French outside Quebec from the French within. The French population of Quebec has turned its attention inward; it does little to support French Canadians outside the province. To date only New Brunswick is an officially bilingual province. Ontario is not although it provides extensive services to its francophone population. All other provinces to the east or west remain largely intransigent to French demands. The government of Quebec tends to be more absorbed with its relationship with the government of France and its own federal government in Ottawa than with French interests in distant provinces. To immigrants to Canada who speak neither English nor French, it is English which often has the greater appeal even when the laws of Quebec force a French education on their children. Finally, Quebec has a very low birth rate, so growth in absolute numbers of speakers of French through some kind of population explosion is severely limited.

Esman concludes his survey of the current language situation in Canada by observing (1985, p. 63):

The constitution of 1982 reflects the institutionalization of the national consensus on language policy and practice which has emerged in the quarter century since the beginning of the Quiet Revolution – bilingualism at the center, unilingualism in the provinces, with limited and pragmatic concessions to official language minorities.

This may indeed be the consensus, but it is not one that many Canadians readily acknowledge, being the worst of compromises rather than the best in the view of many. It does not really satisfy any group: not the people of Quebec, who must look within to protect themselves; not even the French outside Quebec, who appear to have most to gain because time and numbers seem to be against them; not many anglophone Canadians, who have little sympathy for French aspirations in Canada; and not many immigrants, who object to the privileges which the French enjoy but which are denied them. Not even those who were behind the federal legislation of the 1960s can be well pleased: they eschewed 'territorial' bilingualism in favour of a variety of 'personal' bilingualism, but the first has increased more rapidly than the second, and made the second increasingly less appropriate than the first.

Language will continue to be an important issue in Canada but, certain opinions in the United States notwithstanding, language differences are unlikely to lead to the break-up of the country. There are other cleavages than linguistic ones to which Canadian attention is drawn from time to time: regional, economic, and class differences, as well as federal–provincial disagreements. The major political parties also try to compete for support from all segments of the electorate. Consequently, language issues do not get exclusive attention even if they are never far from the centre of the political agenda. Finally, the fact that Canada is officially bilingual in English and French places it in a position which is almost unique in the world. Only Cameroon and Vanuatu are linked like Canada to both the anglophone and francophone world communities in this way.

FURTHER READING

Belgium and Switzerland: Stephens 1976; Belgium: Baetens Beardsmore 1980, Lijphart 1981, McRae 1986, Zolberg 1977; Switzerland: Mayer 1980, McCrae 1983, Schläpfer 1985; Canada: Bourhis 1984, Breton et al. 1980, Joy 1972, Lachapelle and Henripin 1982, Smiley 1977, Wardhaugh 1983.

10

Old States, New Pressures

Along with the resurgence of ethnicity as a factor in language maintenance and resistance to any further spread of dominant languages, another factor has emerged to encourage multilingualism within the boundaries of the modern state: the immigration of people who do not speak the language or languages of the country to which they immigrate, but who insist that the languages they bring with them should be preserved in their new locales. Immigration has become an important factor in Western European life, whether it is the immigration of former colonial peoples to such countries as the United Kingdom or France, countries that are now reaping the crops they sowed in colonial times, or that brought about by the deliberate recruitment of labour from poorer countries by many of the wealthier countries of Western Europe in various *Gastarbeiter* ('guestworker') arrangements.

One important consequence is that countries that appeared to be well on the way to developing quite homogeneous societies so far as language and culture are concerned have suddenly found themselves faced with a new diversity of languages and cultures without any real plans for dealing with these. There is an important psychological difference between countries such as France and Germany on the one hand and the United States, Canada, and Australia on the other. The first set of countries do not see themselves as countries of immigration nor do the people who arrive tend to see themselves as immigrants, certainly not in the same way as in the second set. This attitude creates difficulties in coming to terms with the kinds of demographic changes that have occurred in recent years. The United Kingdom is somewhere in between: it has immigrants in the traditional sense but does not quite know what to do with them, particularly when they come in new colours and speaking strange tongues. Héraud describes (1963, p. 97) the consequences of such immigration as follows:

L'immigration intensive métamorphose un pays. Les nouveaux venus apportent leurs mœurs et leurs habitudes qui, la plupart du temps, diffèrent des modes locaux de comportement. L'aspect et la tenue des lieux publics s'en ressentent. Lorsque l'immigration prend la proportion d'une invasion, la situation devient pour les vieux habitants exceptionnellement douloureuse: ils se retrouvent étrangers dans leur propre pays.

Intensive immigration transforms a country. Newcomers bring their customs and habits which, most of the time, differ from local ways. The effects are readily seen in public places. When immigration comes to resemble an invasion, the old inhabitants find the situation extremely painful: they find themselves strangers in their own country.

The kind of feeling that Héraud mentions has been very apparent in recent years.

An influx of immigrants is also likely to lend support to the aspirations of existing groups that have not been completely assimilated – not direct support, to be sure, since alliances are not easily forged in most cases, but support for the view that modern states can just as easily be multilingual and multicultural as they can be unilingual and unicultural. The result has been some serious conflict in many Western democracies as various groups, both major and minor, have been forced to come to try to come to terms with new realities. That they have sometimes not succeeded in doing so is unfortunately all too apparent.

Even traditionally immigrant societies have faced similar problems. The United States, Australia, and Canada are such societies. Each was founded as an immigrant society and each has been built through continued immigration. However, that pattern of immigration was not one which allowed anyone at all to enter the country. There were certain assumptions about who were the most desirable immigrants and who were not at all desirable. There were also assumptions about what kind of cultural mix was desirable in each new state and how immigrants should relate to that mix. In particular, there were strong assumptions, sometimes written into law as in the case of Canada, about the language or languages that were to be used in the new society and the responsibilities immigrants had to accept if they wished to participate fully in the receiving society. Again, as migration patterns have changed in the last several decades, many of these assumptions have been challenged, old issues have been revived, and each of the three countries just mentioned has had to confront the issue of how to deal with other languages than those that are dominant, and with cultural traits that do not fit easily into the existing order.

THE UNITED KINGDOM

The 1981 Census figures for the United Kingdom revealed that over 6 per cent of the population had been born overseas. Out of a total population of slightly under 54 million about 3.6 million had been born elsewhere. (For England alone the corresponding figures were 45.8 million and 3.1 million.) Of these about 19 per cent had been born in one of India, Pakistan, or Bangladesh, about 18 per cent were Irish-born, over 5 per cent were German-born, and Jamaica accounted for another 5 per cent. Other countries such as the United States, Kenya, Italy, Poland and Cyprus each accounted for at least 2 per cent of the foreign-born. Those born abroad had brought with them a wide variety of languages, although knowing the country of birth is not a very good indicator of precisely which language or languages a particular individual may have brought.

Such immigrants also brought with them a variety of racial and cultural types. Given also the modern propensity for immigrants to settle in urban rather than rural areas and to settle, at least initially, among or near those who have preceded them, the appearances of many of England's cities have changed considerably as a result of this recent immigration. Today, London, for example, is a strikingly different city so far as language and racial composition is concerned from what it was 30 or so years ago. About one-third of the foreign-born in England live in the Greater London area.

The British Isles have always attracted immigrants. One of the most influential groups was, of course, the Normans, who through their invasion in 1066 profoundly changed the course of history there. But the Normans were not the first immigrants nor the last. The Danes had preceded the Normans, the Anglo-Saxons had preceded the Danes, and the Celts had come even earlier. The difference between these migrants and those who were to come later was that the former established the social, political, and linguistic framework into which later groups were required to fit.

When later immigrants came, they usually settled into the receiving society and became assimilated rather quickly in most respects. Most sought certain opportunities in Britain that were denied them elsewhere. Flemings, Huguenots, and Jews in earlier times, Germans still later, and more recently refugees from war-torn Europe found their way to Britain seeking some combination of economic, political, or religious freedom. Being almost exclusively of European origin, they constituted an invisible minority, particularly if they were willing to make certain sacrifices to fit into the new society. One of the easiest sacrifices for many was the sacrifice of the languages they brought with them.

The Irish are the largest immigrant group in England but it is impossible to estimate the total size of this group because of the extent to which they have been assimilated. Much of the Roman Catholic population of the country is of Irish descent and one estimate of this population is that it comprises about one-tenth of the total population. The Irish are still largely working-class and to some extent still settle in 'Irish' areas, particularly in the Midlands. If they have not always found it easy to assimilate because of their religion and their social-class origins, language has not proved to be an obstacle to the Irish, since they speak English. Therefore, they have always been easy to absorb linguistically.

Another group, the Jews, are even more integrated than the Irish. Not only do they speak English but they play a prominent role in the political, social, and cultural life of the country. Other groups are more obvious than the Irish or the Jews because of their languages. For example, there is a large Italian group. England has always been hospitable to Italians, and over the last century or so many Italians have come to the country and assimilated to its language and culture. Since World War II, however, there has been a new wave of immigrants from Italy, many of whom have settled around Bedford, Britain's brick-making capital. These new Italians are quite conscious of their differences from the society in which they have settled and, although some have deliberately tried to integrate themselves as quickly as possible into that society, for example by marrying into it, many wish to see Italian ways and the Italian language perpetuated. In this desire they are like many of the other recent immigrants to the British Isles. Whereas once immigrants to England were quite cut off from the lands of their origin and saw their future in quick assimilation with its consequent 'invisibility', now they seek to preserve some of what they have brought with them. One particular right many have claimed is the right to have their children educated in their mother tongue.

A considerably more unsettling factor to many British people than certain groups of immigrants wanting other European languages taught in the schools and recognized through the expenditure of public funds was the influx of immigrants from the 'New Commonwealth', i.e., the Indian subcontinent, Hong Kong, Malta, Cyprus, and the Caribbean, that began in the 1950s. Suddenly there was a noticeable presence in many major English cities of people who looked quite different and who spoke unrecognizable tongues. Those who drew most attention were from either the West Indies or the Indian subcontinent; they spoke either a very different variety of English or quite exotic languages. The Office of Population Census and Survey estimated that in 1983 about

4.1 per cent, i.e., some 2.2 million, of the population of the United Kingdom consisted of immigrants from the New Commonwealth, with, in decreasing order, Indians, West Indians, Pakistanis, East African Asians, and Bangladeshis comprising the largest groups.

These people are also very noticeable because they are not white. Today, about half of the members of these groups are actually British-born and many more by now are citizens. This segment of the population also provides nearly 5 per cent of the current school enrolment. It is also a fertile population, estimated to reach about three million in number by the beginning of the next century with over two-thirds of that number actually born in the United Kingdom. It is this group of immigrants that has drawn most of the public's attention in recent years. The United Kingdom government has also deliberately tried to reduce its growth by confining it as much as possible to natural increase. For example, with the Commonwealth Immigrants Act of 1968 the government adopted a citizenship policy designed to remove certain traditional rights enjoyed by Commonwealth citizens to live in the United Kingdom, but did this in such a way as to make the new restrictive rules applicable to countries of the New Commonwealth rather than those of the Old Commonwealth.

Before 1945 the United Kingdom did have a small black population but this was mainly confined to some of the seaports. There were also a few Chinese and a few Indians. People from all over the world did visit England, particularly London, and some of the universities, particularly the University of London, attracted students from everywhere. In general, however, non-whites in England were rare and barely visible. They certainly had no political and social influence.

This situation changed almost overnight. In the 1950s there was a tremendous upsurge in the British economy which created a need for new sources of labour. Particularly necessary were people to fill many menial jobs in society, jobs that the English themselves did not want because better jobs had become available. Other Western European countries faced with the same situation decided to recruit workers from the less wealthy areas of Europe and bring them in on a system of temporary work permits, their 'guestworkers'. The United Kingdom turned to the Commonwealth as its source of cheap labour. Moreover, citizens of the Commonwealth had a right to live and work in Britain, so it was only a question of organizing the flow of labor from the poorer parts to the rich centre. Since it was not possible to recruit from the quickly developing old 'white' Commonwealth – many Britons actually were leaving at the same time for countries such as Canada and Australia – that new labor force had to come from the non-white part, particularly the West Indies and the Indian subcontinent. Such immigrants now play a significant, perhaps even crucial role in the transportation, engineering, catering, hospital, and garment industries in England, and they also provide a considerable source of unskilled labour.

They have settled mainly in cities and towns where their labour was needed or where they could supply each other with the resources and support needed for life in a new environment. Greater London, the Midlands, West Yorkshire, and South Lancashire have particularly large concentrations of such immigrants and their descendants, with perhaps as many as three-quarters living in Greater London and the West Midlands. Cities like Birmingham, Leeds, Bradford, Leicester, and Wolverhampton each have large minorities. Settlements in areas such as Tyneside, Merseyside, and Northern Ireland are sparse in comparison because these are areas of high unemployment and they have not been at all attractive to immigrants, being indeed areas from which many natives have emigrated.

One important consequence of post-World War II immigration to the United Kingdom, whatever its sources, is that there is now a profusion of languages spoken in many of the towns and cities of England as well as some new varieties of English itself. Several attempts have been made to assess the extent to which languages other than English and varieties of English other than those indigenous to the country are to be found in the schools. For example, the Linguistic Minorities Project (1985), established by the Institute of Education of the University of London in 1979, tried to assess the linguistic situation in such areas as Bradford, Coventry, Peterborough, Haringey, and Waltham Forest. It found a considerable amount of bilingualism in the school population. This finding is hardly surprising for it is well known that there are Local Education Authorities (LEAs) in which more than half the school population is of immigrant origin and that in some cases the proportion in certain areas has gone as high as 80 per cent.

No consensus exists about the kinds of policies that are needed to deal with this new immigration. Some see the solution as one of assimilating immigrants as quickly as possible. Immigrants should be prepared to forgo the languages and cultures they have brought with them and participate fully in 'English' life by exploiting the opportunities that are there for all to enjoy. They point to the way in which previous groups have been so absorbed or, as in the case of certain post-World War II immigrants from Eastern Europe, are being absorbed in spite of their diversity and numbers.

For many of the immigrants from the New Commonwealth colour seems to be an effective bar to this solution, in the short term at least. Moreover, there is today a widespread belief that people have a right to maintain their languages and cultures not only in the places in which they were born but also in those places to which they move by force of circumstance. So the new minorities exert what pressure they can on the authorities in the United Kingdom to give them concessions, above all concessions that would allow them to preserve their languages and important cultural characteristics. It used to be the case that religious and political freedom were the goals that immigrants sought most and that after arrival they also found a large measure of economic opportunity. Now these freedoms and that opportunity are not enough. Currently, immigrants insist that linguistic and cultural freedom be added to the list.

It is these demands that upset a number of people in the receiving society, particularly when made by immigrants who look so very different. They regard English as not only the dominant, even 'natural', language of the United Kingdom but also as the most important language in the world so far as international influence is concerned. They tend to see little place for other languages, particularly on home ground, and they observe the readiness with which children of immigrants acquire English. In this view, it seems wasteful that valuable resources should be spent on encouraging languages which must inevitably disappear.

There has been no nationwide systematic attempt to deal with the issues posed by immigration from the New Commonwealth other than through attempts to restrict the continued flow of immigrants, to change the requirement for citizenship, as in the British Nationality Act of 1981, and to provide a measure of protection against overt racism. The prevailing language policy has been one of tolerance at best for the new diversity of languages. The education system in the United Kingdom is also highly decentralized, and initiatives from the centre, i.e., from the Department of Education and Science (DES), have been few. Most initiatives in education are usually left to Local Education Authorities, which have considerable freedom in this respect, subject only to the 'policing' of the central school inspectorate. These initiatives have, therefore, varied considerably, with some LEAs doing almost nothing and some being extremely innovative. In the first years the major concern, when there was any concern at all, was with teaching English to the new immigrants. Sometimes, however, it was assumed that they would just pick up the language and that little help was needed. It was not until the mid-1970s that there was any real discussion of institutional support for bilingualism and that people began to question the English-only policies that had existed to that time. For example, the 1975 Bullock Report argued that no child should be expected to cast off the language and culture of the home on crossing the school threshold, nor to live and act as though school and home represented two totally separate and different cultures which had to be kept firmly apart.

About this time the United Kingdom became a member of the European Economic Community (EEC), membership in which also required that the country subscribe to certain social policies as the member states developed such policies. One of the proposed policies dealt with the rights of migrant workers to their languages in the countries of their employment. The original 1976 draft called for 'tuition in the mother tongue and culture of the child within the normal school curriculum'. Such a policy was important to most of the Western European countries that employed 'guestworkers', because either they saw such workers returning to their home countries some day or they wished to preserve the myth of such a return. The government of the United Kingdom objected to the proposed legislation on the grounds that most migrants to the country were not guestworkers at all. They were also protected in ways unknown to guestworkers on the continent, for example in having the right to full citizenship within a short period of time, a right completely lacking elsewhere. Anyone born in the United Kingdom was also at that time automatically accorded citizenship. Furthermore, the government believed that it would be unwise in the existing social climate to single out the children of those from EEC countries for special treatment. The United Kingdom also had a highly decentralized education system and the government claimed that such a directive from the centre was entirely inappropriate. Furthermore, there just simply were not the resources available to carry out the proposed policy changes.

The Directive that the Council of the European Communities finally adopted in 1977 recognized all these objections. It required member states to teach children of immigrant workers from other member states the official language of the host state, or one of its official languages, and also to take appropriate measures to promote the teaching of the mother tongue and culture of the country of origin 'in accordance with national circumstances and legal systems'. The Directive came into effect in 1981 and in that year the DES sent out guidelines for its interpretation and implementation to all LEAs. According to the Directive, these authorities 'should explore ways in which mother tongue teaching might be provided, whether during or outside school hours, but ... they are [not] required to give such tuition to all individuals as of right'. The message is quite clear: maintaining the status quo is acceptable and local authorities can do as little – or as much – as they please to satisfy local requests for instruction in and through languages other than English. Together, the 1975 Bullock Report and the Directive did lead to the development of classes in which mother tongues are taught, research projects, the employment of new personnel, conferences, reports, etc. There has been a lot of activity but it has been localized and sporadic in nature.

The Linguistic Minorities Project has clearly indicated that many parents of children who bring other languages than English to school with them want to have these languages taught. They certainly do not want to see them lost, and all fear that they will be lost unless some kind of official recognition is given to them in the school system. But, since the school system in the United Kingdom is highly decentralized and the central government cannot change that fact nor would do so just to preserve something as un-English as other languages in the country , it is quite unlikely that any kind of large-scale support will be provided for those other languages. Instead there will continue to be local attempts to develop bilingual programmes and materials and some time and effort will be given to fostering multicultural understanding. The predominant emphasis is likely to be on the teaching of English and on what are seen to be the problems involved in the process of assimilation.

The success of all of these develoments and programmes may in part be judged by what those who are closest to them have to say. They are still forced to be advocates, still forced to point out what they see to be the benefits of programmes that should be adopted, and still forced to try to persuade those who are in control to change their errant ways. Such outpourings indicate more than anything else how little success has been achieved in all of this effort in swimming against the tide of the English language and the majority culture of the United Kingdom. England is still very much an English-speaking country and is likely to remain so. Its culture is only marginally affected – but many would argue to the better – by its most recent immigrants. It is they who have had to make major cultural adjustments, although it is the English themselves who have protested most loudly against making the few adjustments that have been required of them in order to enjoy the undoubted benefits that such immigrants have brought.

FRANCE

The United Kingdom has not been alone in having to come to terms with large numbers of people who do not speak the language of the country. Other Western European countries have had to face the same problem in recent years. The United Kingdom is different in that most of those who came arrived as immigrants with a right to stay permanently and become citizens. In most other Western European countries those who came did so as 'temporary guestworkers' at a time when there was an urgent need for labour. They generally came from the poorer parts of· Europe, typically under short-term agreements made with the originating countries and with the assumption on both sides, initially at least, that they would one day return to those countries of origin. Many guestworker arrangements were controlled by official accords negotiated between governments. For example, both France and Germany signed a series of bilateral agreements with countries like Greece, Portugal, Spain, Morocco, Turkey, etc. in the 1960s and early 1970s. The receiving countries defended such guestworker arrangements on various grounds: the workers would develop useful skills; they would also acquire some capital; balance of payment problems would be reduced; and there would be a reduction in unemployment in the originating countries.

Many millions of these guestworkers arrived in countries such as France, West Germany, Switzerland, Belgium, the Netherlands, and Sweden from Portugal, Italy, Spain, Yugoslavia, and Turkey. France also has a large group from North Africa, particularly from Algeria. Many have not returned and have no wish to return, for even if life is difficult at times in their new locations, it is much better than it would be if they went 'home'. They may, however, cling to the myth of returning some day, as many Turks do in West Germany, but many have sent for their families and often their children know no other life than the one they have experienced in their new country. Estimates of this population in Western Europe now run in excess of 13 million, with well over four million in each of France and West Germany and close to a million in each of Belgium and Switzerland.

In recent years, then, certain Western European countries have had to attempt to deal with two issues concurrently: the linguistic and other demands that regional minority groups have been making, and the need to develop appropriate language and social policies for migrant workers and their dependants. Not all countries have had to confront both issues. For example, West Germany is spared the problem of dealing with one or more discontented indigenous minorities; West Germany's major problem has been entirely that of trying to decide how to deal with the large Gastarbeiter minority in its midst which cannot be returned to the various countries of origin. What was until very recently an almost completely unilingual state, which denied that it is a 'country of immigration', has become one in which it is quite usual to hear other languages than German spoken in large cities and to see large areas of those cities, particularly West Berlin, populated by non-Germans. West Germany has even experimented with paying people to leave but its repatriation plan – like the one in France – has met with little success.

The European Economic Community developed the previously mentioned policy of providing instruction in the different vernaculars in order to meet some of the educational requirements of migrant workers. Migrant workers who originate outside the EEC countries have also tried to benefit from the various EEC decisions. They have met with varying success. One obstacle in the way of success is the myth that the existence of such minorities is only a temporary phenomenon: they will disappear in time as they return home either as their contractual obligations are fulfilled or through some form of inducement. Alternatively, the problem will disappear as minorities become assimilated. They lack the territorial bases of the indigenous minorities where these exist, their children do learn the major language to some extent, and their grandchildren certainly will. Time will take care of the problems and generous arrangements in such matters as linguistic accommodation will serve only to slow down a process which will be less painful if it is quick. However, in the way of this approach there are cultural differences that persist, there is endemic prejudice, and there is also the making of a new permanent underclass in parts of Europe which is ethnically different from the classes above. Many people who have concerned themselves with the issues regard such consequences as alarming, and believe the only truly viable solutions to be either complete assimilation with full opportunity and equality, or the adoption of policies that guarantee linguistic and cultural pluralism.

France has felt these problems very acutely. Or, alternatively, many French people have made a serious problem out of recent immigration to France. No election occurs without some discussion about what should or should not be done about recent migrants to France, who along with their descendants total well over four million people. Indeed, they are partly the stuff of extreme right-wing victories at the polls. They are also a frequent source of incidents that have led to various allegations about a growing intolerance in France of things that are obviously non-French in origin. The whole issue is also compounded by the fact that the birth rate among French citizens has been for many years below that necessary to maintain the current population level; considerable immigration is necessary if France's population is to be maintained at current levels.

There was continual immigration to France in the nineteenth century from Belgium, Italy, Germany, and Spain, mainly into the adjacent areas of France, but cities such as Paris, Lyons, and Marseilles also benefited from this spontaneous, unorganized influx of mainly skilled labour. In the late nineteenth century more organized immigration occurred as jobs were filled in the new factories and mines, and migrants were brought from more distant places under various types of contracts, with northern Italy being a prime source of such labour. Later, agricultural workers came to France under local government auspices and in the twentieth century the Maghreb became a handy source of such labour.

There was a tremendous influx of foreign workers in the 1920s and by 1931 more than 7 per cent of France's population were immigrants. The French thought it necessary to introduce controls to reduce this proportion and did manage to bring about some reduction. The next great surge of immigration occurred following the end of World War II. The new industrial growth required large amounts of labour, particularly to fill poorly paid service positions. The foreign-born population of France began to grow once more and by 1985 the proportion of foreign-born had reached an all-time high of about 8 per cent. Entirely new groups had become prominent among these immigrants: the 1.5 million Algerians, Moroccans, and Tunisians of 1983 were more numerous than the 1.2 million Portuguese and Spaniards, and much more prominent if colour and cultural differences are used as the major defining characteristics.

Although the French effectively put a stop to immigration in 1974, this move did nothing to reduce the numbers of the foreign-born in France. Most immigrants had decided to stay where they were. Family reunification in France was permitted and the numbers continued to increase as whole families put down new roots in France. By 1983 70 per cent of the foreign-born in France had lived there more than 11 years and very few had any real desire to leave. French cities had begun to take on a new look and even the French language itself was under assault from a new direction. The Jacobinian view of a unified France ruled from the centre and with a uniform language and culture came under a new attack.

One way of assessing the impact of immigration on French society is to look at the numbers of students enrolled in French schools and examine their backgrounds. In the 1979–80 school year there were nearly one million 'foreign' students in the schools of France: about 9 per cent of the primary school population and 6 per cent of the secondary school population, or 8 per cent of the 12 million pupils actually in school. These percentages would also increase during the 1980s since more than 10 per cent of new births in France in the late 1970s were in families in which one or both of the parents was foreign-born. In the mid-1970s about one-third of the 'foreign' children attending school in France were of either Algerian, Moroccan, or Tunisian background, 22 per cent were of Portuguese background, and about 14 per cent each of Spanish and Italian background. The greatest concentrations of such pupils are in the large urban areas, particularly in Paris itself, where as much as one-third of the total school population is of this background. In these areas too there is a definite pattern of migrants preferring to live with people of similar background so that some schools become almost exclusively populated by students of one or two nationalities other than French.

Educational policy in France has none of the flexibility of that of neighbouring West Germany. In the latter country, in Bavaria for example, the children of guestworkers are very often educated in the language of their home country and receive little exposure to German in their segregated schooling. In contrast, in West Berlin, children of Turkish background are not allowed to ghettoize the schools, and are pushed as fast as possible to acquire facility in German by being educated alongside German-speaking children. The French school system is highly centralized and relies exclusively on the use of the French language as the medium of instruction except, as we saw in an earlier chapter, in very limited circumstances with indigenous minorities. It is not surprising therefore that studies have shown that children of 'foreign' origin sometimes lag behind their French counterparts and that the language difficulties they experience account in part for the differences in performance that have been observed. But the low socioeconomic background of many of the immigrants may possibly be even more important in accounting for such poor performance in school than the linguistic background alone. Immigrants tend to form an underclass in France and the performance in school of the children of that underclass is only what might be expected of any underprivileged group regardless of its linguistic background. One study (Bastide 1982, p. 201) concluded that, even if language is a problem for a time for many of them, on the whole foreign-born pupils in France do not really have any more problems than French pupils once socioeconomic differences are taken into account.

Whether or not the children of immigrants to France create a serious problem for the educational system, many French people perceive with horror any move that makes their country less 'French'. There are constant pleas to keep the language pure, whether it is from the influence of English or from the attempts made by any but the thoroughly well educated to speak the language. All other languages than French receive little or no recognition in the schools of France, except as 'foreign languages'. If immigrants from outside the EEC and refugees from a variety of sources wish to see their languages preserved, then they must provide the resources themselves. Those who come from within the EEC have a right to education in the vernacular but it is not a right that is easily granted. When the other languages are also accompanied by distinctively 'non-French' ways of life that makes the situation doubly difficult. In times of economic unrest that difficulty also quickly breeds racial antagonism.

In France, as in the United Kingdom, just when it appeared that a single language and a single culture would dominate the state and the last vestiges of other languages were about to disappear, those last vestiges got a new life. But each state, too, had its unitary language policy assailed from still another direction. Each found itself taking in millions of people who did not speak the language of the state or who spoke it very differently. Many of these same people also brought with them cultural traits that differed considerably from the ones they found in the receiving societies. The general 'liberal' political and social climate of the times was also favourable for the newcomers in that it was possible to question assumptions that had gone unexamined before, particularly the assumption that immigrants should voluntarily discard certain of their baggage on arrival in the new society, with language one of the first pieces to go.

France has found immigration from the Maghreb a particularly difficult issue to deal with. During the 1970s local elections were often fought on issues that involved immigration from North Africa, particularly from Algeria, in one way or another, and in 1983 immigration became one of the key issues in a nationwide election. The results of that election showed that many French people can be roused by claims that there are too many immigrants in France, and that they contribute heavily to unemployment and crime, ghettoize the cities, drain the social services, cannot be assimilated, and pose a serious threat to French ways. For example, Jacques Chirac declared in 1976: '*Il ne devrait pas y avoir de problème de chômage en France, puis qu'il y a 1 million de chômeurs et 1 million 800,000 travailleurs immigrés.*' ('There should not be an unemployment problem here in France since there are a million unemployed and 1.8 million immigrant workers'). A 1985 publication (Le Gallou 1985) was even more insistent on the rights of the French people to impose their language and culture on all those who wanted to settle in their country. The back cover of the book states the position as follows:

Pour sauvegarder leur identité et leur souveraineté, les Français doivent pouvoir réaffirmer avec vigueur le principe de la Préférence nationale qui légitime les nécessaires différences de droits politiques et sociaux entre citoyens et étrangers; ils doivent pouvoir défendre les valeurs qu'ils ont héritées de leur histoire et refuser le modèle d'une France multiculturelle contraire à leurs traditions; ils doivent revaloriser leur droit de la nationalité: acquérir la nationalité française doit cesser d'être une simple formalité pour redevenir un honneur réservé à ceux qui font l'effort de maîtriser notre langue, de connaître notre culture et d'adopter nos mœurs et nos lois civiles; ils doivent enfin préparer le retour dans la dignité des étrangers qui ne peuvent pas ou ne veulent pas s'assimiler.

In order to protect their identity and their sovereignty, the French must be able to reaffirm vigorously: the principle of *National Preference* which legitimizes the necessary differences of the political and social rights between citizens and foreigners; they must be able to defend the values that they have inherited from their history and reject the model of a multicultural France contrary to their traditions; they must reevaluate their right of nationality: acquiring French nationality must no longer be a simple formality but become an honour reserved to those who make the effort to master our language, to get to know our culture and to adopt our customs and our civil laws; finally, they must prepare for the dignified return of foreigners who are unable or unwilling to be assimilated.

Jacobinism is obviously a strong force in modern France and one that can be called upon to support measures taken by parties right across the political spectrum so long as these claim to enhance France itself.

As we have seen, both the United Kingdom and France have been forced to confront the issue of the place that English and French have within their respective borders and what linguistic rights, if any, migrants bring with them. At a time when English is spreading quite rapidly in the world, any reduction of its influence in its original territory does not sit lightly on some observers in the United Kingdom. At a time when French finds itself competing unfavourably with other languages abroad, particularly English, any further linguistic assault on French within France is not at all welcome. Those who find it unwelcome in France are probably more vocal than those who deplore what is happening in the United Kingdom, if for no other reason than the very strong role the French language has played in creating and sustaining French identity.

THE UNITED STATES OF AMERICA

The rights of minorities have become an issue not only in countries such as the United Kingdom and France but also in some of the newer countries of the world, specifically in countries such as the United States, Australia, and Canada, which seemed for a long time not to have significant problems of this kind. The United States was supposed to be a 'melting pot' into which various groups disappeared soon after their arrival, and all came out eventually speaking English and subscribing to a common set of values. Australia was not only a 'whites-only' country, but one in which the English language and English cultural characteristics were virtually unopposed. Canada did have a language problem, but this was entirely a problem of sorting out how English and French would relate to each other. Immigrants who came bringing with them other languages and ways were supposed to fit into the 'cultural mosaic' that was proclaimed to exist in the new country, but in reality they usually ended up speaking English within two generations of arrival and showing many other signs of assimilation to the English-speaking community in Canada. It was only continued immigration that maintained the myth of the cultural mosaic.

Although English is not the official language of the United States, which has no official language, it is nevertheless the language of the Constitution itself and the language that is used almost everywhere in the country for just about all official purposes. While it has long been held that a requirement that English be the official language of the United States would violate constitutional rights to freedom of speech guaranteed under the Constitution, there is no doubt that English is de facto if not de jure the official language of the United States. It is also the language of those who have emerged from the melting pot. However, there are some who assert that the melting-pot myth is not really appropriate for what has happened to many groups within the United States. For example, in their book *Beyond the Melting Pot*, Glazer and Moynihan (1963, p. v) assert of the melting pot that 'the point ... is that it did not happen'. It may have happened to groups like the large German group who came to the United States for reasons peculiar to the group and the time of arrival, but it did not happen to such groups as Negroes, Puerto Ricans, Jews, Italians, and the Irish, particularly in a city like New York. Each of these groups has preserved certain distinctive ways even if it may not have succeeded too well in preserving its distinctive language when that was a possibility.

It is Glazer and Moynihan's thesis that immigrants were not submerged in the melting pot but that ethnic groups were transformed as they entered American life by the conditions of that life. In that transformation any distinctive language and culture were largely lost, making any dream of a 'culturally pluralistic' state impossible. Ethnicity has, however, persisted as a force in American life because members of such groups as Polish Americans and Italian Americans see similarities among themselves, similarities that distinguish them from other groups in Amerian life and also from acquaintances in the old countries. Fishman (1985) has also offered some telling comments on this process. For example, he has pointed out that ethnicity itself is now very much a part of American life. It has been taken into American life and adapted to, and been adapted to, the conditions of that life. He says (p. 269) that 'there are various ways of "being American" and, in the current phase of American reality, non-English language ethnic-community institutions are very much within the normal range of "being American." Relative to other periods in American history there are proportionately fewer who would contest this claim and fewer yet who would deny it, either to themselves or others'. Fishman says (p. 59) that immigrants have undergone a process of relinguification and reethnicification 'in a context relatively innocent of laws requiring such relinguification and reethnification take place'.

In colonial America English was the language of the original colonists and pockets of speakers of other languages, such as the Dutch of New Amsterdam (New York), were soon absorbed into the English-speaking environment. It was also English that spread westward as that part of the country was settled. Nevertheless, at the time of the Declaration of Independence a number of other languages were still spoken in different places: Dutch, German, French, Spanish, Swedish, numerous native languages, and not a few African languages. Just about all would be overtaken by English during the course of the following century and a half, with German, Spanish, and French being the principal victims so far as numbers of speakers were concerned. Each of these languages has had a continuous history in the United States dating back to the very origins of that country, but none has been able to mount an effective challenge to the supremacy of English. German speakers gave up their language in favour of English, with two world wars playing an important role in the process. French has struggled hard to survive in Louisiana and New England. Spanish has always been under attack – even the indigenous Spanish of Puerto Rico, a United States possession since 1898. We can see one aspect of this policy in the way that states such as Louisiana and New Mexico did not come into existence until there was a dominant anglophone population in each. Hawaii has only recently achieved statehood, again only after English was secure there and the Hawaian language had become moribund. And, of course, Spanish-speaking Puerto Rico is still not a state.

As a nation of immigrants, too, the United States built up its population through welcoming people to its shores and through the natural increases that followed as their descendants prospered and multiplied. Large numbers of immigrants arrived in the late nineteenth and early twentieth centuries, mainly from Europe, and considerable effort went into americanizing them, an effort which made the teaching of English and of American ways its principal focus. At first, in the early nineteenth century, there was considerable tolerance for the various languages and cultural characteristics that immigrants brought with them and there was even occasional encouragement given to teaching other languages than English in the schools that came into existence. But by the late nineteenth century attention was increasingly focused on the teaching of English in the public schools of the country and on trying to mould the new arrivals into the existing social framework.

By 1906 it was necessary under the Nationality Act of that year for an alien to speak English in order to become a citizen. Actions such as this began a period in which English was deliberately promoted and other languages actively suppressed. By the 1920s groups such as the National Security League, the American Legion, and the National Americanization Committee spearheaded moves to promote English, loyalty, and American ideals. States responded by restricting instruction in languages other than English, and the restrictive national immigration policy that came into effect in 1921 imposed still another curb. Immigrants were to be americanized, linguistic and cultural diversity was to be resisted, and the melting-pot myth had come into being.

Most recently new waves of migrants have come to the United States and no longer is Europe the major source. Now, speakers of Spanish, with their origin in either the Caribbean, Mexico, or other parts of the Americas, and of more exotic languages than the familiar European ones predominate. There is also a growing concern for what is to happen to the languages brought by these new arrivals. That concern is increased by the patterns of settlement that have occurred, patterns which have, for example, turned whole areas of the United States from English-speaking areas into Spanish-speaking ones even to the extent of 'reclaiming' territories for Spanish that were once lost. No longer do the new migrants rush to be 'melted down', if they ever did. Certain legislative and judicial initiatives seem also to offer rights that immigrants wish to exercise, and the right to preserve the languages which they bring appears to be one such right, or at least the right to be educated for a while through the use of those languages.

Such claims do not, however, go unopposed. To many Americans the English language is the great unifier of the American people and any move toward multilingualism in the state seems to pose a considerable threat to the concept of 'one nation'. It is not surprising, therefore, that there have been moves in recent years to counter what appears to be the rising tide of multilingualism. Waggoner (1981) has produced statistics that indicate the extent to which the United States has become a multilingual country. These show that even in 1940 there was a considerable amount of multilingualism. At that time 22 million white Americans reported mother tongues other than English, i.e., 16.8 per cent of the white population. Of these claimants, 60 per cent were native-born and half were 'second generation' Americans. The largest group – nearly 5 million – were speakers of German, with speakers of Italian, Polish, and Spanish following in that order, but even languages like Yiddish and French had over a million claimants each. In 1970, 33 million persons out of the entire population, white and non-white in this case, reported a non-English mother tongue with three out of four claimants born in the United States and two out of five being 'second generation' Americans. In 1970 the largest group – some 8 million strong – was Spanish-speaking. This group was followed in descending order of group size by speakers of German, Italian, French, Polish, and Yiddish. In addition, about 1.5 million persons claimed an Asian or Near Eastern language as the mother tongue.

In 1975 a Survey of Languages Supplement to the July Current Population Survey asked the mother-tongue question of persons aged 14 and older. Nearly 28 million persons claimed mother tongues other than English in the population aged 14 and older. This group constituted 17.8 per cent of the 14 and older persons in the United States, i.e., something more than one person in every six. A comparison with statistics from the 1970 census suggests, however, that this 17.8 per cent indicates a decline from 1970, when the corresponding percentage was 19.8 per cent. But whereas three out of four non-English mother-tongue claimants aged 15 or over in 1970 were native-born, only seven in ten of like claimants aged 14 and over in 1975 were native-born, the result of a new wave of immigration beginning in the late 1960s and early 1970s. In 1975 Spanish speakers, with 22 per cent, comprised the largest language group followed by German speakers with 15 per cent. Languages such as Chinese, Filipino, Japanese, and Korean all showed strong gains between 1970 and 1975, increasing their total percentage from less than 3 per cent to 5 per cent in that short time.

Further data from the same survey indicated that one person in eight aged 4 or older in the United States in 1975 lived in a household in which a language other than English was spoken, a total of 25.3 million people. One person in ten aged four or older spoke a language other than English in such a household. More than one-third of the persons who spoke languages other than English spoke those languages as their usual languages, and among persons aged four or older 1.6 million did not speak English at all. In households with a non-English language in just under two out of five instances that other language was Spanish. In 11 per cent of cases it was Italian, and it was 9 per cent each for German and French. Asian languages accounted for 6.6 per cent of the persons in such households. One important consequence was that in 1975 there were 7.7 million school-age children in households in which languages other than English were spoken, and 3.3 million – well over 40 per cent – were in Spanish-speaking households.

The 1980 United States Census showed that of the 226.5 million people counted, nearly 23 million persons five years or older spoke languages other than English at home, of whom almost half were speakers of Spanish. Of the 11.1 million who spoke Spanish at home, 8.3 million considered themselves to be bilingual since they also reported that they spoke English either well or very well. Spanish speakers were also clustered heavily in the Far and South West, in New York, and in Florida. Among the 11.8 million who reported a language other than either English or Spanish as the language of the home, 10.3 million indicated that they also spoke English either well or very well. Consequently, it would appear that of the nearly 23 million people who reported a language other than English as the language of the home, 18.6 million considered themselves to be bilingual. Of interest too is that over a quarter of the population of each of four states – New York, Texas, California, and Arizona – reported that they spoke a language other than English in the home. Such homes also contained 8 million school-age children and another 2.6 million children under the age of five. It would also appear that several million residents of the United States either did not speak English at all or spoke it with some difficulty. But perhaps that is not surprising, for the Census reported that there were 14 million foreign-born in the United States and that 23 per cent of these had arrived between 1975 and 1980 with most of these coming from either Latin America or Asia. New York City alone was estimated to have 2.1 million of its total 7.1 million population born overseas.

The above statistics are revealing not so much because each set of numbers exactly confirms each other set of numbers. Indeed, they do not because the surveys and censuses from which they come did not ask identical questions of identical groups. There is also reason to suppose that the various surveys and censuses may have produced inflated figures so far as ability in other languages than English is concerned, because of the way the questions were phrased so as to invite claims of ability to speak another language without offering criteria that specified what was meant by 'speaking' another language, i.e., what level of ability was to be required. The statistics are revealing because they indicate the extent to which multilingualism prevails in the United States and how the phenomenon appears to be a growing one rather than one that is diminishing. The 1980s have seen no decline in migration to the United States. If anything, Spanish-speaking migrants have increased their numbers as have those from Asia. The pattern of settlement for immigrants is also much as it has always been: immigrants tend to settle amongst or near those of similar background. They also prefer to settle in urban areas. The result has been that whole areas of towns and cities and even of populous counties have become Spanish-speaking or that service areas have been created for pockets of speakers of other languages, e.g., pockets of Vietnamese in California.

Faced with what to do about the 'problems' that those who do not speak English have created, the United States government decided to promote 'bilingual education'. With the exception of emergency programmes during wartime, virtually no effort had been spent on the teaching of languages other than English between World War I and the 1960s except as high-school or college subjects and then confined only to a very few languages of 'culture'. In 1968 Congress passed the Bilingual Education Act as Title VII of the Elementary and Secondary Education Act. This law, further continued in 1974 and 1978, provided financial assistance to educational agencies that established programmes of instruction using native languages for children of limited proficiency in English. Another act, the Equal Educational Opportunity Act of 1974, also supported bilingual instruction by requiring educational agencies to 'take appropriate action to overcome language barriers that impede equal participation by its students in its instructional programs'. The *Lau* v. *Nichols* decision of the Supreme Court of January 1974 also reinforced such provisions since it declared that the Constitution guaranteed non-English-speaking students the right of access to a meaningful education. However, it did not guarantee such students the right to bilingual education, although it did allow such education as one possible avenue to the ultimate goal of a meaningful education.

In 1975 an amendment to the Voter Rights Act provided for bilingual voting and registration materials when any minority exceeded 5 per cent of the relevant electoral district. In 1978 the Court Interpreters Act specified that anyone with an inadequate knowledge of English has the right to an interpreter in a federal court, but little attempt has been made to specify exactly what is meant by 'inadequate' or to provide the necessary facilities. The federal government also makes available information concerning Social Security, Medicare, and civil rights in a wide variety of languages. The 1980 Census provided bilingual forms to Spanish-speaking residents. Individual states have also added services in various languages: for example, California has an extensive set of laws requiring the use of languages other than English in certain telephone services, government offices, and educational and social agencies.

In the 1980s, however, there has been a noticeable reaction to bilingual education and to the provision of any further facilities that might encourage the maintenance of languages other than English. Funds have been cut back at both the state and federal levels and many prominent politicians, including President Reagan himself, have spoken out against it. For example, in a speech before the National League of Cities on 2 March 1981 Reagan stated that it was 'absolutely wrong and against American concepts to have a bilingual education program that is now openly, admittedly, dedicated to preserving their [students'] native language'. Such criticisms are made even though most evaluations of bilingual education programmes have showed that they were above everything else programmes designed to encourage the learning of

English rather than to maintain other languages. As Fishman has observed of the Bilingual Education Act (1981, p. 518), 'the act is basically not an act *for* bilingualism, but, rather, an act *against* bilingualism. It may contribute not merely to displacing non-English mother tongues from the instructional process, but to replacing them entirely'. Language maintenance has not been the goal of bilingual education in the United States whatever its critics might have said. Again, in Fishman's words (p. 522): 'Language maintenance in the USA is not part of public policy because it is rarely recognized as being in the public interest.'

In the United States bilingual education is usually placed in the context of compensatory education. Children who come to school speaking any other language than English are presumed to be at a disadvantage. Moreover, a knowledge of English is assumed to be necessary for all children if they are to be able to participate fully in the American way of life. Such knowledge will also ensure their loyalty to that way of life. Bilingualism is therefore regarded somewhat suspiciously because it suggests divided loyalty or at least something less than full devotion to the state, one in which ideological issues play a very important role in public life. Children must therefore be educated in English. If foreign languages have a place in school, it is as subjects of instruction only. So, on the one hand, foreign languages are eliminated in the primary schools while, on the other hand, they are taught with a conspicuous lack of success in the secondary schools.

The current climate in the United States is not one that favours public support for the maintenance of languages other than English. While many levels of government – federal, state, and local – feel obliged to make certain of their communications accessible in languages other than English, with Spanish the principal beneficiary, such a policy often meets with strong criticism. Some Americans fear for the balkanization of the state, and in support of their views have pointed to the 'problems' that Canada and Belgium have faced in recent decades when there is more than one language in a state. They have warned about giving any official status at all to Spanish. Articles and editorials have been published in very important newspapers and magazines, e.g. the *New York Times* and *Newsweek*, criticizing any further recognition of other languages than English, and attacks on any kind of bilingualism are now quite frequent.

A proposal has also been placed before Congress that the Constitution be amended to declare English the official language of the United States. This English Language Amendment, first proposed by Senator Hayakawa in 1981 and then taken up by Senator Huddleston and Congressman Shumway in 1983, would also prohibit the government from mandating multilingual publications and from establishing bilingual education as a general entitlement. As one supporter (Will, 1985, p.78) has said, such an amendment to the Constitution:

> would end the pernicious practice of providing bilingual ballots, a practice that denies the link between citizenship and shared culture. ... The promise of America is bound up with the virtues and achievements of 'Anglo culture', which is bound up with English. Immigrants, all of whom came here voluntarily, have a responsibility to reciprocate the nation's welcome by acquiring the language that is essential for citizenship, properly understood.

Furthermore, 'Bilingualism is a gratuitous intensification of disintegrative forces' and the amendment seems necessary 'to preserve the linguistic unity that is as important as the Constitution to a harmonious national life'.

While English is still not the official language of the United States, it is the official language of certain of the individual states. Six states – Georgia, Illinois, Indiana, Kentucky, Nebraska, and Virginia – had declared English as their official language before November 1986, at which time voters in California decided to amend the state constitution to join their number. The November 1986 referendum on this issue in California showed that there was a growing resistance to the use of languages other than English in that state and that even Spanish groups were willing to allow English to dominate so long as the gains they had made elsewhere were not threatened. Six years before, in 1980, voters in a similar referendum made English the de facto official language of Dade County, Florida, by prohibiting the spending of county funds for 'the purpose of utilizing any language other than English or promoting any culture other than that of the United States', even though there were well over a half million Hispanics living in the county. Those who supported 'monolingualism' and 'United States culture' prevailed over those who favoured some form of pluralism and providing financial support to Spanish-language services in the county.

This concern for making English the official language of particular jurisdictions in the United States has been prompted mainly by the growth of the Hispanic segment of the population, many of whom still speak Spanish. In 1984 it was estimated that about 17.5 million residents of the United States were of Hispanic background and that by the year 2000 this figure would perhaps double. In that case as much as 12 per cent of the population would be of this background and Hispanics would surpass blacks as the the largest minority group in the United States. About half of those who speak a language other than English in the home in the United States are of Hispanic origin and the language they speak is Spanish. That language is also being reinforced constantly through current immigration, both legal and illegal. In 1980 it was estimated that 60 per cent of Hispanics were of Mexican origin, 14 per cent of Puerto Rican origin, 6 per cent of Cuban origin, 8 per cent from various other South and Central Amerian countries, and the rest from elsewhere.

Hispanics are also clustered in certain states such as Texas, California, New Mexico, Arizona, and Florida. Certain cities too now have large numbers of Hispanic residents: Los Angeles is said to be the second largest Mexican-Spanish city in the world; New York City is said to have more speakers of Puerto Rican Spanish than San Juan, and to contain a quarter of the population of Puerto Rico; and Miami is second only to Havana as a Cuban-Spanish city. It is settlement patterns such as these that have prompted moves to reaffirm that English is the language of the United States and that those who come to that country must be prepared to learn English and use it in their official dealings with governments. There is an almost complete rejection of the idea that there should be territorial pockets in which Spanish has equal status to English. Since the United States has also found itself almost powerless to stay the flood of Hispanic immigration in the late 1970s and 1980s, the threat to English has appeared to be a growing one. When Lamm and Imhoff (1985, p. 77) declare that 'America's culture and national identity are threatened by massive levels of legal and illegal immigration', they have Hispanics in mind, and they quite clearly see as one part of the solution the need to affirm an 'English-only' language policy for the United States.

Such is the current linguistic climate of the United States. In the last few decades, there has been a great influx of other languages than English as immigrants have arrived from throughout the world, and the possibility has arisen that some of these languages could be continued into succeeding generations of native-born Americans if certain conditions were to exist. As a result too of the upsurge in ethnic consciousness, language minorities have been encouraged to give considerable attention to language and cultural maintenance. For a while at least certain legislative and judicial initiatives also encouraged such efforts at maintenance, although there are those who believe that this kind of support was an historical aberration which Americans are now seeking to correct. Today, a conservative climate in the United States seems to require a renewed emphasis on the 'American way of life', though somewhat more liberally interpreted than once was the case, and to do so through the medium of the English language. This view also appears to be rather strongly held by those who currently have the greatest influence in public life.

The long-term results are harder to predict. The pressures to assimilate in the United States are considerable and it is unlikely that small scattered linguistic groups will be able to resist them. However, some groups are neither small nor scattered. Hispanics, for example, control whole tracts of land in areas such as New York City, Florida, and the Southwest, and in many other places they are strongly enough represented to make their wishes decisive in the electoral process. Whether they will be strong enough and unified enough to use that influence to preserve the Spanish language in the United States remains to be seen. Many other groups in the United States, e.g., Poles, Italians, and Jews, have managed to retain a considerable part of their identity and much of their influence while giving up their languages in favour of English. It remains to be seen whether the same historical process will also lead to the eventual decline of Spanish. Languages other than English are tolerated in the United States but they are not encouraged. There is more than a hint that they are somehow 'un-American'. General opinion seems to hold that English is the 'natural' language of the country and the language that all those who live in the country should aspire to master as rapidly as possible.

AUSTRALIA

Australia is another country that is now confronted with a diversity of languages and cultures. It had long been not only an English-speaking country but also a 'white' country. After an initial flirtation with almost unrestricted immigration during the gold-rush years following the discovery of gold in 1851, the country adopted policies and practices which favoured those who were white and who either already spoke English or who would quickly learn the language, a 'white-Australia' policy that lasted well into the 1960s and which met its official demise only with the passing of the 1975 Racial Discrimination Act. These policies and practices effectively excluded all others. For example, one of the very first Acts passed into law when the Commonwealth of Australia came into existence was the Immigration Restriction Act of 1901. While this Act did not specifically prohibit Asian immigration, it empowered immigration officers to administer dictation tests in any European language to would-be immigrants and these tests were used when necessary to keep out 'undesirables'.

By the early years of the twentieth century Australians felt that they were united by a common Anglo-Saxon, or, as it came to be called later, Anglo-Celtic, bond. Their government was British in style and English was the common language. Groups who tried to preserve other languages were persuaded or coerced to give them up. In particular, those Germans who had immigrated to Australia and who had tried to maintain their language through instruction in German in the schools that they had established were compelled in 1916 during World War I either to close those schools or to use English. A unilingual, unicultural ideology came to prevail and was to last for many decades. Particularly harshly treated were the aboriginal peoples.

Hick (1984, p. 125) explains the consequences of such measures in the early twentieth century:

This marked the beginning of a deliberate attempt to make English the exclusive national language, and by implication, the Anglo-Australian culture the norm. When migrants arrived they were expected to conform, to speak English and to be like other Australians. Nearly all the migrants were of British stock and found little difficulty in meeting these requirements. The remainder simply had to adjust, and so the policy of assimilation was born.

Not all migrants, of course, were of British stock, but almost all were Northern European in origin. Other languages than English were to be found in use in Australia but none received any kind of recognition. It took another world war for significant changes to occur in these policies.

The end of World War II was followed by a period of considerable immigration to Australia. Australians realized during that war how underpopulated their country was and how vulnerable it could be. So immigration was encouraged as soon as hostilities ceased. To the traditional British and Northern European immigrants were added large numbers of refugees and immigrants from south and southeast Europe, with Italy, Greece, and Yugoslavia contributing well over a half million of these by 1971. The Italians and Greeks, in particular, tended to settle near those who had preceded them in earlier migrations and this chain migration led to the formation of cultural enclaves in certain cities. Many Australians opposed this pattern of settlement taking the view that the establishment of clearly defined ethnic communitites in which languages other than English would be fostered would prove to be a divisive force in the state. Concurrently, the 'white-Australia' policy was also slowly abandoned, and by the end of the 1960s about 10,000 non-Europeans were being admitted to the country each year.

Throughout the 1960s there was an almost unquestioned insistence that all newcomers should learn English, and that new Australians had a duty to see that their children quickly acquired the language of their new country. However, there was a reduction in the emphasis on assimilation; the new approach was to be one that stressed integration. But it was never made precisely clear how integration was to differ from assimilation: for example, there was no reduction in the insistence that immigrants had to learn English if they were to fit into Australian society. Anglo-Celtic hegemony would be preserved in matters of language. The new policy of integration, however, did mean that some attention could be given to the kinds of problems that immigrants were confronting in their new land, and to possible contributions that they could make to it because of the special characteristics they had brought with them.

By the 1970s it was apparent that existing policies did not serve the immigrant communities at all well. Various reports had shown that such policies had not allowed immigrants to realize their full potential. For example, they were poorly represented in the professions and higher-status occupations, and they compared unfavourably with native-born Australians on a variety of indices concerned with such matters as education, housing, income, and health. Although they had tried to do certain things for themselves without government support, e.g., they had established a variety of ethnic schools, a concerted public effort was required if ethnic harmony was to prevail in Australia.

During the 1970s there was considerable debate in Australia about the changes taking place in Australian society. One of the most widely discussed documents was the Galbally Report of 1978 to the Commonwealth Government entitled *Migrant Services and Programs*. This report proposed an 'integrated package of measures for introduction over a period of three years, to enable the Commonwealth government to take further steps to encourage multiculturalism'. The report opened up the whole issue of multiculturalism in Australia and, following its publication, a considerable amount of effort has gone into trying to decide what form a 'multicultural Australia' might take.

The Australian government immediately accepted the recommendations in the Galbally Report. Australia was to become a multicultural society in which all individuals would have an equal opportunity to realize their full potential. Individuals would be able to retain their culture and would be encouraged to try to understand the cultures of others. Immigrants' needs would be met through the normal programmes and services available to the whole community but special services and programmes would be established when these were necessary to ensure equality of access and provision. The clients of these services and programmes would also be consulted in establishing such services and programmes so that they could become self-reliant as quickly as possible. Areas of special need were identified such as the law, income security, employment, and health. One important acknowledgment was that many immigrants were seriously disadvantaged by their lack of knowledge of English; they should receive the help they were entitled to through dealing with officials who were bilingual. An Australian Institute of Multicultural Affairs was also established in 1979 as a research, advisory, and dissemination institution.

In a 1982 report the Commonwealth Government acknowledged that well over one million Australians regularly used a Community Language Other Than English (CLOTE) in their daily living, with Italian, Greek, German, and Serbo-Croatian being the most frequently used languages. The Schools Commission has suggested that provision should be made for teaching these languages – CLOTEs in Australian parlance – and that children should be given the opportunity to attend bilingual schools if their parents so wished. But little progress has been made. While official policy promotes the image of the country as one which favours multiculturalism, evidently the vast majority of the Australian-born population, some 83 per cent, believe that 'having a lot of migrants has not been so good for this country'. This feeling also extends to the teaching of CLOTEs; while bilingual, multicultural education is something that many Australians are prepared to talk about at some length, it actually exists in rather small quantities.

That this is so should not be surprising. In spite of vast post-war immigration Australia is a country in which an Anglo-Celtic culture and the English language are firmly entrenched. The majority see little need to accede to the wishes of the minority, even though that minority is no longer a small one and does have certain kinds of symbolic support. Many Australians feel that the country will have nothing to gain by proliferating languages. They are also sceptical of claims that Australians can become personally bilingual in English and one of the CLOTEs and that this will give Australia some special edge in the world. They may admit that much might be gained by diversifying Australian culture but claim that such diversity does not require any proliferation of languages. Promoting CLOTEs and encouraging ethnic-group affiliation also raises the thorny issue of endowing groups with special privileges and rights because of language or ethnic differences. The majority of Australians regard English as the language of equality and the majority Anglo-Celtic culture as providing equality of opportunity in spite of a considerable body of evidence to the contrary. While this myth of equality prevails – and there seems to be no reason to suggest that it will not continue to prevail – there seems to be little likelihood that Australia will cease to be a bastion of the English language.

CANADA

As indicated earlier in chapter 9, the major linguistic controversy in Canada has been that of the relative statuses of the English and French languages. The two languages are official languages at the federal level of government and enshrined as such in the 1982 Constitution. However, English is the language of the majority of Canadians. It is also the official language of nine of the ten provinces. French is also an official language in two of the provinces, in Quebec where it is the sole official language (although English has certain constitutional guarantees there), and in New Brunswick, where both French and English are official languages.

The English and French languages are divided on a territorial basis in Canada. Most francophones live within Quebec or in the adjacent 'bilingual belt', and most anglophones live in the rest of the country, and all available evidence suggests that this separation is increasing rather than decreasing. This further separation of the the languages is also occurring at a time when the Constitution commits the federal government to promoting policies to encourage the use of French in the non-francophone part of the country. These policies are designed to allow francophones there the opportunity to deal with the federal government and its agencies through the medium of French. They also require that where numbers warrant, certain educational opportunites be provided to francophone children in anglophone Canada just as anglophone children in Quebec have long been guaranteed an education through the medium of English.

Like the United States and Australia, Canada is a nation of immigrants, but in this case those immigrants have had to enter a country split linguistically between the English and French languages. (The descendants of the original aboriginal peoples, numbering about a half million in the 1981 Census, are now largely anglophone with 72 per cent of them reporting English as the language of the home in 1981.) In one view, the French view, Canada is a country built by two equal founding nations; in the other view, the English view, it is a country built through conquest, of the French by the English, and then developed to fill the empty spaces to the north of the United States. In neither view is it a country intended to be multilingual and multicultural, and recent moves to declare that it is such a country have met with little enthusiasm from the majority of Canadians.

The traditional pattern of innmigration has been one that brought immigrants to the English-speaking part of 'Canada. Quebec has never been attractive to immigrants, and it early acquired and then kept a reputation for xenophobia. Immigrants settled in Ontario and the provinces to the west. They built farms and populated the cities. They brought a variety of European languages with them, mainly those of Northern Europe at first, because immigration policy was deliberately selective. Later, people were allowed into Canada from central Europe and still later from the Mediterranean area, but orientals were rigidly excluded on racial grounds.

It is part of the Canadian myth that these new immigrants were invited to form part of the 'cultural mosaic' that existed in the country, that is, that they were encouraged to maintain many of their cultural characteristics in their new land. According to the myth, it is this fostering of a diversity of cultures and the lack of pressure to conform to a single ideal that above all characterizes the Canadian approach to immigrants. Many Canadians claim that such an approach is quite different from the one practised by Canada's southern neighbour, the United States, with its 'melting-pot' approach to immigrants out of which a single nation emerges (*E pluribus unum*). In actual practice, it seems that from the very beginning a policy of Anglo-conformity prevailed in English Canada: English was taught in the schools, the Union Jack was saluted, 'English' virtues and values were lauded, and the British monarchy was glorified. Such a policy was particularly evident at the turn of the twentieth century when immigration to Canada was at its peak.

One consequence was that immigrants found it very difficult to maintain the languages they brought with them. Isolated attempts to found schools in which these languages would be used as languages of instruction had to be abandoned. The developing school systems of the provinces began to insist on English as the only language of instruction and to disfavour much of the cultural baggage that many immigrants had brought with them. Even the French who resided outside Quebec fell victims to this same insistence on English and English ways, suffering a particularly severe defeat in Manitoba, where all languages except English were virtually wiped out of the schools.

Until the period of immigration after World War II, little consideration was given to immigrants and their special needs. They were a source of labour and were particularly useful in filling in the many empty spaces that the country had. They could be praised for their quaint ways of dressing and foods, but any special ambitions they had, particularly linguistic and cultural ones, were not to be taken seriously. If anything, immigrants were often regarded as posing 'problems' of one kind or another: they sometimes harboured 'radical' ideas, they were suspect in their loyalties in times of war – the French too fell into this category because of their lack of enthusiasm for being conscripted to fight wars on behalf of the English – and they were sometimes regarded as breeders of disease in the terrible conditions in which many were forced to live in the rapidly growing Canadian cities.

Following World War II, Canada gradually liberalized its immigration policy. Overt racial discrimination was ended, and in the prosperous 1950s and 1960s immigrants began to arrive from many different parts of the world. Not only did people come from traditional sources such as the United Kingdom and other Western European countries, but large numbers also arrived from Italy, Greece, and the Portuguese Azores. West Indians and various Asiatic peoples were also well represented among the immigrants. About half settled in Ontario, and about half of these in Toronto so that by 1981 38 per cent of the population of that city had been born outside the country. In general, this later wave of immigrants to Canada came mainly to live in the cities. But the vast majority avoided French-speaking Quebec, except for the city of Montreal, the most English of that province's cities.

Renewed effort was placed on teaching English to the new immigrants. This was the only language that their children encountered as a language of instruction in the schools of their new country. Even those immigrants who settled in Montreal tended to opt for their children to be instructed through the medium of English, choosing to send their children to the English schools of the city rather than to the French schools. They might be Catholic in religion, the people with whom they worked might be speakers of the local variety of French, but they recognized that success in the new country, even in Montreal itself, required that one should speak English. Therefore, it was to the English schools that they sent their children in spite of the Protestant denominational persuasion of those schools.

By the 1960s language had become a major issue in Canada. The French were discontented with what had happened to their language outside the province of Quebec. Even within Quebec itself French was being eroded through a combination of factors: a falling birth rate, continued out-migration, immigration and the immigrants' choice of English for their children, and the spread of bilingualism, e.g., into the workplace. Immigrants themselves were also quite familiar with the patterns of language loss that all arriving groups had experienced in Canada. In general, in the absence of continued immigration an immigrant language had a lifespan of less than three generations in the new country. The children of immigrants became bilingual, and their children nearly always became unilingual in English. With minor variations this pattern of loss has applied to all immigrant languages in Canada. Languages survived only when those who spoke them managed to isolate themselves on the prairies or receive transfusions from new immigrants. In the 1960s there was a fairly widespread feeling that a valuable cultural resource was going to waste in Canada and that something should be done to arrest the decline of immigrant languages.

The Royal Commission on Bilingualism and Biculturalism established in 1963 effectively turned its back on the issue of the non-official languages of Canada. In legislation that followed publication of the Commission's report in 1969 the government of Canada dealt with the issue of the relationship between the English and French languages, and tried to put them on some basis of equality through passage of the Official Languages Act of 1969. Concurrently, various administrations in the province of Quebec began to deal with the issue of the French language within that province through legislation designed to curb the influence of English there, particularly among immigrants. Both solutions were to create considerable controversy in the years that followed and still today provide Canadians with an important item on the internal agenda of their country.

In 1971 the government of Canada announced a policy to take into account the new ethnic composition of the country. By that time those of neither English nor French origin – some 27 per cent of the total population – had come to number almost as many as those of French origin in the country – about 28 per cent – and those of English origin had actually become a minority in Canada. Catholics had come to outnumber Protestants in many places. Some large cities, even Canada's largest city, Toronto, had become places in which the majority of residents had been born somewhere else; a large minority had actually been born in another country and did not have English as the native tongue. Often, too, differences in skin colour would be quite noticeable in these same cities. In recognition of all these developments the government of Canada proposed in 1971 to support a policy of 'multiculturalism within a bilingual framework'. Canada was to have two official languages but no official culture; it was to be 'multicultural', whatever that meant.

This policy was designed to allow the various ethnic groups that had come to Canada the opportunity to preserve the 'best' in what they had brought with them to their new country. The languages they had brought were part of this heritage and deserved support. However, that support has been only token in nature. The federal government has actually spent very little money on its multicultural programmes, and the minister in charge of multicultural matters has always been a political lightweight. Critics often complain too that what money has been spent has gone largely to window-dressing of various kinds, to buying-off or co-opting ethnic entrepreneurs, and to promoting the image of the government of the day in ethnic newspapers. Provincially-sponsored multicultural programmes have been no different.

Federal efforts to promote multiculturalism are undoubtedly superficial. That they should be so is not at all surprising. The major linguistic effort of the federal government must necessarily be directed toward working out the ongoing relationship between the English and French people and their languages in Canada. The French are particularly resistant to the idea that other languages should get any attention until the needs of the French and their language have been satisfied. They also object strongly to the French language itself outside Quebec often being placed in the same category as Ukrainian, Italian, and so on, i.e., being subsumed under a policy of multiculturalism rather than one of bilingualism. For their part, speakers of languages other than English or French outside Quebec often resent what they feel to be the entirely undeserved position that French has today in Canada. It is less spoken in some parts of Canada than certain other languages, particularly Ukrainian, but those who speak it have access to resources the others lack. Perhaps the federal government's lack of enthusiasm and leadership in multicultural matters is entirely understandable in the circumstances: it would be in a no-win situation if it tried to do more.

Trying to do more also would not guarantee that the particular federal government that did so would increase its electoral support through its efforts. In general, Canadians have shown little enthusiasm for multiculturalism, and show little willingness to support the spending of public money on teaching through the medium of languages other than English or French. Education is, of course, a provincial matter in Canada and educational provisions for minorities vary from province to province. Several provinces have made some provision for the teaching of what are called the 'Heritage Languages' in Canada as part of an 'enrichment' process in education. That is, it is possible to find schools in Canada in which some attention is given to maintaining the languages that immigrants to Canada have brought with them. Considerable controversy has surrounded some of these programmes, e.g., in Toronto where there has been resistance to making them part of the normal daily school programme, and how successful they have been is also a matter of dispute. The issue of teaching these language tends to be overshadowed by the issue of teaching French. There is much more enthusiasm and money for 'French-Immersion' programmes than there is for the teaching of Heritage Languages. Apparently, many Canadians see much more merit in programmes designed to encourage bilingualism in English and French than in programmes which aim to preserve minority languages and to foster multiculturalism. It is apparently enough to encourage folk dancing and ethnic foods; using public money and part of the school day to maintain 'exotic' languages and customs is quite another matter!

It seems safe to predict that the influx of new languages to Canada has done little to change either the balance or distribution of languages in the country. The fundamental language issue continues to be that of the relationship between English and French. The English and French communities within Canada place all other languages firmly into that context. They are, however, a little more generous about cultural matters than they are about linguistic ones. Racial issues also do not figure as large as they do in certain other countries. In the immigrant communities the traditional patterns of language loss continue. The decline these languages experience may become even more noticeable in the near future because in recent years Canada has ceased to be a country in which immigration is an important factor in population growth, although there are signs in the late 1980s that the doors for immigrants are to be opened a little wider than they had been in the previous decade.

In an era of equality and the assertion of rights, minority groups in Canada will make themselves heard whenever they become numerous enough to affect the political balance. In some places, e.g., Toronto, some groups have both the necessary numbers and the desire that must go with these if those numbers are to be effective. In such circumstances they can make local gains. Individuals, however, may well choose not to identify with their ethnic groups and prefer to work within an overall system that clearly favours individual rights over group rights. Internal conflict within both ethnic groups and individuals may well arise from the tensions that such a situation is likely to produce. The dominant English and French languages in Canada will continue to absorb speakers of other languages just as they have always done. Canada may develop certain characteristics of multicultural societies but Canadians will demonstrate these characteristics to one another through the medium of either the English or French languages. The real issue in Canada is still the relationship between speakers of these two languages. Whatever diversity of languages immigrants bring to Canada, their descendants are likely to find themselves very quickly aligned on one side or the other of the fundamental English–French cleavage. Those who have sought the development of some kind of 'third force' in Canadian life, one that might even play some kind of meliorative role in English–French relations, are almost certain to be disappointed.

FURTHER READING

Western Europe in general: Castles 1984, Miller 1981, Skutnabb-Kangas 1981, 1984; the United Kingdom: Cropley 1983, Jeffcoate 1984, Linguistic Minorities Project 1985, Martin-Jones 1984, Reid 1984; France: Cordeiro 1983, Gaspard and Servan-Schreiber 1985, Le Gallou 1985, Richer 1986, Les Temps Modernes 1984; Australia: Bullivant 1984a, 1984b, Clyne 1982, Foster and Stockley 1984, Poole 1981; the United States: Ferguson and Heath 1981, Fishman 1966, 1985, Gleason 1984, Thernstrom 1980; multiculturalism: Corner 1984.

Bibliography

Abdulaziz Mkilifi, M. H. A. 1978: Triglossia and Swahili–English bilingualism in Tanzania. In Fishman 1978: 129–49.

Afoloyan, A. 1984: The English language in Nigerian Education as an agent of proper multilingual and multicultural development. *Journal of Multilingual and Multicultural Development*, 5 (1): 1–23.

Alexandre, P. 1972: *An Introduction to Languages and Language in Africa*. London: Heinemann.

Allardt, E. 1984: What constitutes a language minority? *Journal of Multilingual and Multicultural Development*, 5 (3 and 4): 195–205.

Altbach, P. G. and Kelly, G. P. (eds) 1984: *Education and the Colonial Experience*, 2nd edn. New Brunswick, N. J.: Transaction Books.

Ansre, G. 1974: Language standardisation in Sub-Saharan Africa. In Fishman 1974: 369–89.

Baetens Beardsmore, H. 1980: Bilingualism in Belgium. *Journal of Multilingual and Multicultural Development*, 1 (2): 145–54.

Bailey, R. W. and Görlach, M. (eds) 1982: *English as a World Language*. Ann   Arbor: University of Michigan Press.

Baker, C. 1985: *Aspects of Bilingualism in Wales*. Clevedon: Multilingual Matters.

Bamgbose, A. (ed.) 1976: *Mother Tongue Education: The West African Experience*. London: Hodder and Stoughton.

Banton, M. 1983: *Racial and Ethnic Competition*. Cambridge: Cambridge University Press.

Barth, F. (ed.) 1969: *Ethnic Groups and Boundaries*. Boston: Little, Brown.

Bastide, H. 1982: *Les Enfants d'immigrés et l'enseignement français*. Paris: Presses Universitaires de France.

Bec, P. 1986: *La Langue occitane*. Paris: Presses Universitaires de France.

Beer, W. R. and Jacob, J. E. (eds) 1985: *Language Policy and National Unity*. Totowa, N.J.: Rowman and Allenheld.

Bengtsson, S. 1968: *La Défense organisée de la langue française: étude sur l'activité de quelques organismes que depuis 1937 ont pris pour tâche de veiller à la correction et à la pureté de la langue française*. Uppsala: Almqvist and Wiksells.

Berghe, P. L. van de 1981: Protection of ethnic minorities: a critical appraisal. In Wirsing, P. G. (ed.), *Protection of Ethnic Minorities: Comparative Perspectives*. New York: Pergamon Press. 1981: 343–55.

Berthet, E. 1982: *Langue dominante, langues dominées*. Paris: Edilig.

Betts, C. 1976: *Culture in Crisis: The Future of the Welsh Language*. Upton: The Ffynnon Press.

Blancpain, M. and Reboullet, A. (eds) 1976: *Une Langue: le français aujourd'hui dans le monde*. Paris: Hachette.

Bostock, W. W. 1983: *The Organisation and Coordination of La Francophonie: A Research Report*. Hobart: Department of Political Science, University of Tasmania.

Bourhis, R. Y. 1982: Language policies and language attitudes: *le monde de la francophonie*. In Ryan, E. B. and Giles, H. (eds), *Attitudes Towards Language Variation: Social and Applied Contexts*. London: Edward Arnold. 1982: 34–66.

Bourhis, R. Y. 1984: *Conflict and Language Planning in Quebec*. Clevedon: Multilingual Matters.

Breton, R., Reitz, J. G., and Valentine, V. F. 1980: *Cultural Boundaries and Cohesion in Canada*. Montreal: Institute for Research on Public Policy.

Breton, R. J.-L. 1981: *Les Ethnies*. Paris: Presses Universitaires de France.

Breuilly, J. 1982: *Nationalism and the State*. Chicago: University of Chicago Press.

Brosnahan, L. F. 1963: Some historical cases of language imposition. In Spencer, J. C. (ed.), *Language in Africa*. London: Cambridge University Press. 1963: 7–24.

Bullivant, B. M. 1984a: Ethnolinguistic minorities and multicultural policy in Australia. In Edwards 1984: 107–40.

Bullivant, B. M. 1984b: *Pluralism: Cultural Maintenance and Evolution*. Clevedon: Multilingual Matters.

Calvet, L.-J. 1974: *Linguistique et colonialisme: petit traité de glottophagie*. Paris: Payot.

Calvet, L.-J. 1981: *Les Langues véhiculaires*. Paris: Presses Universitaires de France.

Castles, S. 1984: *Here for Good: Western Europe's New Ethnic Minorities*. London: Pluto Press.

Chabot, J.-L. 1986: *Le Nationalisme*. Paris: Presses Universitaires de France.

Clyne, M. G. 1982: *Multilingual Australia: Resources – Needs – Policies*. Melbourne: River Seine Publications.

Cobarrubias, J. and Fishman, J. A. (eds) 1983: *Progress in Language Planning: International Perspectives*. Berlin: Mouton.

Cohen, A. 1976: *Two-Dimensional Man: An Essay on the Anthropology of Power and Symbolism in Complex Society*. Berkeley and Los Angeles: University of California Press.

Conférence des Ministres de l'Éducation des États d'Expression Française 1986: *Promotion et intégration des langues nationales dans les systèmes éducatifs: bilan et inventaire*. Paris: Librairie Honoré Champion.

Connor, W. 1977: Ethnonationalism in the First World: the present in historical perspective. In Esman 1977a: 19–45.

Connor, W. 1978: A nation is a nation, is a state, is an ethnic group, is a . . . *Ethnic and Racial Studies*, 1 (4): 377–400.

Conrad, A. W. and Fishman, J. A. 1977. English as a world language: the evidence. In Fishman et al. 1977: 3–75.

Cooper R. L. (ed.) 1982: *Language Spread: Studies in Diffusion and Social Change*. Bloomington: Indiana University Press.

Corbett, E. M. 1972: *The French Presence in Black Africa*. Washington, D. C.: Black Orpheus Press.

Cordeiro, A. 1983: *L'Immigration*. Paris: Éditions La Découverte.

Corner, T. (ed.) 1984: *Education in Multicultural Societies*. London: Croom Helm.

Coste, D. (ed.) 1984: *Aspects d'une politique de diffusion du français langue étrangère depuis 1945: matériaux pour une histoire*. Paris: Hatier.

Cropley, A. J. 1983: *The Education of Immigrant Children: A Social-Psychological Introduction*. London: Croom Helm.

De Vos, G. 1975: Ethnic pluralism: conflict and accommodation. In De Vos, G. and Romanucci-Ross, L. (eds), *Ethnic Identity: Cultural Continuities and Change*. Palo Alto: Mayfield Publishing Company. 1975: 5–41.

Deniau, X. 1983: *La Francophonie*. Paris: Presses Universitaires de France.

Deutsch, K. W. 1975: The political significance of linguistic conflicts. In Savard and Vigneault 1975: 7–28.

Dorian, N. C. 1981: *Language Death: The Life Cycle of a Scottish Gaelic Dialect*. Philadelphia: University of Pennsylvania Press.

Durkacz, V. E. 1983: *The Decline of the Celtic Languages: A Study of Linguistic and Cultural Conflict in Scotland, Wales and Ireland from the Reformation to the Twentieth Century*. Edinburgh: John Donald   Publishers.

Eastman, C. M. 1983: *Language Planning: An Introduction*. San Francisco: Chandler and Sharp Publishers.

Edwards, J. (ed.): *Linguistic Minorities, Policies and Pluralism*. London: Academic Press.

Edwards, J. 1985: *Language, Society and Identity*. Oxford: Basil Blackwell.

Ellis, P. B. 1974: *The Cornish Language and Its Literature*. London: Routledge and Kegan Paul.

Esman, M. J. (ed.) 1977a: *Ethnic Conflict in the Western World*. Ithaca: Cornell University Press.

Esman, M. J. 1977b: Perspectives on ethnic conflict in industrialized societies. In Esman 1977a: 371–90.

Esman, M. J. 1985: The politics of official bilingualism in Canada. In Beer and Jacob 1985: 45–66.

Fabian, J. 1986: *Language and Colonial Power: The Appropriation of Swahili in the Former Belgian Congo 1880–1938*. Cambridge: Cambridge University Press.

Fasold, R. 1984: *The Sociolinguistics of Society*. Oxford: Basil Blackwell.

Ferguson, C. A. 1977: Sociolinguistic settings of language planning. In Rubin et al. 1977: 9–29.

Ferguson, C. A. and Heath, S. B. (eds) 1981: *Language in the USA*. Cambridge: Cambridge University Press.

Fishman, J. A. 1966: *Language Loyalty in the United States*. The Hague Mouton.

Fishman, J. A. (ed.) 1972a: *Advances in the Sociology of Language: Vol. II, Studies and Applications.* The Hague: Mouton.

Fishman, J. A. 1972b: *Language and Nationalism: Two Integrative Essays.* Rowley, Mass.: Newbury House Publishers.

Fishman, J. A. (ed.) 1974: *Advances in Language Planning.* The Hague: Mouton.

Fishman, J. A. 1977: Language and ethnicity. In Giles 1977: 15–57.

Fishman, J. A. (ed.) 1978. *Advances in the Study of Societal Multilingualism.* The Hague: Mouton.

Fishman, J. A. 1981. Language policy; past, present, and future. In Ferguson and Heath 1981: 516–26.

Fishman, J. A. 1983: Sociology of English as an additional language. In Kachru 1983: 15–22.

Fishman, J. A. 1985: *The Rise and Fall of the Ethnic Revival: Perspectives on Language and Ethnicity.* Berlin: Mouton.

Fishman, J. A., Cooper, R. L., and Conrad, A. W. (eds) 1977: *The Spread of English: The Sociology of English as an Additional Language.* Rowley, Mass.: Newbury House Publishers.

Fishman, J. A., Cooper, R. L., and Rosenbaum, Y. 1977: English the world over: a factor in the creation of bilingualism today. In Hornby, P. A. (ed.), *Bilingualism: Psychological, Social, and Educational Implications.* New York: Academic Press. 1977: 103–39.

Fishman, J. A., Ferguson, C. A., and Das Gupta, J. (eds) 1968: *Language Problems of Developing Nations.* New York: John Wiley and Sons.

Foster, C. R. (ed.) 1980: *Nations Without a State: Ethnic Minorities in Western Europe.* New York: Praeger.

Foster, L. and Stockley, D. 1984: *Multiculturalism: The Changing Australian Paradigm.* Clevedon: Multilingual Matters.

Friedrich, C. J. 1966: Nation-building. In Deutsch, K. W. and Foltz, J. (eds), *Nation-Building.* New York: Atherton. 1966: 27–32.

Gallagher, C. F. 1966: Language and identity. In Brown, L. C. (ed.), *State and Society in Independent North Africa.* Washington, D. C.: Middle East Institute. 1966: 73–96.

Gaspard, F. and Servan-Schreiber, C. 1985: *La Fin des immigrés.* Paris: Éditions du Seuil.

Gellner, E. 1983: *Nations and Nationalism.* Ithaca: Cornell University Press.

George, P. 1984: *Géopolitique des minorités.* Paris: Presses Universitaires de France.

Gérard, A. S. 1981: *African Language Literatures: An Introduction to the Literary History of Sub-Saharan Africa.* Harlow: Longman Group.

Giles, H. (ed.) 1977: *Language, Ethnicity and Intergroup Relations.* London: Academic Press.

Giles, H., Bourhis, R. Y., and Taylor, D. M. 1977: Towards a theory of language in ethnic group relations. In Giles 1977: 307–48.

Glazer, N. 1983: *Ethnic Dilemmas, 1964–1982.* Cambridge, Mass.: Harvard University Press.

Glazer, N. and Moynihan, D. P. 1963: *Beyond the Melting Pot: The Negroes,*

Puerto Ricans, Jews, Italians, and Irish of New York City. Cambridge, Mass.: M.I.T. Press.

Glazer, N. and Moynihan, D. P. (eds) 1975: *Ethnicity: Theory and Experience.* Cambridge, Mass.: Harvard University Press.

Gleason, P. 1984: Pluralism and assimilation: a conceptual history. In Edwards 1984: 221–57.

Gordon, D. C. 1978: *The French Language and National Identity (1930–1975).* The Hague: Mouton.

Grandguillaume, G. 1983: *Arabisation et politique linguistique au Maghreb.* Paris: Éditions G.-P. Maisonneuve et Larose.

Greenbaum, S. (ed.) 1985: *The English Language Today.* Oxford: Pergamon Press.

Grosjean, F. 1982: *Life with Two Languages: An Introduction to Bilingualism.* Cambridge, Mass.: Harvard University Press.

Harzic, J. 1976: Le Français et les autres langues de communication. In Blancpain and Reboullet 1976: 148–61.

Haugen, E. 1966: *Language Conflict and Language Planning: The Case of Modern Norwegian.* Cambridge, Mass.: Harvard University Press.

Haugen, E., McClure, J. D., and Thomson, D. (eds) 1981: *Minority Languages Today.* Edinburgh: Edinburgh University Press.

Heath, S. B. and Mandabach, F. 1983: Language status decisions and the law in the United States. In Cobarrubias and Fishman 1983: 87–105.

Hechter, M. 1975. *Internal Colonialism: The Celtic Fringe in British National Development, 1536–1966.* London: Routledge and Kegan Paul.

Heggoy, A. A. 1984: Colonial education in Algeria: assimilation and reaction. In Altbach and Kelly 1984: 97–116.

Héraud, G. 1963: *L'Europe des Ethnies,* 2nd edn. Paris: Presses d'Europe.

Hick, D. 1984: The emergence of cultural diversity in Australia. In Corner 1984: 117–36.

Horowitz, D. L. 1985: *Ethnic Groups in Conflict.* Berkeley and Los Angeles: University of California Press.

Isajiw, W. 1980: Definitions of ethnicity. In Goldstein, J. E. and Bienvenue, R. M. (eds), *Ethnicity and Ethnic Relations in Canada: A Book of Readings.* Toronto: Butterworth, 1980: 13–25.

Jeffcoate, R. 1984: *Ethnic Minorities and Education.* London: Harper and Row.

Joy, R. J. 1972: *Languages in Conflict: The Canadian Experience.* Toronto: McClelland and Stewart.

Kachru, B. B. (ed.) 1983: *The Other Tongue: English Across Cultures.* Oxford: Pergamon Press.

Kahane, H. and Kahane, R. 1979: Decline and survival of Western prestige languages. *Language,* 55 (1): 183–98.

Kelly, G. P. 1984: Colonialism, indigenous society, and school practices: French West Africa and IndoChina, 1918–1938. In Altbach and Kelly 1984: 9–32.

Kennedy, C. (ed.) 1983: *Language Planning and Language Education.* London: Allen and Unwin.

Khleif, B. B. 1985: Issues of theory and methodology in the study of ethnolinguistic movements. In Tiryakian and Rogowski 1985: 176–99.

Kwofie, E. N. 1979: *The Acquisition and Use of French as a Second Language in Africa (Sociolinguistic, Historical-Comparative and Methodological Perspectives)*. Grossen-Linden: Hoffmann Verlag.

Lachapelle, R. and Henripin, J. 1982: *The Demolinguistic Situation in Canada: Past Trends and Future Prospects*. Montreal: Institute for Research on Public Policy.

Ladefoged, P., Glick, R., and Criper, C. (eds) 1972: *Language in Uganda*. London: Oxford University Press.

Lamm, R. D. and Imhoff, G. 1985. *The Immigration Time Bomb: The Fragmenting of America*. New York: E. P. Dutton.

Landman, R. H. 1978. Language policies and their implications for ethnic relations in the newly sovereign states of sub-Saharan Africa. In du Toit, B. M. (ed.), *Ethnicity in Modern Africa*. Boulder: Westview Press. 1978: 69–90.

Laponce, J. A. 1984: *Langue et territoire*. Quebec: Les Presses de l'Université Laval.

Le Gallou, J.-I. 1985: *La Préférence nationale: réponse à l'immigration*. Paris: Albin Michel.

Lebesque, M. 1970: *Comment peut-on être breton? Essai sur la démocratie française*. Paris: Éditions du Seuil.

Leclerc, J. 1986: *Langue et Société*. Laval: Mondia Éditeurs.

Lewis, B. 1966: *The Arabs in History*. New York: Harper and Row.

Lewis, E. G. 1982: Movements and agencies of language spread: Wales and the Soviet Union compared. In Cooper 1982: 214–59.

Lieberson, S. 1981: *Language Diversity and Language Contact*. Stanford: Stanford University Press.

Lieberson, S. 1982: Forces affecting language spread: some basic propositions. In Cooper 1982: 37–62.

Lijphart, A. 1977: *Democracy in Plural Societies: A Comparative Exploration*. New Haven: Yale University Press.

Lijphart, A. (ed.) 1981: *Conflict and Coexistence in Belgium: The Dynamics of a Culturally Divided Society*. Berkeley: Institute for International Studies.

Linguistic Minorities Project 1985: *The Other Languages of England*. London: Routledge and Kegan Paul.

Linz, J. J. 1975: Politics in a multi-lingual society with a dominant world language: the case of Spain. In Savard and Vigneault 1975: 367–425.

McCrum, R., Cran, W., and MacNeil, R. 1986: *The Story of English*. New York: Viking.

Macnamara, J. 1971: Successes and failures in the movement for the restoration of Irish. In Rubin and Jernudd 1971: 65–94.

McRae, K. D. 1983: *Conflict and Compromise in Multilingual Societies: Switzerland*. Waterloo: Wilfid Laurier University Press.

McRae, K. D. 1986: *Conflict and Compromise in Multilingual Societies: Belgium*. Waterloo: Wilfrid Laurier University Press.

Makouta-Mboukou, J.-P. 1973: *Le Français en Afrique noire (histoire et méthodes de l'enseignement du français en Afrique noire)*. Paris: Bordas.

Manessy, G. and Wald, P. 1984: *Le Français en Afrique noire: tel qu'on le parle, tel qu'on le dit*. Paris: Éditions L'Harmattan.

Martin-Jones, M. 1984: The new minorities: literacy and educational issues. In Trudgill 1984: 425–48.

Mayer, K. 1980: Ethnic tensions in Switzerland: the Jura conflict. In Foster 1980: 189–208.

Mayo, P. E. 1974: *The Roots of Identity: Three National Movements in Contemporary European Politics*. London: Allen Lane.

Mazrui, A. A. 1975: *The Political Sociology of the English Language: An African Perspective*. The Hague: Mouton.

Megarry, J., Nisbet, S., and Hoyle, E. (eds) 1981. *World Yearbook of Education 1981: Education of Minorities*. London: Kogan Page.

Mencken, H. L. 1919. *The American Language: A Preliminary Inquiry into the Development of English in the United States*. New York: Alfred A. Knopf.

Merad, A. 1984: *L'Islam Contemporain*. Paris: Presses Universitaires de France.

Miller, M. J. 1981: *Foreign Workers in Western Europe: An Emerging Political Force*. New York: Praeger.

Morgan, K. O. 1981. *Rebirth of a Nation 1880–1980* (History of Wales, volume 6). Oxford: Oxford University Press.

O'Barr, W. and O'Barr, J. (eds) 1976. *Language and Politics*. The Hague: Mouton.

Ohannessian, S. and Kashoki, M. E. (eds) 1978. *Language in Zambia*. London: International African Institute.

Philip, A. B. 1980: European nationalism in the nineteenth and twentieth centuries. In Mitchison, R. (ed.), *The Roots of Nationalism: Studies in Northern Europe*. Edinburgh: John Donald Publishers. 1980: 1–9.

Platt, J., Weber, H., and Ho, M. L. 1984: *The New Englishes*. London: Routledge and Kegan Paul.

Polomé, E. C. and Hill, C. P. (eds) 1980: *Language in Tanzania*. London: Oxford University Press.

Poole, M. E. 1981. Educational opportunity for minority groups: Australian research reviewed. In Megarry et al. 1981: 254–78.

Price, G. 1979: Minority languages in Western Europe. In Stephens 1979: 1–17.

Price, G. 1984: *The Languages of Britain*. London: Edward Arnold.

Pride, J. (ed.) 1982: *New Englishes*. Rowley, Mass.: Newbury House Publishers.

Reboullet, A. 1976: Images et réalités de la langue française. In Blancpain and Reboullet 1976: 1–11.

Reid, E. 1984: The newer minorities: spoken languages and varieties. In Trudgill 1984: 408–24.

Richer, L. 1986: *Le Droit de l'immigration*. Paris: Presses Universitaires de France.

Richmond, E. B. 1983: *New Directions in Language Teaching in Sub-Saharan Africa: A Seven-Country Study of Current Policies and Programs for Teaching Official and National Languages and Adult Functional Literacy*. Washington, D. C.: University Press of America.

Royce, A. P. 1982: *Ethnic Identity: Strategies of Diversity*. Bloomington: Indiana

University Press.

Rubin, J. and Jernudd, B. H. (eds) 1971: *Can Language be Planned? Sociolinguistic Theory and Practice for Developing Nations*. Honolulu: University of Hawaii Press.

Rubin, J. and Jernudd, B. H. 1979: *References for Students of Language Planning*. Honolulu: East–West Center Culture Learning Institute.

Rubin, J., Jernudd, B. H, Das Gupta, J., Fishman, J. A., and Ferguson, C. A. (eds) 1977: *Language Planning Processes*. The Hague: Mouton.

Rubin, J. and Shuy, R. (eds) 1973: *Language Planning: Current Issues and Research*. Washington, D. C.: Georgetown University Press.

Rustow, D. A. 1975: Language, nations, and democracy. In Savard and Vigneault 1975: 43–60.

Savard, J.-G. and Vigneault, R. (eds) 1975: *Les États multilingues: problèmes et solutions*. Quebec: Les Presses de l'Université Laval.

Schermerhorn, R. A. 1978: *Comparative Ethnic Relations: A Framework for Theory and Research*. Chicago: University of Chicago Press.

Schläpfer, R. (ed.) 1985: *La Suisse aux quatre langues*. Geneva: Éditions Zoé.

Scotton, C. M. 1972: *Choosing a Lingua Franca in an African Capital*. Edmonton: Linguistic Research.

Scotton, C. M. 1982: Learning lingua francas and socioeconomic integration. In Cooper 1982: 63–94.

Seton-Watson, H. 1981: *Language and National Consciousness*. London: British Academy.

Shiels, F. L. (ed.) 1984: *Ethnic Separatism and World Politics*. New York: University Press of America.

Simpson, J. M. Y. 1981. The challenge of minority languages. In Haugen et al. 1981: 235–41.

Skutnabb-Kangas, T. 1981: *Bilingualism or Not: The Education of Minorities*. Clevedon: Multilingual Matters.

Skutnabb-Kangas, T. 1984: Children of guest workers and immigrants: linguistic and educational issues. In Edwards 1984: 17–48.

Smiley, D. V. 1977: French–English relations in Canada and consociational democracy. In Esman 1977a: 179–227.

Smith, A. D. 1981: *The Ethnic Revival*. Cambridge: Cambridge University Press.

Smith, L. E. (ed.) 1981: *English for Cross-Cultural Communication*. London: Macmillan.

Stephens, M. 1976: *Linguistic Minorities in Western Europe*. Llandysul: Gomer Press.

Stephens, M. (ed.) 1979: *The Welsh Language Today*. Llandysul: Gomer Press.

Stevens, P. B. 1983: Ambivalence, modernisation and language attitudes: French and Arabic in Tunisia. *Journal of Multilingual and Multicultural Development*, 4 (2 and 3): 101–14.

Les Temps Modernes 1984: *L'Immigration maghrébine en France*. Paris: Denoël.

Thernstrom, S. (ed.) 1980: *Harvard Encyclopedia of American Ethnic Groups*. Cambridge, Mass.: Harvard University Press.

Tiryakian, E. A. and Rogowski, R. (eds) 1985. *New Nationalisms of the*

Developed West: Toward Explanation. Boston: Allen and Unwin.

Todd, L. 1982: English in Cameroon. In Pride 1982: 119–37.

Todd, L. 1983: Language options for education in a multilingual society: Cameroon. In Kennedy 1983: 160–71.

Tougas, G. 1967: *La Francophonie en Péril.* Ottawa: Le Cercle du Livre de France.

Toumi, M. 1982: *Le Maghreb.* Paris: Presses Universitaires de France.

Touret, B. 1973: *L'Aménagement constitutionnel des états de peuplement composite.* Quebec: Les Presses de l'Université Laval.

Treffgarne, C. 1981: Language Policies in West and East Africa. In Megarry et al. 1981: 198–208.

Trudgill, P. (ed.) 1984: *Language in the British Isles.* Cambridge: Cambridge University Press.

Trudgill, P. and Tzavaras, G. 1977: Why Albanian-Greeks are not Albanians: language shift in Attica and Biotia. In Giles 1977: 171–84.

Turcotte, D. 1981: *La Politique linguistique en Afrique francophone: une étude comparative de la Côte d'Ivoire et de Madagascar.* Quebec: Les Presses de l'Université Laval.

Turcotte, D. 1983: *Lois, règlements et textes administratifs sur l'usage des langues en Afrique occidentale française (1826–1959).* Quebec: Les Presses de l'Université Laval.

Valdman, A. (ed.). 1979: *Le Français hors de France.* Paris: Éditions Honoré Champion.

Viatte, A. 1969: *La Francophonie.* Paris: Librairie Larousse.

Waggoner, D. 1981: Statistics on language use. In Ferguson and Heath 1981: 486–515.

Wakelin, M. F. 1975: *Language and History in Cornwall.* Leicester: Leicester University Press.

Wardhaugh, R. 1983: *Language and Nationhood: The Canadian Experience.* Vancouver: New Star Books.

Weber, E. 1976: *Peasants into Frenchmen: The Modernization of Rural France, 1870–1914.* Stanford: Stanford University Press.

Weinreich, U. 1966: *Languages in Contact: Findings and Problems.* The Hague: Mouton.

Weinstein, B. 1980: Language planning in francophone Africa. *Language Problems and Language Planning,* 4 (1): 55–75.

Weinstein, B. 1983: *The Civic Tongue: Political Consequences of Language Choices.* New York: Longman.

Whiteley, W. H. 1969: *Swahili: The Rise of a National Language.* London: Methuen.

Whiteley, W. H. (ed.) 1971: *Language Use and Social Change: Problems of Multilingualism with Special Reference to Eastern Africa.* London: Oxford University Press.

Whiteley, W. H. (ed.) 1974: *Language In Kenya.* London: Oxford University Press.

Will, G. F. 1985: In defense of the mother tongue. *Newsweek,* 8 July: 78.

Williams, C. H. 1984: More than the tongue can tell: linguistic factors in ethnic separatism. In Edwards 1984: 179–219.

Withers, C. W. J. 1984: *Gaelic in Scotland, 1698–1981: The Geographical History of a Language*. Edinburgh: John Donald Publishers.

Yinger, J. M. 1981: Toward a theory of assimilation and dissimilation. *Ethnic and Racial Studies*, 4 (3): 249–64.

Young, C. 1976: *The Politics of Cultural Pluralism*. Madison: University of Wisconsin Press.

Zolberg, A. R. 1977: Splitting the difference: federalization without federalism in Belgium. In Esman 1977a: 103–42.

Index

Index

DATE DUE